VOLMA...
MY JOURNEY

One Man's Impact on the Civil Rights Movement in Austin, Texas

D1564461

By Carolyn L. Jones

EAKIN PRESS ★ Austin, Texas

FIRST EDITION

Copyright © 1998
By Carolyn L. Jones

Published in the United States of America
By Eakin Press
A Division of Sunbelt Media, Inc.
P.O. Box 90159
Austin, TX 78709
email: eakinpub@sig.net

2 3 4 5 6 7 8 9

ISBN 1-57168-218-X

Library of Congress Cataloging-in-Publication Data

Jones, Carolyn L.
    Volma--my journey : one man's impact on the civil rights movement in Austin, Texas. --1st ed.
        p.   cm.
    Includes bibliographical references and index.
    ISBN 1-57168-218-X (alk. paper)
    1. Overton, Volma. 2. Afro-American civil rights workers--Texas--Austin--Biography. 3. Civil rights workers--Texas--Austin--History--20th century. 5. Austin (Tex.)--Race relations.
6. National Association for the Advancement of Colored People--Biography. I. Jones, Carolyn L. II. Title.
F394.A99N46 1998
323'.09764'31--dc21   98-10628
                                                            CIP

To my wife, Warneta B. Hill Overton,
for her selflessness in raising our four children—
Florence Jean, Volma Robert, Jr.,
Sharlet, and DeDra Estell—
while I sought justice in the streets during
the Civil Rights Movement.

VOLMA R. OVERTON

Volma Overton, President Emeritus of the Austin branch National Association for the Advancement of Colored People.

CONTENTS

FOREWORD

This book is about a tall Texan—Volma Overton.

In his quest for service through excellence, Volma exhibited the tenacity and patience learned from Job, the commitment and dedication of Abraham, and the skill and finesse displayed by King Solomon.

After I decided to get to know the Austin population by giving service, I chose the NAACP as my avenue. There I met Volma Overton, president of the Austin branch NAACP.

Mr. Overton's knowledge and skill as president of the Austin branch NAACP were clearly visible in his guidance of the organization. In one session I was informed of the next meeting, which committee needed help, who to contact, how much time was required, and of the great need to have an impartial observer. Not only was Mr. Overton the welcoming committee, an involvement specialist, family man, and city, district, county, state and national NAACP representative, but he also became my friend.

His leadership and networking resulted in my appointment to the state of Texas District IX Grievance Committee. Mr. Overton encouraged others to grow and develop while his personal development continued to rise meteorically. He led and attended numerous NAACP workshops, and those held by other organizations as well. The financial world also benefitted from his knowledge and skill as he helped establish the NAACP Credit Union (currently the

East Austin Community Federal Credit Union). He became the organization's director and financial officer.

His activities in the financial realm paralleled his rise in his own profession, working for the U.S. Postal Service. He rose from postal clerk to postmaster in the city of Cedar Creek.

He also developed his skills in other areas. As a skillful golfer, he recruited students and awarded scholarships for golf lessons. His love of dancing extended to lessons, contests, club membership, fraternity functions, and other limitless networking partnerships.

I hope in reading this book you will see how Mr. Overton, a tall Texan with tenacity, commitment, skill, and finesse, managed to accomplish so much and influence so many.

—CECIL Y. WRIGHT

PREFACE

When Volma Overton and his brothers and sisters were children running barefoot through the rich black earth of the small, rural, central Texas community of Maha during the 1930s and 1940s, they often looked around at the farmhouses of a dozen or so Overton relatives situated amid a sea of cotton fields, corn fields, and maize.

Long before *Roots* author Alex Haley traced his family lineage from his hometown of Henning, Tennessee, back six generations to the village of Juffure, the village in the Gambia, West Africa, where Kunte Kinte, his great-great-great-great-grandfather was abducted by white slave traders in 1767 and sold to a plantation owner in Virginia, Volma's younger brother Roscoe wondered about the Overton family's roots.

"Where did we come from?" Roscoe asked his Uncle Mike Overton one Sunday when the two stayed home from church.

"Ros, I don't know," Uncle Mike answered. "But they tell me we came from Tennessee."

It was not until the mid-1960s when Roscoe Overton had completed a bachelor's and a master's degree at Texas Southern University and Tennessee State University that he took a job in Nashville and later Memphis. He began to notice that the name Overton was all over the place . . . a high school, a museum, a park.

During the mid-1980s, in anticipation of the second

Overton family reunion to be held in Memphis, Roscoe used his experience as an investigator for the Tennessee State Department of Commerce and Insurance to start researching the Overton family history. He felt there was a link between his own family in Maha, Texas, and the Tennessee Overtons. His research took him from the libraries in Memphis and Nashville to the State Archives Library and Travis County Courthouse in Austin, Texas. He also visited Travellers Rest, the Overton plantation in Nashville.

He researched the names of slaves in all ninety-six counties in Tennessee before he determined that the Overtons lived in Davidson County in Nashville. He obtained the names of the former Overton slaves and compared them to individuals who purchased property in Texas after the Civil War.

He also studied the holdings of Judge Overton and his son Col. John Overton, well-to-do members of the Tennessee aristocracy who owned fifty-three slaves in 1860 and more land than other property owners in the area. He found that Colonel Overton had the reputation of a good and generous man who treated his slaves kindly.

Contrary to his first impression that most whites owned slaves, Roscoe found that slave owners had to be wealthy because they had to feed and maintain their slaves as well as pay taxes on them.

After five years of research, Roscoe felt he had all the information he needed to prove there was a connection between the Tennessee and the Texas Overtons. But he knew he had to convince the historians at Travellers Rest Plantation of his findings—that former slaves of the Tennessee Overtons, George, Alfred, Jim, and Amanda (probably sired by Col. John Overton and the slave girl Emmaline) were among the family of Overton's former slaves who settled in Maha, Texas, just south of the state capital at Austin after the Civil War. He felt strongly that Oscar, Henry, and Cora were also among the Overtons who travelled to Texas from Tennessee—but he couldn't prove they came with the original group.

There was also the question of Emmaline. Roscoe could not connect her to the rest of the family and could not find her in the Austin history. But according to history passed down orally through aunties and parents, Emmaline existed.

The late Anna Glover, an aged Overton cousin affectionately called Mutz, often spoke of Emmaline and her light skinned children. Looking at a picture of the slave family, Roscoe saw they were the spitting image of his own father and uncles who lived and farmed around Maha, Texas.

Roscoe theorized that the family left Tennessee, went down the Mississippi River and crossed over to New Orleans in about 1867 or 1868. They headed west, travelling through the oil and swamp country around Beaumont and Houston and finally settled outside of Austin in a small community called Maha.

State Archives records indicate that in 1871, George Overton purchased sixty-three acres of land for $600, a large amount of money for a slave. Since they could not go to a bank and borrow money, Roscoe theorized that their old master, Col. John Overton, gave Emmaline and her children money to make a new start after slavery ended.

Roscoe discovered headstones for Oscar, Alfred, and Henry in Williamson Creek Cemetery on Highway 290 just beyond South Austin. But he never found Emmaline's headstone.

The historians at Travellers Rest Plantation in Nashville, interested in Roscoe's paper trail, combed the records he presented—land purchase deeds and census documents reproduced from microfilm.

The Overton family reunion, held in Memphis, Tennessee, in 1991, drew over 275 relatives from Texas, Tennessee, Florida, California, Missouri, Oregon, Virginia, Washington, Illinois, Ohio, and Pennsylvania. A special part of the reunion festivities included a bus trip to Travellers Rest where the family had lunch on red and white tablecloths under the shade of stately trees, and met some of their white Overton relatives. The governor of Tennessee sent a resolution honoring the Overton family, and Roscoe's search was the subject of several newspaper articles. He was also a guest on a television talk show.

Despite his extensive research, the historians at Travellers Rest found that Roscoe's documents did not prove conclusively that the former slaves of Col. John Overton of Tennessee settled in Texas and started the Texas Overtons.

The homes of the Overton family that once dotted the open fields of Maha are only a memory. The ravages of time, the Depression, and World War II combined to make farming economically unfeasible. Like many rural families, when the older Overtons died out, the young ones packed up and moved to urban cities where it was easier to make a living.

When he travels from his home in Memphis to visit his relatives in Austin once or twice a year, Roscoe Overton drives down to the old homeplace at Maha where a growing community once thrived. He remembers Sunday afternoon conversations with his Uncle Mike, who didn't like to go to church, and his own five-year search for the Overton family's roots. He remains convinced that his father and uncles are direct descendants of the slave girl Emmaline and the Old Colonel.

—CAROLYN L. JONES

CHRONOLOGY

1865-1867	Emmaline, matriarch of the Overton family, and her children leave Col. John Overton's Travellers Rest Plantation in Nashville, Tennessee, after the Civil War puts an end to slavery. They settle in Maha, Texas.
1909	The National Association for the Advancement of Colored People (NAACP) is founded by influential whites after a race riot in Springfield kills many Blacks and forces others to flee the city.
1910	*Crisis Magazine* founded. Edited by W. E. B. DuBois, the magazine highlights the achievements of Blacks in the arts, business, and other fields.
August 1919	John R. Shillady, the white executive director of the NAACP, is severely beaten on Austin streets after he journeyed there to investigate why Texas officials subpoenaed the records of the NAACP. Texas Governor W. P. Hobby applauds the action, widely believed to have been done by Judge Pickle.
September 26, 1924	Volma Robert Overton is born at home in Maha, Texas.

1942	Volma Overton enlists in the segregated Marine Corps.
June 1944	Sherman Overton, Volma's brother, is killed while serving in a service unit in the military overseas during World War II.
1946	Heman Marion Sweatt, a Houston postal worker, files a lawsuit under the sponsorship of the NAACP to gain admission to The University of Texas School of Law. UT's refusal to admit Sweatt is based solely on his race.
April 14, 1946	Volma Overton marries the former Warneta Hill.
1947	Volma Overton is asked to give up his seat on a bus in downtown Austin, Texas, so whites can sit down.
1951	Community activist and journalist Arthur B. DeWitty narrowly misses being elected the first Black on the Austin City Council. Afterwards, the council changes the election method to the place system, making it difficult for a minority to win a seat.
1952	Volma Overton accepts a position as a mail clerk at the post office in Austin, Texas.
May 17, 1954	The Supreme Court hands down a ruling in *Brown v. Board of Education* outlawing "separate but equal."
December 1, 1955	Rosa Parks refuses to surrender her seat on a Montgomery, Alabama, bus to a white passenger and is jailed, sparking a boycott of the public bus system by Montgomery Blacks led by the Rev. Dr. Martin Luther King, Jr.

1955-56	School year in which thirteen African-American students make history in Austin. They attend three previously all-white schools.
Fall 1956	The University of Texas at Austin completes integration of graduate and undergraduate classes, but does little towards achieving integration in other areas of campus life.
1962	Volma Overton assumes the presidency of the Austin branch NAACP. He is mentored by Madam U. V. Christian and Arthur B. DeWitty.
September 1962	The Austin branch NAACP joins with other groups to picket the segregated Austin Ice Palace, which eventually closes down.
Fall 1962	Mississippi Governor Ross Barnett stands in the doorway as twenty-nine-year-old James Meredith attempts to enroll.
Summer 1963	Volma Overton, a group of Boy Scouts, and several friends become the first Blacks to use the facilities at Bastrop State Park without being asked to leave because of their race.
June 1963	Mississippi NAACP Chairman Medgar Evers is shot to death at his home in Jackson, Mississippi.
July 1963	Black activist B. T. Bonner stages a sit-in in Texas Governor Connally's office in Austin.
August 28, 1963	Volma Overton attends the March on Washington; hears Martin Luther King's "I Have A Dream" speech.
November 1963	The University of Texas at Austin lifts color bar on everything except housing (including sports).

Nov. 21, 1963	Volma Overton resigns his position as president of the Austin branch NAACP after doctors diagnose bleeding ulcers.
Nov. 22, 1963	President Kennedy is shot to death as he rides in a motorcade in Dallas, Texas. Lyndon Baines Johnson, a Texan, assumes the presidency.
January 1964	Twenty-third Amendment to the U.S. Constitution outlaws the poll tax.
April 1964	Volma Overton and NAACP demonstrators hold a "read in" at Austin City Council chambers in protest of the council's vote against establishing a Human Relations Commission to address complaints of discrimination.
July 1964	The Civil Rights Act of 1964 is passed under the watchful eye of President Lyndon Baines Johnson. The act outlaws discrimination in public accommodations as well as jobs.
September 1964	The Austin Independent School District (AISD) begins integrating teachers in a "crossover plan."
August 6, 1965	President Johnson signs the Voting Rights Act.
_____1967	Volma Overton decides to run for a place on the Austin City Council, then changes his mind when he finds it conflicts with his employment.
September 1968	The Austin City Council approves an ordinance creating a Human Relations Commission, which Overton sees as little more than an advisory board.
December 1968	The Austin branch NAACP presents the DeWitty Award to Volma Overton.

1969	The Department of Health, Education, and Welfare approves the NAACP's charter for a credit union.
August 7, 1970	Lawsuit filed by U.S. Justice Department after administrative hearing by the department of HEW finds AISD out of compliance with Civil Rights Act of 1964.
August 25, 1971	A motion to intervene in the Austin ISD School Board's desegregation suit is granted to DeDra Estell Overton.
September 4, 1970	Judge Jack Roberts signs desegregation order closing Anderson High School, Kealing Junior High School, and St. Johns Elementary School.
December 14, 1970	AISD Board adopts desegregation resolution policy. Includes provisions that staff members should be assigned so that the racial composition of the staff does not indicate that a school is intended for one racial group.
December 16, 1970	Conference held for about 500 "crossover teachers" at Reagan High School cafeteria. Produces reports dealing with differences in discipline, administrative requirements, varied facilities and supplies, ethnic adjustments, language barriers, and lack of parental involvement.
April 30, 1971	Supreme Court issues unanimous ruling in *Swan v. Charlotte* in Mecklenburg, North Carolina. Ruling says busing is a legal, viable tool to use in desegregating school districts.
June 14, 1971	Six-day AISD desegregation trial begins in Judge Jack Roberts' court.
June 28, 1971	Judge Roberts rules in Austin desegregation

case that no discrimination against Mexican Americans in Austin schools occurred due to school board policy.

July 19, 1971	Judge Jack Roberts orders AISD's desegregation plan be implemented. He also strongly criticizes HEW, saying cross-town busing such as in the plan submitted by HEW is unreasonable.
January 1972	Volma Overton, president of the Austin branch NAACP, writes letter to HEW office of Civil Rights in Dallas requesting an investigation into student fighting at Reagan High School.
May 1, 1972	Strong rumors of student riots result in little activity except some minor altercations.
August 1, 1972	Austin branch NAACP submits its own plan developed by Dr. John A. Finger, Jr., of Rhode Island.
August 2, 1972	Ruling from the Fifth Circuit Court of Appeals in New Orleans overturns U.S. District Judge Jack Roberts' original decision which held that no discrimination against Mexican Americans exists in Austin. The ruling orders a new hearing.
August 1, 1973	Judge Jack Roberts issues court order for desegregation of Austin schools, mandating eight sixth-grade centers.
August 16, 1973	Judge Jack Roberts' school desegregation ruling is appealed a second time by the Justice Department, the NAACP, and MALDEF. The Fifth U.S. Circuit Court of Appeals in New Orleans is scheduled to hear the case for the second time.
May 13, 1976	U.S. Fifth Circuit Court of Appeals hands down order in AISD desegregation case, charging

Judge Roberts with overseeing implementation. Also orders Kealing Junior High School reopened.

May 19, 1976
Austin School Board trustees vote 4-3 to file an appeal to the Fifth Circuit Court of Appeals decision in the desegregation case.

December 6, 1976
Supreme Court overturns lower court decision of May 13, 1976, in Austin desegregation case that would have required massive busing of forty percent of AISD students.

November 21, 1977
U.S. Fifth Circuit Court of Appeals rules that the Austin Independent School District is guilty of intentionally segregating Mexican-American students. Judge Minor Wisdom issues a twenty-five-page opinion, sending the case back to U.S. District Judge Jack Roberts for rehearing.

_____1977
Volma Overton retires from the army reserve at the rank of lieutenant colonel.

June 22, 1979
Volma Overton is appointed postmaster at Cedar Creek, Texas.

July 2, 1979
Supreme Court denies Austin School Board's appeal for a hearing in its nine-year-old deseg-regation suit. The court upholds the lower court ruling that the Austin School Board intentionally discriminated against Mexican Americans.

January 3, 1980
Judge Roberts gives final approval to the con-sent decree.

_____1983
Volma Overton tells NAACP members that he will not run for another term as president.

Do not take the path where the trail leads, but go instead where there is no path and leave a trail.

Author Unknown

INTRODUCTION

I often noticed him sitting quietly in meetings or talking in low tones with the myriad of people who were drawn to the National Association for the Advancement of Colored People (NAACP). Just about everyone knew Volma Overton, and I was to find out later that he was considered something of an institution in Austin.

One day during a Black history program, he spied me madly scribbling notes in shorthand. He leaned over my shoulder and whispered "If you can do that, the branch can use you."

I smiled. He seemed like such a nice, quiet-natured gentleman. But when I started talking to people about Mr. Overton, I found out that he can be gentle as well as extremely reserved. I also found that he had a persistence in the face of adversity that was almost unequalled.

I later started doing volunteer work for the Austin branch NAACP, and in the process got to know about Mr. Overton and the many things he has done for the Black community in Austin. This was just about the time I became serious about becoming a writer.

I had written a few articles for one of the Black weeklies in East Austin, assignments for which I felt I was grossly underpaid. But I was to learn quickly that this is the fate of beginning writers.

One day as Mr. Overton and I sat talking, it suddenly struck me that here was living, breathing history, and no one had written down a word of his biography. I hazarded to broach the subject with him, casually asking him if he intended to begin on his autobiography soon. No, he said, although he had thought about it. He was too busy improving his golf game and learning ballroom dancing. He also volunteered the lion's share of his day to the NAACP Credit Union (now the East Austin Community Federal Credit Union).

"Why don't you let me do it?" I asked flatly.

He looked at me and considered what I said for a time, never changing his expression. I was to find out later that he never jumped into any kind of a decision quickly. He weighed the factors carefully, and would give you an answer by and by.

But he finally agreed, and I happily set out to interview dozens of people who had known him most of his life. In the process, I found that biography is one of the most difficult kinds of writing there is. Over the next five-year period, I interviewed what seemed like hundreds of his friends and acquaintances, combed the Austin History Center for clippings on the Civil Rights Movement, and read dozens of books.

The result of my research appears in this book.

Preserving our living, breathing history has become a goal for me. Mr. Overton played a unique part in Austin's history and changed the course of the city's future with his persistence and determination for equality for all people.

Shedding light on our past is the goal of this book.

—CAROLYN L. JONES

1

Council Shutdown

The man, his wife, and their youngest daughter, a plump three-year-old, were about to walk out of the front door of their home that morning when he remembered that he needed something to read. He retraced his path across the living room, his footsteps silent against the tufted carpet and the stillness of the early morning. It was a few minutes past eight.

The man was cocoa colored and wore the closely cropped haircut popular with Black men during the early sixties. He had to bend his six-foot frame to read the titles of the books on the lower bookshelf. He knew he should be more concerned about selecting a book. But his mind lingered on the meeting the night before, and the coming meeting later that morning.

He ran his fingers over the hard backs of several books, then absently pulled out John Howard Griffin's *Black Like Me*, a slim tome chronicling Griffin's travels with his skin darkened to experience what it was like to be a Black man in the South. The man had begun reading the book several months ago, but had put it aside half finished. He stuffed the book in the pocket of his jacket and joined his family in the car, a two-tone green 1952 Pontiac.

Sunlight poured from a clear sky as he drove down Springdale Road. He absently glanced at the homes that

1

made up Cedar Valley, the subdivision where he purchased a home after returning from World War II. Some forward-thinking entrepreneur had constructed the subdivision in far East Austin after foreseeing the potential for growth in the area and the influx of returning veterans who wanted new homes. Of course, East Austin was predominantly Black. Returning Black veterans, restricted to the east side of the expressway, except for a few neighborhoods in south and west Austin, soon bought up all the homes in Cedar Valley.

At the same time that the young man with the book stuffed in his pocket and his wife and child drove through the streets of Cedar Valley, about twenty other people climbed into automobiles and drove through other East Austin neighborhoods towards downtown.

It was Thursday.

Some of the travellers passed through the McKinley Heights neighborhood where the flower beds of neat A-frame houses and brick homes held the first buds of spring. It was one of the best neighborhoods for Blacks who were financially able to purchase and maintain upscale homes to live.

Others turned into the Rosewood and Salina neighborhoods, where paved avenues gave way to unpaved streets lying in the shadow of rows of tumbling down shotgun houses. The wind blew paper cups, bits of newspaper, and empty motor oil containers along the hard-packed dirt streets.

The Blackland neighborhood lay further north. In several years, its close proximity to The University of Texas campus would make its real estate a prime target for the school's burgeoning growth, much like it had swallowed up Wheatville, once a thriving Black neighborhood in what became the heart of the university's campus.

Some of the travellers passed by Doris Miller Auditorium and Rosewood Park, white Austin's concession to its Black residents. It was tacitly understood that city "fathers" constructed Rosewood Park during the

1930s for the enjoyment of Blacks in East Austin, and to keep their Black brothers out of white Austin's parks.

Others passed the George Washington Carver Library at the corner of Rosewood Avenue and Angelina Street. Until the early 1950s, it was the only library Austin's Black population could use. The city "fathers" opened all the city's libraries to everyone after a reasoned plea before the city council for racial equality by W. Astor Kirk, an instructor at Tillotson College and former president of the Austin branch NAACP.

Some of the travellers drove down San Bernard Street, an area where elegant homes with neatly manicured yards sat behind fancy wrought iron fences. It was the street settled by Austin's Black bourgeois. Black doctors, lawyers, business owners, and a dentist lived along its wide avenues.

Others drove by the red brick classrooms and football stadium of Old Anderson High School, the only high school Black students could attend until the late 1950s.

The jupe joints, small night clubs, and chicken and ribs cafes scattered along "the cuts," the slang name for East 11th Street, lay quiet after a night of heady blues, soul music, and rock and roll. The automobiles that jammed the side streets of "the end," the term denoting East 12th Street, were but a memory. The sweating faces of bass guitar and saxophone players that filled the smoky bars and clubs scattered along both streets were gone like the darkness before the sunlight.

Music lovers journeyed to the east side to hear the bands that were part of the lifeblood of East Austin. Some of those bands brought white faces across the interstate to the IL Club, once called Charlie's Playhouse, the premiere entertainment spot on "the cuts."

As the neighborhoods of East Austin gave way to the wide avenues of Interstate Highway 35, the facades of buildings took on the conservative look of banks, office buildings, retail stores, and other business establishments. The flowing greenery of acres and acres of parks, coupled with neatly maintained houses and apartment buildings, marked it as a better area of town, the area where custom and practice dictated that Blacks could not buy homes, rent apartments, or use the public parks.

The group didn't want to attract attention to themselves as they parked their cars near Congress Avenue and along West Eighth and Colorado streets in downtown Austin.

Some found parking places just across Eighth Street near the city government building that was home of the regular Thursday meetings of the Austin City Council. Others parked along Congress Avenue, the main downtown thoroughfare where city buses picked up and discharged passengers in the shadow of the Texas state capitol. Some of the group walked past the Piccadilly Cafeteria, the landmark eating establishment in downtown Austin where aged patrons sat in a reception area fronted by a large picture window. Passers-by often glanced idly at the white customers served on a cafeteria serving line by a predominantly Black staff who could do everything to keep the cafeteria one of the best in the city. But they could not sit down in its large dining room and have a meal.

Others passed the brick facade of White's Pharmacy, the drugstore that stuck by its Jim Crow segregation practices, even in the face of student lunch counter sit-in demonstrations. The pharmacy went so far as to take the tops off its bar stools so Blacks could not take a seat.

They walked in the shadow of the staid banks that often turned down applications for loans submitted by Black customers, a continuation of a practice begun in Jim Crow-era Austin. These same banks often "redlined" customers, a practice wherein residents of low income areas, often having large concentrations of minorities, were not granted loans for revitalization. It would be another five years before Blacks would unite under the NAACP and form their own credit union, the first in East Austin.

Further up Congress Avenue stood two movie theaters, the Paramount and the State. Both refused service to Black customers. But if Blacks walked further up Congress Avenue and turned east on Sixth Street, they found the Ritz Theater, where they were welcomed to come in and watch a movie, but only from the confines of the upstairs balcony. White patrons sat downstairs.

They passed Nixon Clay Business College, an institution that did not admit Blacks as a matter of course until the Civil Rights Act of 1964 became law. Individuals aspiring to federal employment descended on the small business college to take the civil service test in such numbers that observant newspaper reporters often phoned civil rights leaders to see if there was a protest going on that they didn't know about.

The members of the group, about twenty people in all, walked unobtrusively into the front door of the municipal building and down the hallway to the chambers of the Austin City Council.

There was B. T. Bonner, a tall, slender young man who had been a part of the Civil Rights Movement since its early beginnings. He was probably the most outspoken member of the group. He would chain himself to a chair in city council chambers and later stage a sit-in in Governor John Connally's reception room.

Wesley Sims, a local minister, was among the group, as well as Mary Wadley, an attractive housewife of about forty who served as vice president. Faye Willis, a pert, pretty woman, and staunch supporter and veteran fighter for equal rights, was there, along with Mrs. Hattie Pinkston, an older woman who dropped her work for the day to support the cause. J. Phillip Crawford, a Black attorney who frequently did legal work for the organization, also came along. Claude Allen was the only Anglo in the group, and worked as an instructor at Huston-Tillotson College in East Austin.

As the days passed, others would also join the group. Arthur B. DeWitty and Mrs. U. V. Christian, veteran civil rights activists from the 1940s, would become part of the audience. Bertha Means, a school teacher who also worked with the local branch, listened on her car radio as she drove out of town.

Three members of the group remained outside the building with protest signs reading "NAACP—Rights, Remedy, Relief in Austin."

Council chambers were already filled when they arrived for the 10:00 A.M. session. The group's leader, the young man with the book in his pocket, exchanged pleasantries with three members of his church who were already seated in the audience. When council members finally took their seats and began the day's session, the group waited for the agenda item on utility refunds for subdivision contractors to be called for discussion.

The group's leader was primarily concerned that everyone be seated when the meeting began. He didn't want council members to have any argument about the members of the group speaking.

When the item was called, he asked for the floor.

Before the practice was changed, the person who gained the floor to address the city council held sway until he decided to yield to someone else. Bored council members sat back in their chairs listening to the man who billed himself as president of the Austin branch of the National Association for the Advancement of Colored People, or simply the NAACP.

They were familiar with the young man by now. When strong March winds blew children's kites high into the treetops, he had begun addressing council sessions on behalf of creating a Human Relations Commission. Tired of the ingrained discrimination in hiring and firing, and being refused service at hotels, restaurants, and movie theaters, the NAACP felt a city ordinance outlawing these practices would bring them to an end. The group also wanted the ordinance to assess a monetary penalty for those who refused to comply.

Although council members were familiar with the subtle and full-blown discrimination still practiced in the capital of the state of Texas, they were also aware of the strong streak of conservatism that ran through the city. Many agreed privately that there was a need for a city ordinance that would provide the authority of law to hear complaints of discrimination. But some felt that the young man's remedy simply went too far.

Councilwoman Emma Long felt his proposed ordinance assessing a penalty of $200 for those businesses found in violation of anti-discrimination laws was harsh and arbitrary. Other council members felt the group should wait for passage of the Civil Rights Act of 1964, the most far reaching civil rights law ever proposed. It was currently being debated in a divided Congress under the watchful eye of President Lyndon Baines Johnson, a native of the Texas Hill Country. Even a petition of 3,000 signatures collected by the Austin City Council's Special Committee on Human Relations urging the council to set up a nine-member Commission on Human Relations failed to sway council members. The measure was tabled.

But the young man knew that the real crux of the matter lay in the powerlessness of the city's minority population to make changes in the way they were governed. Because of the ingrained discrimination that had existed for so many years, Blacks in Austin were boxed into their own neighborhoods with their own schools and businesses. Consequently, they had no real power. But the community also lacked the cohesiveness that might have garnered them some political clout. They were more often than not divided on issues, and so far had not been able to field a successful political candidate.

The local branch NAACP seemed to be a reflection of the political aspirations of the city's Blacks. Prior to the early 1960s, the local branch was basically dormant. Their meetings attracted few members and it had virtually "died on the vine."

The young leader of the Austin branch NAACP took over the organization in 1962. Gradually, the few faithful members turned into a trickle. Many Blacks came to recognize representatives of the organization as East

Austin's spokespeople. However, the more radical student element found the NAACP too passive, and branded them as Uncle Toms. The organization's goal of working within the court system to achieve legal changes throughout the country was much too slow for student protesters, whose motto was "Freedom Now!"

Volma and branch members often discussed the need for a Human Relations Commission. Time and again, individuals seeking work or looking for a place to live walked into the NAACP office on East 12th Street. They told of being turned down for leasing or purchasing homes or apartments, passed over for selection for jobs, not promoted, or the humiliation of seeing other less experienced co-workers promoted ahead of them.

Volma met behind closed doors with the NAACP Board of Directors on several occasions in late March 1964. Board members, seasoned NAACP veterans well schooled in methods used by the organization to achieve legal changes through the courts, often talked long past the 9:00 P.M. closing time of the Howson Community Center on Angelina Street in East Austin. Sometimes the group stood talking under starry skies until someone finally noticed the lateness of the hour.

As April rolled around and the council took no further action, the group was poised for action.

They held a clandestine meeting at Lott Lumber Company, a family-owned business located near East Seventh Street and Webberville Road in East Austin. About twenty protesters and their families, along with Attorney J. Phillip Crawford, the law partner of Virgil Lott, filled the small office. They went over strategy and rehearsed their speeches for the city council chambers the next day.

In city council chambers, Volma asked for and was given permission to address the city council at about 10:30 A.M. He reached into his pocket for the book.

Council members who had been skeptical of the young man's threats to disrupt the meeting began to take notice.

Something in the young man's tone sounded odd. Two or three of the council members leaned forward in their chairs. Protest groups of all kinds regularly descended on council chambers to remind bored city fathers of their shortcomings. They were used to it. But this young man was different. It sounded like he was reading. He was. Volma Overton, president of the Austin branch NAACP, stood before a crowded city council chamber and read from *Black Like Me*. And he steadfastly refused to yield the floor to anyone except members of his group for the next two weeks.

When it became apparent to council members that some sort of protest was going on, Mayor Lester Palmer began the first of two previously scheduled public hearings. Speaking in low tones, council members passed an ordinance.

At 11:00 A.M. Volma again refused to yield the floor, and a local attorney who had come to council chambers for a hearing on zoning said he would yield the floor.

"Let's have order in this room so we can hear Mr. Overton," the mayor said to a room that was described by the Austin daily as "quiet and orderly for the most part."

From time to time, Volma paused in his reading to direct the council's attention to some miscarriage of justice. He said that city tax money was being spent on authorization of a refund contract for water and sewer mains in University Hills, a subdivision in northeast Austin which he said excluded Negroes. Mayor Palmer responded that subdividers had put up the money, not the city.

Later Volma paused to say "the city fathers should quit giving aid and comfort to those who practice segregation."

In the meantime, Austin Police Chief Bob Miles had a contingent of officers on standby at the police station on East Seventh Street. "I hope the only thing I have to do with these officers today is to pay them overtime," Miles told the press.

The speak-in continued for the remainder of the day, a

total of eleven hours. Volma's reading was followed by Claude Allen, a white English professor at Huston-Tillotson College, who read from *Nobody Knows My Name*.

Later Thursday afternoon, over 200 young people joined folk singer Joan Baez as she sang protest songs and strummed her guitar on the sidewalk in front of city hall.

Speaking to the city council, Allen asked members to visit East Austin to see first hand the "ravages of poverty."[1]

Taking up the cause again the next day, Allen told the news media that the NAACP was willing to get together with the council to work out details of a compromise ordinance to ban discrimination. He said the NAACP would be willing to accept a compromise between a nonpolitical agency suggested by the city attorney, and a model ordinance called the El Paso Ordinance.

The city attorney suggested that the city of Austin contract with an outside agency to "receive, investigate and process specific charges of racial discrimination."[2] The suggestion included a five-member commission to oversee hearings. However, the commission would not have authority to set fines or determine remedies. It also would not have subpoena powers. Allen suggested cases involving compromise be given to corporation court for dispensation if a penalty was called for.

On the second day, Allen spoke for thirteen hours. He then turned the podium over to Rev. Wesley Sims, a local Black minister who put a different spin on the world's problems.

Speaking for almost two hours, Reverend Sims said the nation's problems stemmed from man not having learned how to love.

The next day, Wednesday, April 8, 1964, the newspaper blared the headline "Mayor in Hospital Near Collapse." The mayor's wife reported that "her husband returned home from a marathon civil rights filibuster at City Hall 'exhausted and near collapse.'"[3] The NAACP's speak-in evidently prevented the mayor, who suffered from a heart condition, from getting his daily several hours of rest.

The mayor remained in the hospital for several days while the speak-in and council members plodded along, each with their respective business.

The council and civil rights protesters recessed Wednesday while council member Louis Shanks met with the Junior Chamber of Commerce to hear the group's proposal for a citywide referendum on the proposed discrimination ordinance.

The daily newspaper said Councilman Shanks stated he found it hard to believe that the filibusterers represented the real Negro structure of the community, and suggested the protest might become a rallying point for "non-militant, moderate Austin Negroes" to express their feelings.

The next day, Thursday, found the remaining council members stymied by the NAACP's tactics. When Reverend Sims again refused to yield the floor—this time to Councilwoman Long who wanted to place a motion on the floor that the council recess until Mayor Palmer returned from the hospital—the entire council walked out en masse.

Reverend Sims then sat down in the mayor's chair to the voice of an NAACP backer declaring him "mayor pro tem of the city of Austin." Perturbed, Councilman Shanks said "You get up there by ballots, not bullets. If they don't like the way we run this council, they ought to turn us out at the polls. Not this sort of thing."[4]

"This City Council has worked itself to the point of exhaustion over this situation," Councilman LaRue said. "We could not improve anything by sitting any longer. We could only impair."

Councilman Shanks said, "If they say we have not listened to them, that is the understatement of the century. We're at our wits end."

However, the NAACP saw the situation differently. Veteran NAACP member Arthur DeWitty told reporters for the Austin daily, "Mayor Palmer told us he would not adjourn until he had heard all we had to say." He felt that the council was not officially adjourned.

Volma refused to tell members of the press the group's future plans. He simply said they would remain at city council "all day long."

Volma cut into Reverend Sims' reading of "What's Right with Race Relations" long enough to say, "Since the mayor is ill and the mayor pro tem and other council members have deserted their duties, Rev. Wesley Sims will take on himself to be the mayor pro tem of Austin, so the city won't be void of government at this time."

Before recessing, Volma had Reverend Sims say a prayer. Reverend Sims bowed his head and asked for forgiveness for "this sinful city," and promised to pray for the "irresponsible city council." He asked that "their eyes and minds be opened to understanding."[5]

The next day, as Mayor Pro Tem Travis LaRue urged a period of calm, Volma issued the following statement to the press:

> On Thursday, April 9, the City Council walked out of chambers with a citizen on the floor in protest of a refund contract to a private developer for the continuation of a segregation policy in regard to houses in a certain subdivision.
>
> It is with sincere regret that other matters entered into this protest. But in as much as they did, the City Council and the City of Austin is hereby put on notice that legal proceedings will be instituted in any attempt to circumvent action, if any is taken by the City Council in a private kangaroo session to pass on any business included on their agenda that included this business.
>
> The matter of an ordinance forbidding racial discrimination with a penal ordinance will still not be compromised regardless of the position taken on this refund contract.[6]

Mayor Pro Tem LaRue responded, "The City Council will not hold any secret sessions. We will not resort to this sort of thing, and we will meet openly in City Hall."

In the meantime, members of the Junior Chamber of Commerce and others banded together to form a 220-man volunteer organization. The group circulated 500 petitions asking the city council to call a referendum on the proposed ordinance.

Although opposed to any ordinance that would prohibit discrimination by owners and operators of hotels, motels, restaurants and theaters which serve the public, the Jaycees said "these legal steps were necessary to give the council the right to call a referendum on what the majority of Austin citizens want."

But an editorial in *The Daily Texan* took issue with the Jaycees stance. "We would rather see them [the Jaycees] spending more time advertising that their particular businesses are open to persons of all flavors than to take up time and effort fighting something that won't be passed anyway," the editorial stated.

While Mayor Palmer still languished in the hospital with no sign of improvement, three members of the city council, LaRue, White, and Long, vowed to meet and conduct the city's business. They did just that. However, business was conducted behind a line of fourteen uniformed Austin policemen while three demonstrators were ejected from chambers.

Booker T. Bonner, Rev. Wesley Sims, and UT graduate student Brad Blanton were bodily ejected from the council meeting when Bonner attempted to continue the filibuster while council members tried to conduct city business.

City hall chambers were filled to capacity with a variety of onlookers, some having business before the council, and others who did not.

The following day, Volma issued a statement: "It's going to be a long, hot summer with all kinds of demonstrations. We certainly will be back."[7]

Then Volma hinted at the possibility of something that neither he nor the NAACP espoused. He told reporters for the Austin daily that he approved of tactics which inconvenienced those making decisions, tactics such as stall-ins, sit-ins, and speak-ins. But until the council took some action on an ordinance, "the potential for violence is ever present."

It seemed as if everyone had an opinion on the "read-in." *The Daily Texan*, student newspaper of The University of Texas at Austin, released a lead editorial condemning the NAACP: "We have time and again espoused the need for Negro rights . . . (but) we have come to the conclusion that those militant Negroes who appear at City Hall are not representative . . . We are beginning to think their principal interest is in headlines, and for this reason they refuse to compromise."[8]

The following Sunday saw a mixed crowd of over 150 people descend on Givens Park in East Austin for a Freedom Rally sponsored by the Austin branch NAACP. Speakers from in and around Austin pressed for action from the city council on creating a Human Relations Commission. They said there was a possibility that demonstrations would begin all over again at the next council session on Thursday.[9]

The Austin branch NAACP wanted to get every facet of the community involved in integration. Since the Black church was the spiritual leader of the Black community, the branch invited ten area ministers to speak at the Freedom Forum Rally in Givens Park.

*   *   *

Mayor Lester Palmer returned to city hall the following Tuesday, after having spent eleven days recuperating from his much publicized exhaustion. Palmer was eager to get on with the business of the city since no council sessions had been held for the preceding two weeks. He expressed a desire to "investigate a proposal made by one of the NAACP spokesmen indicating a possible solution." That proposal was for a compromise between the city's plan and the El Paso Plan espoused by Claude Allen and the NAACP.[10]

The following week, as Mayor Palmer agreed to a meeting with Volma and a committee of the NAACP, twenty-five students held a sit-in at Kinsolving Dormitory on The University of Texas campus. The students protested the university's policy of segregation in the dormitories. The sit-in was called "impromptu" by the city's daily and came after a forum on the West Mall of the campus. Some demonstrators promised to return.[11]

The Monday night meeting between Volma, his committee, and four members of the city council held some hope for both groups. Volma told the Austin daily, "After having met with four members of the city council, the NAACP feels there are some areas of agreement."

However, the four city council members, Travis LaRue, Louis Shanks, Mayor Lester Palmer, and Mrs. Emma Long, all favored a voluntary approach to end discrimination. LaRue and Shanks, along with Councilman Ben White, who did not attend the meeting, stated they would never vote for the penal ordinance pushed by the NAACP.

Councilman Ben White, who represented South Austin, staunchly refused to attend meetings with the NAACP. His comments summarized the feelings of many business owners as well as ordinary citizens towards proposed methods designed to end discrimination:

> I am opposed to all ordinances, especially ordinances with penal clauses. A penal ordinance would infringe on the rights of private businesses and private citizens. I have a responsibility to 200,000 citizens in this town, not a handful of demonstrators. Had these demonstrations not taken place, Austin would have been fully integrated in six months. We were already 90 percent integrated.
>
> I asked these people to wait until Congress had acted, but they refused.
>
> I am not going to any meeting.[12]

City attorney Doren Eskew proposed a plan that the

city contract with an outside agency to "review, investigate and process specific charges of investigation."[13]

Mayor Palmer proposed the Community Council for the job, drawing the ire of Councilwoman Emma Long. She shot back, "If the City Council deals with the Community Council on this I will resign. This is our obligation and responsibility." Long, along with Mayor Palmer, suggested that a special commission be set up.

Volma didn't want to be hasty in passing judgment on either suggestion: "We are not saying that this is totally acceptable or that we will go home and rest and be easy. We are going to study this proposal. Perhaps we will be back. We hope to continue to communicate."

Concerning the proposal by the city attorney, Volma said, "In the opinion of the committee, [it] needs improving upon. There are still some vital areas that must be resolved to protect the dignity of the Negro in Austin . . . it is our express hope that the City Council will correct these iniquities so that an acceptable proposal will emerge."[14]

Early May brought news that President Lyndon Johnson was scheduled to attend graduation exercises at The University of Texas at Austin. The news media went into action when remarks by Rev. Wesley Sims indicated the NAACP planned to picket the president during his visit.

"We have never had any intention of picketing the President," Volma told the press, adding that he wanted to make it "really clear" that earlier reports that the president would be picketed in Austin were wrong.[15]

While the university completed preparations for President Johnson to speak at commencement exercises, they also made progress towards alleviating the lily-white image that had been a part of its makeup since time immemorial.

Dr. Ervin Perry, a Black civil engineer, was hired by UT as an assistant professor. He became what the *Austin Statesman* termed "the first Negro to be appointed to the faculty of the University, [and] is also the first Negro to be appointed to professorial status in any major university in the South."[16]

The Austin branch NAACP and Austin Blacks had traditionally held The University of Texas in very low esteem. They remembered Heman Sweatt's struggle to gain admission to UT's law school during the 1950s. However, times were changing and UT officials probably saw the writing on the wall. In May 1964 the UT Board of Regents voted to eradicate racial barriers in campus housing.

Volma was to have many dealings with UT officials before full integration became a policy at the school. But for now, the prospect of implementing a Human Relations Commission occupied the full attention of the Austin branch.

By the May 11th council meeting, four members of the city council had agreed on establishing a Human Relations Commission which would deal with problems relating to "the broad field of civil rights" on a voluntary basis. The council would appoint the seven members of the commission as well as the chairman. The plan did not contain a penal clause. Only voluntary complaints would be heard by the commission, which had authority to use mediation, conciliation, and persuasion to arrive at solutions.[17]

Two proposals by Councilwoman Long went down in defeat. She proposed that the commission be given a $10,000 budget to obtain the aid of a trained sociologist. Long also wanted to give the commission authority to appoint "sub-committees chosen from the community at large to deal with other problems, such as housing welfare, youth and job opportunities."[18]

Councilman Ben White still "refused to attend any meetings dealing with civil rights." He felt the establishment of a Human Relations Commission was the "first step towards a strong ordinance on public accommodations."

"I am not opposed to this actual commission, and I hope that it works, because it takes the voluntary approach," White said. "I believe in equal rights for everybody. But I don't believe I have the right to make everybody else believe the way I do. I don't believe I have the right to make somebody else operate his private life and business, and to hire and fire the way somebody else happens to want him to."[19]

The NAACP considered the establishment of the Human Relations Commission a feather in its cap. But city council members began to drag their feet again when the time came to make appointments to the commission. Two weeks had elapsed since the council approved a Human Relations Commission.

In a press release, Volma said: "The NAACP feels that far too much time has elapsed since the passage of the so-called ordinance and the appointment of a commission to implement it. Inaction by the council seems to indicate stalling after an indication of good faith."[20]

Perhaps prodded by public criticism, the city council appointed seven members to the Human Relations Commission, six of whom immediately resigned. Attorney Virgil Lott, the first Black graduate of The University of Texas at Austin School of Law, was the sole appointee who remained on the commission. The excuse given for the resignations was that someone questioned the usefulness and balance of the organization.[21]

The resignations played right into the hands of Mayor Palmer, who felt that in light of the U.S. Senate's vote to invoke closure on the pending civil rights bill, the city council would return to executive session at once to start naming new members to the Human Relations Commission. But he warned that "it may well take us several weeks to name the six new members to the commission."[22]

On Wednesday night, June 10, 1964, over thirty Black civil rights demonstrators with the NAACP marched on city hall to encourage the city council to begin naming new members of the Human Relations Commission immediately.

Two days later, nine picketers carrying signs entered council chambers during the morning session. Warneta Overton, Volma's wife, was one of the picketers. Mayor Palmer at first ignored the signs, but later asked that they be lowered so that all persons in the council chamber could see.

However, a perturbed Councilman Shanks questioned why the signs had to be allowed at all. Minutes later, uniformed police officers appeared. When the demonstrators did not voluntarily hand over their signs as requested by officers, they were forcibly "yanked" away. Officers also tore a sign from the hands of Booker T. Bonner.

The Austin daily described the demonstrators as silent during the council session, "except for one brief hysterical outburst from Mrs. Warneta Overton . . . who burst into tears and repeated over and over 'Oh no, oh no.'"[23]

After the signs were removed, the group of demonstrators sat and kneeled with their backs to the council as if they were praying. Councilman Shanks tried to get other council members to make the demonstrators sit down or leave. But he could not get any support.

"I'm heading back to the store," Councilman Shanks, owner of a furniture store, said as he walked out of council chambers. "I won't sit out there with that disturbance. It is an affront to the dignity of the council. I resent City Council chambers being made a mockery of."

While the Austin City Council remained in limbo concerning the appointment of members to a viable Human Relations Commission with the power to hear violations of civil rights, the most far reaching civil rights bill ever to reach Congress moved closer to passage, and amendments proposed by southern senators met defeat.

As the national scene readied for a change in civil rights of drastic proportions, locals in Austin were also quietly going about changing racial practices which had existed for years.

Officials at The University of Texas at Austin announced that "Negro students are living for the first time in some previously all-white dormitories." The announcement came in the wake of a May 18, 1964, decision by the UT Board of Regents "immediately after a suit was dropped in federal court by the attorney of three former Negro students. They were seeking to live in then-segregated dormitories."[24]

The Austin daily reported that during the summer session at The University of Texas at Austin thirteen Blacks lived in Kinsolving Dormitory, two in Simkins, one in Moore-Hill, six in San Jacinto and fourteen in Brackenridge. However, none of the students living in the dormitories had roommates of another ethnic group. "They [Negroes] have not asked for it and whites have not asked for them," F. C. McConnell, director of food and housing, said.

Civil rights clearly had a ways to go, as Volma and supporters of a Human Relations Commission for Austin were discovering anew each day.

Thursday, June 18, 1964, saw Volma, Rev. Wesley Sims, and a group of young people descend on city council chambers. Carrying balloons with the slogan "Freedom Now," the demonstrators filled the front rows before releasing the white balloons. As the balloons nestled against the ceiling, members of the city council continued with their agenda.

Reverend Sims rose to his feet. "I would like to request all in this room who are interested in human dignity to kneel and pray," Sims said. The group of Blacks, sixteen in all, kneeled and began to pray.[25]

While the Austin Police Department's motorcycle squad waited downstairs in the basement, the council continued its agenda until recess.

Not to be deterred, Volma told reporters that the NAACP still wanted a strong anti-discrimination ordinance with a penal code to cover public accommodations, housing, and job opportunites. Until the ordinance was passed, Volma promised that the NAACP would "demonstrate, demonstrate, demonstrate!"[26]

Volma refused to rely on the hope that the national civil rights bill would contain provisions that would cover all the pertinent issues on the local level. He strongly held out for a Human Relations Commission because "the federal civil rights bill does not cover all of the Negroes' demands on a local level."[27]

Just two days later, violence against civil rights workers again surfaced on the national front. Three young civil rights workers, Michael Schwerner and Andrew Goodman, whites from New York City, and James Chaney, a Black from Meridian, Mississippi, were slain. They had been shot and Chaney brutally beaten. Their bodies were found August 4, 1964, in a narrow grave.

The country was saddened that such an atrocity could happen in a country that prided itself on being founded on the ideals of democracy.

*   *   *

On July 2, 1964, President Lyndon Johnson made history. He signed the most far-reaching civil rights act into law that the country had ever witnessed. The Civil Rights Act of 1964 contained provisions guaranteeing Blacks the right to vote and access to public accommodations, such as hotels, motels, restaurants, movie theaters, and places of amusement. It also authorized the federal government to sue to desegregate public facilities and schools, extended the life of the Civil Rights Commission and gave it new powers, and provided for an end to federally funded programs found to be administered discriminatorily.

The law also established a community relations service section of the Justice Department to help in solving civil rights problems. It required the Census Bureau to gather voting statistics by race and authorized the Justice Department to enter into pending civil rights cases.

Blacks nationwide hailed the Civil Rights Act of 1964 as a second Emancipation Proclamation. Many knew that had it not been for the political acumen of President Lyndon Johnson, the law would have never become a reality.

But politically, Johnson paid dearly for his part in the bill's passage. He felt he lost the South in the effort. "Well, I think I've just delivered the South to the

Republican Party," President Johnson told Texas Congressman Jake Pickle.[28]

The passage of the Civil Rights Act of 1964 also had negative repercussions all the way to Austin, Texas. Volma was unable to get enough council members interested in appointing new members to the Human Relations Commission. The uncertainty surrounding enforcement of the Civil Rights Act of 1964, and the resulting white backlash, were prime reasons for council members' reticence. It would be another three years before the issue would resurface at council meetings and the NAACP would push for implementation.

But Volma felt the positives far outweighed the negatives of the bill. Three months after he led a group of fifteen NAACP members to Austin City Council chambers, the future seemed brighter. As he drove through the East Austin neighborhoods of McKinley Heights, Rosewood, Salina, Blackland, and St. Bernard Street, he realized that the dream that Black Austinites could become first class citizens—living where they wanted with full access to hotels, restaurants, and movie theaters as well as equal opportunity in the job market—was more than just a dream. It was a reality.

Each time Volma glanced at his copy of *Black Like Me* on the bookshelf in the family's living room, it reminded him of what was possible in a world of impossibles.

In the meantime, Volma knew that the new civil rights law was only as good as its enforcement. Consequently, he and other members of the branch began making plans to visit all the restaurants, movie theaters, and other public places that refused to serve Blacks.

There were other changes, too. New members flocked to the Austin branch NAACP's monthly meetings. Others who did not come to the meetings were with the group in spirit. And everyone wanted to know more about Volma Overton, the dynamic young man who took over leadership of the Austin branch NAACP and riveted the attention of Austinites on local civil rights issues.

2

EARLY LIFE

The waning days of the summer of 1924 found the little wood-frame house silent and still beneath the early morning mist. Sitting amid a sea of cornfields, cotton-fields, and scattered farmhouses, the small house held the warmth of the family that lived within.

Inside the thin walls of the home that Nicholas Overton, a Black farmer, built with his own hands, a young white doctor's footsteps fell silently against the wooden floor.

Many times, Doc Williamson left his office in the small central Texas whistlestop of Mendoza and drove the five miles to the neighboring community of Maha. Rounding the sharp curve at Maha Loop, he turned south on Eilers Road, his small truck belching and groaning as he shifted gears and turned down the rutted road that led to Nicholas Overton's farm.

Once each week, he left large bundles of laundry that Eliza Overton, Nicholas' wife, washed with her own hands and pressed with the heavy flat iron. Her delicate hands grasped the heavy metal iron and lay it above the flames of the family's large black cookstove. When it was hot to the touch, she lay the heated surface over the fabric of the doctor's shirts and pants. Steam rose from the garment, shrouding Eliza's soft brown skin and touching the thick black tresses on her head.

But today, September 26, 1924, Doc Williamson

wrinkled his forehead, glanced at his watch for the twentieth time, and cast his tired eyes down at the delicate form of the Black woman lying prostrate on the rumpled bed beneath sweat-dampened sheets.

Eliza Edmondson Overton's body lay bathed in the kind of heavy sweat peculiar to women in childbirth. Her face was contorted with the painful contractions that began deep within her swollen belly.

Three times Doc Williamson had driven his little pickup down the rutted road to Nicholas Overton's farm to coax new life from Eliza's slender frame.

Three healthy children of shirttail size, Artie Hazel, Velve, and Sherman, slept in the near bedroom, oblivious to their mother's pain and the sounds of childbirth. Tonight, after Doc Williamson had walked a trail in the floor, and when Eliza's hard contractions reached a regularity that bespoke of a quick birth, a newborn baby boy opened his eyes to the light of day. The baby's cries, delicate at first, reached a crescendo, telling the doctor that his lungs were good and that he was a strong, healthy baby.

As the doctor reached for his bag and turned to leave the Overton farm, Eliza slept and the newborn baby sucked his thumb.

Nicholas and Eliza named their baby boy Volma Robert Overton.

His birth would be followed by the births of Edmondson, Nicholas, Lydia, Roscoe, and Euela. Never to see the inside of a hospital, Eliza Overton would sometimes be attended by one or a series of midwives. Susie Thompson, Mary Patton, Effie Burse, Amy Wilson, and a midwife everyone called "Aunt Callie" came to help the expectant mother.

They allowed no one in the birthing room. Drawing the curtains tightly against the windows, they did not even allow light to enter the room.

Older children were often perplexed by the mystery of childbirth. They were never allowed in the room. But later, when they heard a tiny little squall, they knew what had happened.

Volma grew into a happy, bouncing baby who played on the porch with his brothers and sisters until they were old enough to follow Nicholas Overton into the fields.

Volma found that his father's farm was only a drop in a sea of Overton kin. When they were first married, Nicholas and Eliza lived in a small house on the property.

George and Etta Overton lived in the seven-room house that stood at the corner of Eilers Road and Doyle Road in southeast Travis County. The L-shaped sunporch went around three sides of the house. A swing rocked gently in the shade of the front porch. On hot summer days when guests sitting on the sunporch became too hot, they simply moved to another shady spot and had a drink of cool water from the family's well.

After Nicholas Overton drove the last nail into his own home, he moved his growing family closer to Eilers Road. From there, Volma saw the full expanse of Overton kin. He found he could visit most of his relatives by simply walking or running down the road to their homes.

Volma's Uncle Mileus (called Mike) Overton and his wife Minnie, who was also the teacher at Maha Colored School and the most educated person in the community, lived less than a mile up the road to the west. His Aunt Etta Overton Kavanaugh and her husband Louis lived in the "Big House."

Easter Overton DeWitty, Nicholas' sister, and her husband Frank lived two miles west of the Nicholas Overton farm.

Nicholas' sister Amanda Overton Davidson and her husband Henry, a prominent landowner in St. Mary's Colony and surrounding communities, lived about three miles west.

Nicholas' first cousin, Johnny Patton, and his wife lived two miles east of Nicholas' farm.

Ruby Sneed Prosser, Nicholas' cousin, and her husband George Prosser lived 200 yards west of Nicholas Overton's farm.

Volma spent his early years helping his family work

the blackland soil of the Overton farm. In the springtime, the Overton children chopped the thick rows of cotton. Later in the summer they plucked the fluffy cotton bolls, placing them in cotton sacks made of sturdy ducking that trailed behind them in the cotton rows.

Sometimes they paused at their work to listen to the voice that filled the sun-splashed summer days with longing. While he walked behind Jenny and Big Red, the two broadbacked mules that pulled the hand-drawn plow through the clods of blackland soil, Nicholas Overton's strong baritone voice hung on the stillness of the day. He sang the same songs he would sing again on Sunday at the small Baptist Church for Blacks in St. Mary's Colony, the community just five miles from Maha.

Sunday mornings were special times at the little frame house on Eilers Road. After a breakfast of hot cereal and pork sausage or bacon from the family's smokehouse, they loaded a picnic basket of fried chicken, potato salad, and fresh vegetables, along with a dessert baked by Eliza, into the family automobile and drove to St. Mary's Baptist Church.

Sometimes before the rest of the family was dressed, Volma and his brothers, dressed in their Sunday best, walked out to the highway to catch a ride to church with their Uncle Newey Harden. By the time Nicholas loaded the Overton women and the picnic basket into the car, the boys had left their footprints on the dusty backroad and were playing under the boughs of the cedar trees outside the little church when Nicholas and the rest of the family arrived.

St. Mary's Baptist Church was not only a place of worship, it was also a gathering place for the community's Blacks for miles around. Fiery preachers, on-going revivals, and gospel singing groups filled the little church with worshipers from neighboring communities. The old ones ushered non-members of the church to the "mourners bench," the first pew in the audience.

"They [parents, church members] would come and

get you and put you on that mourners bench if you didn't
go voluntarily," Edward Doyle said of his childhood years
in St. Mary's Colony. "You were going to go. The old folks
saw that you did that."[1]

Most people eventually joined the church, but some
held out for a long time.

"Two old guys sat on that mourners bench for
years," Vivian Prosser Smith remembers. "It like to tore
up the church house when they finally joined."[2]

Nicholas Overton was only one of a myriad of men-
folk—daddies, uncles, cousins—who provided leadership
in the small community. Considered a powerful prayer
leader by people near and far, Nicholas traveled from
community to community for revivals. There was simply
something in the way he bowed his head and called heav-
en that made others stop what they were doing to listen.

Nicholas' son, Roscoe, often travelled to various
churches with him. "I'd hear the men out there talking,
'Man. Nick Overton is getting ready to pray!' They'd be
getting out of their cars going to hear. Even the sinners,
them cats that didn't even go on the inside of the church
. . . they would go to the windows to hear him pray."[3]

Nicholas Overton's other love was fox and raccoon
hunting. Sometimes on moonlit nights after a rain when
the scent of the fox stayed close to the ground, Nicholas
reached for his shotgun and untied his favorite blood-
hound, Joe Louis. Along with his buddies Daniel Ates,
Holland Overton, George Prosser, Jack Landren, Johnny
Patton, Abe Patton, Milton (Boss) Patton, and Simon
Freeman, he went to the woods of St. Mary's Colony,
Cedar Creek or the outskirts of Lockhart after sunset.

Some of the men held the chains of four or five hunting dogs each. Others came empty-handed. They simply
came along to sit and talk under the moonlight, to hear the
hiss of rattlesnakes in the underbrush, to see fireflies light
up the darkness, and to be a part of the little island of easy
banter and gossip about the doings in the community.

As they sat in the woods under a starlit sky, the dogs

trotted into the tree-covered expanse of land that somewhere held a fox or a coon. The dogs sniffed the brush
and undergrowth. Sometimes by the time the dogs picked
up the scent, the fox was over the hill and three or four
pastures away.

During a lull in the conversation, each man strained
to hear the hounds as the sound of their barking grew
fainter and fainter. "That's old Joe Louis leading," someone said between chews of tobacco. The others laughed.
That was no surprise. Joe Louis had a reputation for being
the best hunting dog around those parts.

Joe Louis could pick up the trail of the fox or coon
when other dogs could not. He never chased rabbits. He
was the best dog on the trail. But in the end, it was probably Joe Louis' fame that did him in. One morning when
Volma and the other children went outside to take Joe
Louis a bowl of bones and table scraps, they found his
chain broken and him nowhere to be found. Nicholas
Overton knew someone had stolen his dog. He never saw
Joe Louis again.

* * *

Volma's childhood in Maha and St. Mary's Colony
was filled with all the things that country boys did. The
entire family picked the fat bolls of cotton from rotting
stalks when they were ready. In late summer Eliza and the
children journeyed "down South" to the small communities around Corpus Christi and Robstown to pick cotton.
But unlike other families, Eliza never held the children
out of school until the crops were gathered.

In the early summer, the family celebrated
Juneteenth, the anniversary of Gen. Gordon Granger's
arrival in Galveston in 1865 with the announcement that
the slaves had been emancipated three years before. St.
Mary's Colony held the celebration from the early 1920s
through the early part of the 1940s in Overton's Shady
Grove, a stately expanse of pasture land belonging to the
Overton family. Made up of several acres of pasture land
bordered by stately oak, hackberry, and mesquite trees,

the property was a second home to the area's fishermen. It was part of the original 500 acres of Overton holdings left by the slave girl Emmaline.

Preparations for the Juneteenth celebration began the previous day. Nicholas Overton and the other men of the community prepared the fire for the barbecue and nailed the stands together. While fireflies lit up the night, they barbecued the meat over an open pit covered with chicken wire. Jokes, laughter, and easy banter filled the night as they cleared the land of weeds and brush, while the smoke from barbecued beef, chicken, mutton, and sausage filled the night skies.

Hundreds of people came from miles around to eat free barbecue, watch the softball and baseball games, and see the horse races. "Henry Davidson had race horses and two-wheeled carts," Johnny Mae King remembers of her early years growing up in St. Mary's Colony. "He had trotters and pacers. They would hook them to the two-wheeled carts and race."[4]

But the Blacks who inhabited Maha and St. Mary's Colony found that the prosperity they enjoyed would soon change forever. With the coming of the Depression, the economics of Blacks farmers changed along with the fortune of the rest of the country. Many farmers lost their land along with the only way of life they had ever known.

Volma was just a boy when he and his brothers and sisters were on their way to school. They walked past an uncle's house and found his furniture sitting out on the highway. Nicholas Overton, Jr., said, "I don't remember what year it was. I guess it stayed with me because everybody had to get some of the furniture. We kept some at our house for a long time."[5]

Many Black farmers lost their land in various ways. The spring rains that farmers depended upon for their fields of cotton, corn, maize, sugar cane, and other crops often fell erratically or were slow in coming.

Some farmers became desperate. With large families to feed, they were forced to take measures which were considered drastic for those days. With little formal education and small knowledge of the intricacies of the real estate market, many sold their land for a pittance or practically gave it away for a financial grubstake. The money allowed them to start all over again in the city.

However, Blacks in Maha and St. Mary's Colony did not migrate to the large cities up north at the alarming rate that other southern Blacks moved away to the urban industrial centers that offered jobs and better educational opportunities for their children.[6] Owning their own land made all the difference . . . sometimes.

Other families in Maha and St. Mary's Colony had begun to move away from the rural setting to the state capital at Austin long before the Depression years set in.

They left the land in various ways. Some simply sold their land and moved away. Other Black farmers lost their land through unpaid back taxes. Still others borrowed money against their land, signing documents they could barely read. Some borrowed money to buy stock for their farms. But when the whitefaced cattle and fat sows failed to breed, or died as a result of various diseases and ailments, the farmer could not repay the loan, and the land was lost.

Added to the problem of keeping the land was the passing of the older generation—the old ones whose work ethic and values were much different than their offspring's. When the old ones died out, many of the heirs, young people who often preferred life in the city to country life, sold the property and moved on.

Some settled in the fast growing metropolis of Houston. Others found homes in Austin, just fifteen minutes away.

Then there were those Black farmers who borrowed money from whites whom they knew and trusted. Many Black farmers travelled to Austin to a merchant located just off Congress Avenue who was known to make loans. When the farmers could not repay their debt to the merchant, he took their property. In some instances, they received a mere fraction of what the land was worth. The merchant later resold the land to other whites at a handsome profit. These whites settled down to tilling the soil in what was formerly a colony of Black farmers. In this way the Overton holdings at Maha dwindled down from the original 500 acres. The wonderful pasture called Overton's Shady Grove, where numerous Juneteenth celebrations were held, was lost.

* * *

Thirteen-year-old Volma joined the rest of the seventh graders at Maha Colored School in the annual school closing program. Their voices floated across the sea of Black faces that made up the audience and drifted out of windows propped open with sticks to catch the evening breeze. Young cotton in surrounding fields would not be ready for picking until late summer. But by that time, Volma's life would be changing.

It was May 1937, and he was graduating from the seventh grade at Maha Colored School. When the graduating seventh graders were proudly handed their certificates to the admiring faces of their parents and loved ones, many knew that they would not be continuing school. The small school at Maha went through the seventh grade only. If parents were interested in further schooling for their children, they would have to find a way for them to live in Austin and attend Old L. C. Anderson High School. Austin was just fifteen miles away.

Many of the graduates knew they would not be continuing school. Many would remain on the farm and continue to gather the crops and till the soil. Others would follow their mother and father to their jobs in town where the child might learn to sling hash in a restaurant, iron sheets, cook meals, and care for Miss Ann's children in a private home, or clean and wax the floors in an office building or retail store. But thirteen-year-old Volma knew his future.

In the fall Nicholas and Eliza Overton loaded Volma's belongings into the family's 1928 Chevrolet and headed for Austin. Roscoe Overton remembers that it became tradition in the Overton family that "Everybody went to town to finish school. That was routine. Whoever's relative was in town that we knew, we would be coming to stay with them one way or another."

That first year, Nicholas and Eliza installed Volma in the spare bedroom of Nicholas' cousin, Ethel Harden. The Hardens lived on East 11th Street just across from Holy Cross Catholic Church, a sanctuary erected that same year.

When school started, Volma got his first taste of city living. He joined the stream of Black students headed for Old L. C. Anderson High School. They walked past Father Weber's Holy Cross Church on East 11th Street, north on Angelina Street where the George Washington Carver Library had been built for the town's colored citizens in 1933, and east on Pennsylvania Avenue where the city's only Black high school stood.

He saw shotgun houses standing ghostlike against the early morning sunrise. The houses were built close together, and had become an East Austin trademark.

Emerging from those shotgun houses, many of which contained outdoor privies and no running water, the parents, low skilled and poorly educated, caught the trolley car from East Austin to the private homes and businesses in downtown Austin and beyond.

They sat at the rear of the trolley until they emerged on Congress Avenue or near white neighborhoods such as Enfield and Hyde Park.

Their jobs as housekeepers, janitors, and bootblacks barely paid them enough to feed their families. But if they had a job, they were better off than most of the hordes of unemployed Blacks forced to subsist on handouts from soup kitchens and the good will of friends and family.

For Volma, the excitement of city living was a very different experience. Of course, his classmates and the children in the neighborhood knew he was not a "city boy." They teased him about being from the sticks, something which bothered him at first. But he saw their taunts turn to admiration when he answered questions in the classroom.

His trigonometry teacher, T. C. Calhoun, stood aghast one day as Volma worked through a complicated trig problem and quoted theorems without having reviewed the chapter.

His interests in high school remained purely academic. He did not take up a musical instrument or play sports until his senior year. Even then, when he donned the black and gold football uniform of the Anderson High School Yellow Jackets and sat with the rest of the players on a field that he had only seen from afar, he still was not ready to participate.

Years later, he would tell friends that football was a game in which you had to know the play. You couldn't just go in and block and tackle. You had to know which way the play was going and what you were supposed to do.

On weekends Volma returned home to Maha where he helped with chores around the farm and attended church at St. Mary's Colony with the rest of his family.

He usually returned home during the summers and helped gather the crops before returning to school in the fall.

During his second year in high school, Volma and his older brother Sherman stayed with Nicholas Overton's first cousin near the Rosewood housing projects.

The third year of high school was Volma's roughest.

He roomed with an old woman named Liza who owned a small house on East 10th Street and Prospect in East Austin. The five-dollar-a-month rent was often hard for the farm family to come by. During the months of March and April, Nicholas and Eliza were unable to come up with the rent at all.

Fifteen-year-old Volma came home from school one day to find all his clothing and personal belongings sitting in the grass in the front yard. It was extremely embarrassing to the shy young man. He moved two blocks away to the home of his cousins, George and Walter DeWitty, where he slept on the hard floor until the end of the school year.

During his senior year, he found a job picking turkeys for ten cents each at L. East Produce. Later he worked for Tom Miller Produce downtown on Fourth and Guadalupe streets.

Volma had company during his senior year in high school. His younger brothers, Ed and Nick, finished the little school at Maha and came to town to attend Old L. C. Anderson High School. They rented a two-room house from Mrs. Ella Mae Lane, the mother of the football player Dick "Night Train" Lane, for fifteen dollars a month. No longer dependent on parental support, the brothers cooked for themselves and worked part-time jobs to pay their own rent.

On Volma's graduation day, Eliza Overton planned for him to wear a new suit. But the department store would not honor the family's credit. Volma was forced to borrow a jacket from his cousin.

Volma Overton at graduation from Old L. C. Anderson High School in Austin, Texas, June 1942. Photo courtesy of Overton Family Collection.

He graduated in May 1942 with a class that numbered fifty-six.

* * *

Volma's first job following graduation was with Lamme's Candy Company in downtown Austin. For six months, he helped four other workers make candy. They stirred sugar, butter, and caramel in a big pot to make pralines. He was still working at Lamme's when David Lamme, the owner, came into the store and told the employees that the Japanese had bombed Pearl Harbor. It was December 7, 1941. World War II had begun.

But Volma's mind was not on going to war just then. When he found a better paying job, he left Lamme's Candies.

He accepted a job at Goodfriends, a ladies ready-to-wear store that stood among a beehive of stores, shops, and restaurants in downtown Austin. He earned ten dollars a week in a janitorial job where he was eventually made store superintendent. He wore a shirt and tie and supervised the store's custodial staff, which included Big Baby Warren and Nettie Caldwell.

Each worker had a certain area of the store to keep clean. Volma's responsibility was to see that the custodial employees did their jobs. He found that some workers liked to work and others did not. He had to get on their backs about it when their work was not done.

By the time Volma started working at Goodfriends, Austin's Jim Crow practices had eased somewhat. Blacks still rode in the rear of the street cars and could not eat in restaurants or use restrooms in public places in downtown Austin. But they could shop freely in most stores, although the major ones, such as Scarbroughs, still refused to let Blacks try on garments in the store. They were often told to take the garment home and if it didn't fit, to return it.

Goodfriends was an upscale ladies store where Austin's upper crust shopped for ready-to-wear clothes. Most of the store's clientele included the wives of doctors, lawyers, and professors. Some of Volma's teachers at Old Anderson High School also shopped at Goodfriends.

Although he liked his job at the store, the far horizons beckoned Volma. He wanted to join the military, but was undecided about which branch of service to join. When he visited the recruiting office, they tried to talk him into joining the Navy. But Volma didn't like the bell-bottomed trousers that the sailors wore. Also, he didn't know it then, but he got seasick every time he went to sea.

He found himself enlisting in the U.S. Marine Corps in 1942, a time when Black service in the military, as well as Black employment in wartime industries, had opened up considerably.

During 1941 Black leader A. Phillip Randolph's threat of an all-Black March on Washington pushed the Roosevelt administration to the wall on the issue of race in America. Randolph and other Black leaders were disappointed in the lack of employment of Blacks in jobs in wartime industries.

The Roosevelt administration made some concessions to the increasingly dissatisfied Black population. The administration appointed the dean of Howard University's School of Law, William H. Hastie, to the position of secretary of war. The administration also promoted Col. Benjamin O. Davis to the rank of brigadier general. Mary McLeod Bethune became director of the Division of Black Affairs of the National Youth Administration. She became the impetus for the formation of a "Black Cabinet," an informal group of high profile Washington, D.C., Blacks whose ideas Bethune carried to President Roosevelt.[7]

When President Roosevelt found he could not influence Randolph and other Black leaders to call off the March on Washington scheduled for July 1, 1941—a march that was expected to draw as many as 100,000 Blacks—he issued Executive Order 8801. The Executive Order dated June 25, 1941, was designed to combat discrimination in industry and government departments. It created the Committee on Fair Employment Practices "to receive and investigate complaints of discrimination in violation of the provisions of this order" and "to take appropriate steps to redress grievances which it finds to be valid."[8]

But lost somewhere in the high-level policy making and political maneuvering was a key issue that began as a vital part of Randolph's plan. Its omission was to have an effect on Volma and every other Black who was part of the military service. Roosevelt's executive order did not address discrimination in the military forces.

Consequently, Volma and his buddies joined a Marine Corps that segregated them by race. Brigadier General Hastie was to have a continuing battle with War Department administration officials over the use of Black soldiers.

Unlike other branches of the military, the Marine Corps remained closed to Blacks until 1942 when the demands of war made it imperative that additional troops be found. Volma found that it was not difficult to get into the marines.

He and two buddies travelled to San Antonio to be inducted into the corps. They were provided train tickets to travel to Mumfort Point at Camp LeJeune in North Carolina for basic training.

Their tickets were for a Pullman coach, a private compartment with sleeping berths. But when they changed trains in New Orleans, they were not given a Pullman berth. Although their tickets called for a better class of accommodations, the three buddies were seated in the "Black car." A common Jim Crow practice throughout the South, the Black car was the railroad car pulled along immediately behind the coal car. The first car behind the coal car was traditionally reserved for Black travellers in the South.

By the time Volma and his buddies reached Wilmington, their faces were covered with a thin film of soot. It was then that Volma realized that Jim Crow practices common in Austin extended far beyond the Texas border.

He found that Mumfort Point was the Marine Corps facility for training Black marines. During that summer, they became a part of the first all-Black battalion of enlisted men. However, the corps had no Black officers until after the war, when the first Black lieutenant was commissioned. The NAACP protested that the Marine Corps quota system was unfair to Blacks.

After a rugged boot camp, Volma and his regiment of all-Black marines shipped out to Ellice Island in the Pacific Ocean. The islands were part of the British Crown.

Volma knew that his unit was one of the best in the entire Marine Corps. They practiced endlessly and became a crack fighting team. The only problem was that there was no one to fight. Commanders only reluctantly accepted Black troops, and then only if whites were unavailable. The Black units always seemed to relieve the white boys. But they were never allowed to fight. The brass thought they would turn tail and run at the first sign of trouble.

* * *

When Volma enlisted, his older brother Sherman had already joined military service and shipped off to Europe. But the heartbreaking news came from the War Department in June 1944 that Sherman was killed in the line of duty. He was unloading cargo from a ship, a service job historically assigned to all-Black regiments. The cargo came loose from its bonds, crushing Sherman to death.

Sherman was buried in England. But when the war ended, many families requested the remains of their loved ones be returned home. The military flew Sherman's body home after the war ended. Nick and Eliza's family buried him in Evergreen Cemetery in East Austin.

Volma remained in the islands until the war ended. He rotated back to the states and mustered out of the marines in 1946, the same year that a young Black postal worker from Houston, Heman Marion Sweatt, applied for admission to The University of Texas at Austin Law School. For the next four years, Volma watched the case wind its way through the courts.

The little farm at Maha somehow looked smaller. Nicholas and Eliza had aged, but still had their same enthusiasm for life. The younger children had grown taller. Nick Jr. was enrolled at Huston-Tillotson College in

360th Quartermaster Company, U.S. Army Reserve Unit (segregated) in 1952. Fort Hood, Killeen, Texas. Overton, standing at the far right, has just made lieutenant. Photo courtesy of Overton Family Collection.

Austin while Roscoe attended Texas Southern University in Houston. Both brothers ran track and played sports. Their sister Minerva also attended Huston-Tillotson College in Austin.

After Volma returned from his tour of duty in the marines, he stayed at home in Maha for a short while before moving back to Austin. He eventually returned to his old job at Goodfriends.

He watched the Heman Sweatt case with interest. The University of Texas refused to admit Sweatt to its law school based solely on his race. By the time the case dragged on for four years to its final conclusion, Volma had enlisted in the Army Reserve.

He wanted to join the Marine Corps Reserve, but when they asked if he could cook, it reminded him of segregated military life. The marines didn't have a place for him, so he applied to the Army Reserve.

President Truman's order integrating the army was signed about the same time Volma applied to join the Army Reserve in 1947. He found that the army offered opportunities in fields in which soldiers were already trained. He did not have to accept work as a cook.

Volma stayed in the Army Reserve until his retirement in 1977 at the rank of lieutenant colonel.

Soon after Volma returned home from the Marine Corps, he dressed in his military uniform and caught the public bus downtown to the Veterans Affairs Office in the courthouse to take care of some business. The bus driver, in keeping with the practice of the time, asked the Blacks seated on the bus to move to the back so that white passengers boarding the bus could have their seats.

At first, Volma kept his seat. He had been away in the military so long that he had almost forgotten about the Jim Crow practice of seating Blacks to the rear and asking them to stand while whites took their seats.

The bus driver kept asking for Volma's seat. Angry and defiant, he was amazed that something like skin color could determine a person's seating privilege on a public bus. But he finally decided that his arrest, which police did not hesitate to do, would not serve any useful purpose.

Silently, he rose from his seat. But he did not move to the rear. He got off the bus and stood in the hot Texas sunshine. He determined that he would do something about the ingrained Jim Crow practices common throughout the South.

* * *

Soon after returning home from the Marine Corps, Volma met Warneta Hill on the Huston-Tillotson College campus. Warneta was a native of Yoakum, Texas, and attended Huston-Tillotson. They dated steadily for three months. Warneta thought Volma was the quietest boy she had ever met. She told Volma's cousin, Oneta Overton Batie, "I don't think Volma has said 100 words to me."[9]

They were married on April 16, 1946, in a double ring ceremony on the front porch of Warneta's parents home in Yoakum. They eventually moved into the Rosewood housing projects. The apartments were new and well maintained. They provided a home for the young couple and the first three of their four children. After Volma finished college and earned raises in pay at the post office, the housing authority informed the family that they earned too much money to continue living in the projects and therefore they would have to move.

Volma moved Warneta and the children out to the farm at Maha. He thought about farming the land himself and even tried it for a while. But once he ploughed the back forty, fiddled with an ailing tractor, and did all the chores that went along with being a farmer, he found he was in no mood to go to his post office job. It had to be the farm or the post office. Volma chose the post office.

After he completed college he discovered a new subdivision of homes, aimed at the market of returning veterans, being constructed in East Austin. The subdivision was called Cedar Valley. Volma and Warneta purchased a neatly trimmed home on Springdale Road.

Goodfriends provided steady employment for Volma for the next five years. He took up where he left off as store superintendent and frequently rode the street car to and from East Austin.

Several of his friends had gone to work for the post office in downtown Austin and urged Volma to try to get hired. He passed the civil service examination for postal service. But he was torn between leaving his familiar job at Goodfriends for a job that he didn't know anything about. The Jewish family that owned Goodfriends had always treated him well.

Each time he made up his mind to leave Goodfriends and take a job with the post office, the store raised his pay. The post office continued to send him notices of vacancies, and his friends kept telling him, "Man, they make good money over there."

In 1952, just one year after the city council decided to end segregation in all Austin's public libraries, Volma made up his mind to leave Goodfriends. He accepted a position as a mail clerk at the U.S. Post Office and was placed in a job at the post office facility on West Sixth Street.

He found himself among about 500 postal employees who worked on various shifts in different postal branches.

Warneta Hill and Volma Overton on their wedding day on April 14, 1946. Photo courtesy of Overton Family Collection.

He soon discovered that there were very few Blacks employed at the post office. There were maybe three or four Black letter carriers and three or four custodians. He worked with Jack Fields, Lee Kirk, and Matthew "Boots" Edwards. He also worked with Abe Haywood.

One day not long after Volma began working for the post office, he experienced an incident that brought home to him the fact that discrimination was still alive and well. He and a co-worker, letter clerk Abe Haywood, found seats in the snack bar during their lunch break. Handicapped workers ran the snack bar. Postal employees dined on short orders and snacks such as sandwiches, cookies, ice cream, and soft drinks. Volma noticed that most of the other Black employees placed their lunch orders through a take-out window, but carried the food to the swing room to eat. But he never paid the practice much attention. A blind man approached Volma and Haywood. "You're not supposed to come in here," the blind man said.

At first Volma didn't comprehend his meaning. The incident on the bus that occurred when he returned to Austin from military duty overseas was always somewhere at the back of his mind. But the memory had faded with time.

Being asked to give up his seat on the bus so that white passengers could sit down had so angered Volma that he had not only risen from his seat, but had also gotten off the bus and walked the rest of the way to his destination.

But times were changing. There was still the kind of subtle discrimination that divided the Black postal employees from the whites. When lunch hour rolled around, the white guys who lived in small towns around Austin headed for a little cafe about three blocks away. They never asked Blacks to join them. There was one white guy who had come to the post office from upstate New York who often asked Volma to join him for lunch. But the white guys from Austin never extended an invitation.

Then there was the matter of job classification at the postal service. For Blacks with college degrees, the post office was known as a graveyard. Promotions were all but impossible to come by.

Some of his co-workers who had completed undergraduate degrees worked as postal clerks, carriers, and mail handlers. Volma knew that some of the white supervisors only had high school diplomas, if that.

Volma left the snack bar and headed upstairs. He told two of his friends, both white, who had ties to the postal union, about the incident in the snack bar. They dealt with the matter the same day.

Volma found he could return to the snack bar and have lunch whenever he wanted. But sometimes he studied the blind man, trying to figure out if he was really blind. Volma concluded the blind man must not be too blind if he knew which patrons were Black.

The blind man never said another word to Volma.

The two co-workers that Volma told about the incident were clerks, just like him. They were also members of the union. They had the connections to pull together others who had the power to straighten things out.

Throughout the next several years, Volma would use his penchant for "knowing someone who knew someone" to get results.

It didn't take Volma long to discover that whites and Blacks were treated the same salarywise. But promotions were a different matter. The federal civil service required that employees take a test to be promoted from postal clerk positions into management positions. But there were only so many management positions available.

Volma saw that the inequities in the postal system were ingrained. He knew that he had to do something about it. He was drawn into civil rights work in the early 1950s during his initial employment with the post office. In 1952 he joined the National Alliance of Postal Employees, a union of mostly Black maintenance and janitorial workers, and served as the organization's president for two years. In this capacity, Volma met many local and national leaders, including Congressman J. J. "Jake" Pickle.

From time to time, Pickle attended meetings where Volma represented the concerns of postal workers. Pickle found young Overton "quiet but outspoken." From that beginning, Pickle and Volma shared a friendship that spanned the remainder of their lives.

Volma felt the problems at the post office stemmed from far larger problems which were basically racial in nature. The 1950s held the kind of discrimination in all facets of life that made it difficult for Blacks to progress. Nationwide, Blacks were the last hired and the first fired. The limited number of white collar jobs available to Blacks during the 1950s made the low-skilled postal jobs desirable.

Volma found that the postal service was similar to other businesses throughout the South. Discrimination was ingrained within the system. It was the rule rather than the exception. Volma found himself advocating for the rights of Black employees, sometimes successfully, sometimes not.

His determination to see that Black postal employees were given opportunities equal to that received by whites earned him the reputation as a fighter. It was a reputation that brought him the respect of his Black co-workers and the community.

But in the end, his reputation for dogged determination also branded him as a troublemaker with post office management.

He diligently followed the activities of the fledgling civil rights movement in the newspapers. Austin had two newspapers during that time—the *Austin Statesman*, the evening paper, and the *Austin American*, which came out in the mornings. Blacks appearing within its pages were generally depicted negatively. Volma searched for copies of the *Pittsburgh Courier* and the *Houston Informer*, both published by Black publisher Carter Wesley. The papers covered lynchings, voting rights, and discrimination issues.

When he started reading the *Houston Informer,* Volma became friends with the Austin journalist who wrote Austin's section of the *Informer*. The journalist was Arthur B. DeWitty, a Black man destined to play a major role in the early civil rights struggle in Austin. His convictions and political savvy drew many Blacks to his cause, among them Volma Overton, whom DeWitty mentored until his own death.

Volma was impressed with DeWitty's writings, speeches and political savvy. He was a born leader. DeWitty was a mason, a member of the men's group at Ebenezer Baptist Church, and a mover in the Travis County Voters' League, a group which ultimately helped defeat the white primary in Texas.

When DeWitty decided the time was right to make a bid for a seat on the all-white Austin City Council, Volma pitched in and helped beat the bushes to get Blacks out to the polls. Prominent Austin attorney Ed Wendler, a mover and shaker in political circles in Austin, was DeWitty's campaign manager.

Prior to the 1951 election, candidates for the city council were elected by majority vote. The top vote getters were elected to the council.

DeWitty did well in the polls, attracting Black and white voters alike. He did so well, in fact, that the prospect of a Black on the city council was rumored to be unsettling to a number of whites.

The council formed a Charter Review Committee to redesign the election system for city council members. The committee recommended a place system be implemented. Instead of candidates who garnered the highest amount of votes winning a council seat, candidates were forced to run for a place or a section of Austin. The high votegetters in each place were elected. Austin's Black community was to remain the loser in the place system for years.

Without the help of the white community, East Austin could not field a successful Black candidate. For politically aspiring Blacks, there would be no relief until the early 1970s, when a gentlemen's agreement between Austin's white movers and shakers would allow first one Black, then one Hispanic candidate to win a seat on the Austin City Council each election year thereafter.

Volma's first experience with an election whetted his own appetite for public service, but he would not seriously consider a run for office until many years later.

During the mid- to late 1960s, Volma took a myriad of civil service tests in order to be promoted. He tested for supervisor, a position which no Blacks in the Austin postal region had ever held. He knew that he had to make a top score in order to even be considered for an interview.

His score fluctuated between ninety-five and ninety-seven. But he was never called in for an interview. He knew that guys who made lower scores were granted interviews. He knew this because he managed to see the test scores. But they were all white.

It would be a full fourteen years after Volma accepted a job at the post office in 1952 until he would make the decision to take his case to a higher authority.

Volma's interest in civil rights and better educational opportunities for Blacks provided a gentle reminder that his own education was not yet complete. He always had a desire to go to college and could have chosen from several institutions. But he wanted to stay close to home.

He enrolled in Huston-Tillotson College in East Austin in 1947. Since he was a veteran, he enrolled under the GI Bill. The veterans program paid his tuition, plus ninety dollars a month. He could have attended other colleges. Wiley College in Marshall, Texas Southern in Houston, Paul Quinn in Waco (now located in Dallas), Texas College in Tyler, and Bishop College in Dallas were all established Black schools. But the one college he could not attend was the major college in his own hometown— The University of Texas.

The University of Texas, along with other institutions of higher learning in the South, did not accept Blacks because of their race.

Volma, along with all of Black Austin, watched the case of Heman Marion Sweatt with anticipation. Austin's Blacks saw The University of Texas as a bastion of discrimination. Many journeyed from their homes in East Austin across East Avenue to the cafeterias, dormitories, and classrooms of the university where they held jobs cooking and cleaning—but could not attend school.

Sweatt filed a lawsuit against the university in May 1946, and was supported by the national NAACP. Many local Blacks, including Volma, contributed to a fund designed to help support the young postman and his wife and pay for the numerous trips from their hometown of Houston to Austin for court appearances.

The 126th District Court ordered that Sweatt be provided an education in a state-supported school. In the absence of a Black law school in Texas, UT and Texas A&M University created an undergraduate school which offered courses equal to the ones Sweatt was not allowed to enroll in at UT.

The School of Law of the Texas State University for Blacks opened its doors on March 10, 1947, with two Black attorneys as professors.

But Sweatt refused to attend the makeshift school.

Determined to see the court battle through to the end, Sweatt first went to the Court of Civil Appeals, then to the Texas Supreme Court, and ultimately to the U.S. Supreme Court.

On June 5, 1950, the Supreme Court ruled that Sweatt be admitted to the UT Law School. He enrolled in the fall of 1950, but never graduated, the strain of the court case and class material taking its toll on his physical, emotional, and personal life.

Although UT became the first university in the South to admit Blacks into its graduate level studies, the school still refused to accept Black undergraduates until the fall of 1956. But even then, Blacks were not allowed to participate in school activities such as dramatic performances, band, or athletics until the 1960s, causing the institution to hold on to the lingering taint of racism left from the Sweatt case long after Black students enjoyed the full freedom to participate in all school activities.

Volma enrolled at Tillotson College, East Austin's historically Black college. It was a growing school with many students. Like Volma, there were many veterans attending school at Tillotson. Most classes were full, with an enrollment of thirty to forty students.

Volma worked at the post office at night, and attended classes at Tillotson College during the daytime. He majored in chemistry and minored in math, courses that he considered challenging.

But when he graduated in 1950, he found that other jobs did not compare salarywise to what he earned at the post office. He earned a teaching certificate and began to look for a teaching job. When he could get a day off, he frequently loaded his overnight bag and a change of clothing into the family automobile and headed for interviews with various school systems all over Texas.

In his search for a teaching job, he found himself driving over the country backroads and urban highways of a large part of Texas. He was amazed to see the hovels that served for Black schools in some areas. Frequently, the schools had no running water or indoor toilet facilities. Children brought their lunches from home in a jelly bucket. Volma sometimes found sweltering classrooms in the summertime, and students huddled around pot-bellied wood-burning stoves for warmth in the winter.

Although he had attended school in much the same kind of environment, he was amazed that over the years the quality of education for African-American children had not improved.

As he maneuvered his car through the heavy traffic in the thoroughfares of urban cities, or dodged gullies and ravines that jutted from country lanes with grass growing down the middle of the road, he often looked at the red brick façades of white schools. They frequently had shiny playground equipment and a big yellow bus or two in the school yard.

Volma often found himself wondering what would have to happen to break the cycle of oppression that was systematically applied to the African-American race in America. If something did not happen, and soon, the entire race would be so poorly educated that there would be small hope of competing with other races for better jobs, social status, and better living conditions.

After searching for a teaching job for several months, Volma finally found himself exasperated. The African-American school districts historically paid teachers less than white teachers, salaries that never matched what he earned at the post office. And he would also have to relocate his family. He finally decided that Warneta and the children needed his financial support more than the African-American school districts desperately needed good, quality teachers. He was offered teaching positions in several communities, which he turned down. Volma remained at the post office in Austin, and later in the small communities of Dale and Cedar Creek, until he retired in 1985.

3

A TIME OF CHANGE—
THE SIXTIES

The myriad of churches dotting East Austin were the mainstay of the Black community. Considered the voice of East Austin's conscience by some, and a sad comment on the state of Black activism by others, the churches weathered the racial and economic storms that battered the Black community.

Volma, a member of a small church in East Austin, attended business meetings where they made decisions on church policy. They agreed on making a small change in the order of church service. It would make worship service shorter. Many times the deacons noticed that some members grew bored before service ended. Some even nodded off to sleep.

But when the pastor found out about the change, he became angry that no one had consulted him. He informed them that no change would be made. An argument followed. Volma grew livid. He and the pastor had words that became a heated debate. "If you don't like the way things are run 'round here, brother, why don't you just go some place where you will be happy?" the pastor said to Volma as the other deacons looked on. Asberry Walker, a deacon and Volma's friend, quietly watched the scene.

After the argument, Volma was torn in two directions: remain at the East Austin church he had known as home for most of his adult life, where he knew that confrontations with the pastor would no doubt continue, or move his membership to another church.

Volma took time to make up his mind to try other churches. A friend often invited him to visit his church in downtown Austin. But the friend was white and Volma never seriously considered going to a white church. But in the end, he found his way downtown to the imposing brick church on Colorado Street.

The First Baptist Church was an institution in Austin. The sprawling membership was made up of people from every walk of life. A supreme court judge, highly placed politicians, and educators sat beside university students, families, and the occasional Black face at Sunday morning worship.

Volma found himself returning Sunday after Sunday. He liked the change from the small East Austin church that he thought would be his spiritual home for the rest of his life.

On a beautiful spring Sunday, Volma walked to the front of the congregation and accepted Assistant Pastor Mike Smith's hand, becoming one of only a handful of Blacks who regularly attended services at First Baptist Church.

Volma's disagreement with the minister at the East Austin church was not lost on the deacons who witnessed it. His friend, Asberry Walker, quietly took him aside one day. Rev. J. L. Dawson, the current president of the Austin branch NAACP and also pastor of Davis Chapel Baptist Church in East Austin, was leaving town. He did not wish to leave the NAACP presidency vacant. The organization was practically dormant, its meetings drawing a scant few. But Reverend Dawson was concerned that the organization's goals be carried forward. Walker asked Volma to consider taking the job. John and Betty Crawford, friends and officers in the Austin branch NAACP, also encouraged Volma to accept the presidency. Volma thought seriously about the NAACP and its place in the Austin community before making a decision.

Founded in 1909 by influential whites William English Walling, a socialist, Mary White Ovington, and Henry Muskowitz, both social workers, and joined by Oswald Garrison Villard, the NAACP was at first run by middle and upper class whites. Black educator W. E. B. DuBois joined the organization in 1910 and became the first editor of *The Crisis*, the NAACP's magazine. He was followed by James Weldon Johnson and Walter White, both Black activists who led the organization in new directions.

But problems faced by the nation's Blacks were almost insurmountable. The growing number of Black lynchings, ingrained discrimination, and lack of voting privileges for some Blacks in the Deep South was enough to stymie the organization's leaders. Whenever they tried to get legislation favorable to Blacks through Congress, they were thwarted by members of the Southern Bloc, who often filibustered bills to an early death.

Blacks in Texas also faced many problems. In August 1919, John R. Shillady, the white executive secretary of the national NAACP, journeyed to Austin to investigate the reasons why Texas officials subpoenaed the records of the NAACP. After trying to meet with the governor and the attorney general, Shillady "was detained by a constable, served with a subpoena, and forced to undergo heckling and hostile questioning before a secret court of inquiry. The following morning when he attempted to see the president of the Association's branch, a group of assailants intervened and beat him severely. His attackers included a county judge and a constable."

When the NAACP national office demanded an investigation and punishment for the offenders, they got nowhere with Texas Governor W. P. Hobby. "I believe in sending any narrow-brained, double-chinned reformer who comes here with the end of stirring up racial discontent back to the North where he came from with a broken jaw if necessary," Hobby said. He added that the NAACP could "contribute more to the advancement of both races by keeping your representatives and their propaganda out of this state than in any other way."[1]

Judge Pickle, widely believed to be Shillady's attacker, was openly congratulated in a newspaper article.[2] Shillady never recovered from his injuries. No one was charged in the attack.

Since returning home from military service, Volma followed the progress of the fledgling civil rights struggle in America. Many times after Warneta had bathed the children and tucked them into bed, she found Volma deeply engrossed in the pages of the *Houston Informer* or the *Pittsburgh Courier*, newspapers published by Blacks. Unlike the Austin daily, the newspapers gave substantial space to the progress of the Civil Rights Movement.

He read about the court ruling in the case of *Brown v. Topeka, Kansas Board of Education* handed down May 17, 1954. The ruling struck down the "separate but equal" interpretation of the U.S. Constitution by which African-American students in Austin and many other school districts throughout the nation were required to attend only African-American schools.

At the time Volma wondered what the ruling meant for Austin's African-American community. He knew that some of the city's schools earmarked for African Americans were of little better quality than the little one-room schoolhouse he attended as a child in the rural community of Maha. But he was unsure of how the Supreme Court's ruling would be interpreted by local school districts.

Others were overjoyed. Dr. Everett Givens, a local African-American dentist and mover and shaker in both African-American and white political circles, was elated. Known as the "Bronze Mayor of East Austin," Givens called the high court ruling "The best news since Emancipation."[3]

Volma knew that Austin's conservative establishment would fight the ruling.

Both Gov. Allan Shivers and State Education

Commissioner J. W. Edgar said compliance would "take a long time."[4]

Senator Lyndon Baines Johnson, a Texas hill country politician whom Volma would come to know well in the ensuing years, was not prepared to comment on the Brown ruling. But Johnson noted the final decree of the Supreme Court would take "at least until next fall," giving Texas a chance to "figure it out." Senator Price Daniel hoped "when the final decree is entered, it will take our problems into consideration and give greater consideration to them than the decision . . . has done."[5]

Representative Homer Thornberry, a confidante of Lyndon Johnson who would later become a federal judge, said, "We ought to be allowed to work out the problems among ourselves."[6]

City and county school officials expressed uncertainty. "I have no idea," AISD Supt. Irby Carruth said. "In fact, I imagine that no one anywhere, knows yet."[7]

Deferring to higher officials, County Supt. I. W. Popham said he believed local boards would "wait for a cue to further action from the state school authorities."[8]

Volma read about NAACP President Marcus Cooper's fight to institute integration immediately. Cooper and a delegation of NAACP officials presented a petition to the Austin Independent School District Board of Trustees for "immediate abolition" of segregation in the Austin public schools beginning in the fall. However, the school board took Cooper's petition "under advisement, with President Noble Prentice promising that the board would 'give this matter very careful consideration, as it does all matters that come before it.'"[9] Immediate integration of Austin's public schools, like other civil rights areas, became an uphill battle.

Unperturbed and perhaps still not knowing how to interpret the Brown ruling, Gov. Allan Shivers and other state officials said Texas schools would continue operating next year as in the past, with separate schools for Blacks.

Attorney General John Ben Shepperd expressed his opposition to integration in a letter to Thomas S. Sutherland, director of the Texas Commission on Race Relations:

> I am of the very definite and firm opinion that the state laws of Texas still call for segregated schools. Our Texas laws were not passed on by the Supreme Court. Until the Supreme Court specifically states otherwise, segregation remains the law in Texas. If the court follows precedent, it will leave the date and method of integration up to the local school districts.[10]

Despite opposition, many school districts in Texas proceeded with plans for integration. By August 1955, the *American Statesman* reported "an estimated thirty to forty school districts have voted to put integration into effect during the coming school year." But Governor Shivers' legal committee warned that school districts faced a "distinct possibility of jeopardizing" state educational aid if they prematurely integrated Black students into white systems.[11]

The Austin Independent School District was one of the school districts which decided to proceed with integration. In August 1955 the board ordered Austin's high schools to drop racial barriers beginning in September.[12]

The ruling instituted transfer procedures that made it possible for African-American students to transfer to districts other than the one in which they resided. The ruling also made it possible for both white and African-American students living in predominantly white or Black neighborhoods to transfer to a school of their choice.

The newspaper covered the thirteen African-American students who made history during the 1955-56 school year by being the first to attend the three previously all-white senior high schools in Austin: Stephen F. Austin, William B. Travis, and A. N. McCallum High Schools.

However, the Austin School Board's good intentions stopped with the integration of the city's junior high schools. A fire at Allen Junior High School forced students assigned there to double up at University Junior High School. The board voted to delay integration at the junior high school level "until such time as it will be feasible to accommodate any change in the number of students attending the junior high schools of the city."[13]

If the public schools had a long way to go to complete integration of all of its grades, The University of Texas was still in the Dark Ages.

The University of Texas at Austin, as well as other institutions of higher learning throughout the South, did little more than the law mandated to achieve integration. By the fall of 1956, UT-Austin had integrated graduate and undergraduate classes. But school officials did little towards achieving integration in other areas of campus life.

While students picketed restaurants and lunch counters, Dr. Wilson, a UT regent, said, "there is complete integration with reference to all educational opportunities and facilities . . . For reasons which the Administration and the Board of Regents consider to be sound, forced integration of extra-curricular areas has not been established . . ."[14]

Discrimination at UT continued unabated, with the Cowboy Minstrels, a campus service organization, performing in blackface at a yearly charitable fundraiser. Blacks referred to the show as "Jim Crow campus humor."[15]

To the public, the majority of whom supported full integration at UT, the nine white men who composed The University of Texas Board of Regents bore most of the blame for the slow progress towards integration. Students and faculty at UT initiated petitions during the spring of 1960, asking for integration of dorms and athletics.

But the UT Board of Regents did not foresee full integration of the university as something that would happen soon. "We do not feel the people of Texas are prepared for social integration at the university," Regent W. W. Heath told the Austin daily in an article published July 26, 1961.[16]

Integration of athletics was another thorny issue. Heath said, "There are eight members of the Southwest

Conference, none of which play colored students." He further stated that until a majority of conference schools were ready to integrate athletics, the university could not do it alone.[17]

Heath also said, "We have probably gone further than a majority of the citizens of Texas and of the members of the Legislature would approve." He added that a majority of Black students were probably getting a break from sympathetic professors because of inadequate pre-college education.[18]

East Austinites watched as Black students at the university protested in earnest over discrimination in visiting privileges in the dormitories. Black students were limited to their own dorms, with no privileges in any other dorms.[19]

Black students filed suit against the UT housing policy, the first such suit since Hemann Sweatt filed his landmark case to enter UT's law school since 1946.

Students also picketed the segregated Forty Acres Club and consulted with civil rights leader Dr. Martin Luther King, Jr., when he visited Austin.[20]

Lastly, Volma carefully considered his own personal situation before making a decision. His job gave him cause for concern. He was a government employee with the U.S. Postal Service, a position that offered a steady income and good benefits. But when the time came to push on unpopular issues or go against the grain of the conservative forces which permeated Austin's politics, Volma wondered about the consequences.

Then there was his family. His wife, Warneta, cared for the four Overton children. Taking over the presidency of the Austin branch NAACP would mean many hours away from home and family. There would be countless meetings, appearances before groups such as the city council and school board, as well as representing individuals with complaints against their employer. Much of the time spent with Warneta and the children would be severely curtailed.

There was also the problem of how the public perceived him. Retiring and soft spoken, Volma stood in stark contrast to the giants of the Civil Rights Movement of the day. He did not have the religious fervor and eloquent tongue of a Dr. Martin Luther King, Jr., nor did he have the streetwise hustle of a Stokeley Carmichael.

When Volma entered a room, no one pointed him out or whispered behind their hands. There would be no immediate recognition for the country boy from Maha, Texas, who would go on to lead the organization for the next twenty years.

Considering all this, Volma's last thoughts were on the effect of his presidency on the National Alliance of Postal Employees. For two years, he and other members agitated for better working conditions, more promotions, and fairer opportunities for employees who performed maintenance work at the Austin post office. They met with the postmaster concerning disputes, and pushed for better representation.

Volma found he was able to work effectively as president of the National Alliance of Postal Employees. Why couldn't he do the same thing with the NAACP? After much soul searching, Volma accepted the presidency, and found that his life would never be the same.

His first course of action was to notify the NAACP national office in New York that he was now president of the Austin branch. Several weeks later, an official-looking envelope arrived in the mail from the national office. It outlined the correct procedure for the election of branch officers. Among other things, the Austin branch had not conducted an official election by dues paying members with at least a thirty-day advance notice to the membership. Volma filed the letter away for future reference and got on with the work of the branch.

* * *

As Dr. Martin Luther King's Southern Christian Leadership Conference (SCLC) joined forces with other civil rights groups and grass roots organizations to force desegregation of public facilities in Albany, Georgia, Volma and a core group of NAACP stalwarts went about reorganizing the Austin branch from the ground up. The small group recognized that the greatest challenge to the survival of the organization was to build a strong membership base. The organization also faced the mounting national push for integration and equal public accommodations, not only in schools, restaurants, and movie theaters, but in all public places.

Volma found that lack of education was also a serious handicap for Blacks. The multitude of maids, janitors, bootblacks, chauffeurs, groundskeepers, sales people, and the like who ordinarily boarded public buses to travel to their jobs labored for a pittance. For Volma, it was imperative that Blacks educate themselves so that they could compete for better jobs at better pay.

Voter registration was another issue high on the organization's agenda. The poll tax would not be outlawed by the Supreme Court until January 1964 with the ratification of the Twenty-Third Amendment to the U.S. Constitution.[21]

In the meantime, the poll tax served the exact purpose that disfranchisers in the South and Deep South intended. It kept many poorer Blacks as well as other ethnic groups from exercising their right to vote.

Volma scheduled regular meetings of the Austin branch NAACP where everyone had the opportunity to attend. For a time, the meetings were held at various Black churches in Austin. Later, the organization moved the meetings to the historic Howson Community Center near the George Washington Carver Library on Angelina Street in East Austin.

Volma experienced a wealth of problems during the first year of his presidency. Among them was his first case of overt discrimination. The Austin Ice Palace, a newly opened facility located at Airport Boulevard and Manor Road, billed itself as a family skating rink. Advertisements in the Austin daily urged everyone to come to an open house. Children came home from school with new book-covers advertising the Austin Ice Palace. More advertisements appearing on the sides of public buses invited the general public.

But when Black parents took their children to the new skating rink for an afternoon of ice skating, they found their business was not welcome. The Austin Ice Palace was segregated.

The segregated Austin Ice Palace so incensed Blacks in East Austin that two organizations combatted its racist policies. The Mothers' Action Council was organized by locals to attempt to integrate the skating rink. Also, the Citizen's Coordinating Committee was established, composed of members of the Mothers' Action Council and the NAACP.[22] The Austin Ice Palace eventually closed its doors and was never heard from again.

As time went by, civil rights took on a more prominent role in the national limelight. The fall of 1962 saw twenty-nine-year-old James Meredith attempt to enroll in the University of Mississippi while Gov. Ross Barnett stood in the school's doorway. President John F. Kennedy was forced to federalize the Mississippi National Guard and also send in army troops so that Meredith could enroll.

Volma watched The University of Texas at Austin slowly change with the times. In the summer of 1962, contrary to previous years, Black freshmen were assigned campus housing during summer orientation sessions. In the fall the UT Regents also announced that Edmund Guinn was the first Black to qualify for the Longhorn band. Facets of a provisional admissions program were also made public. The program allowed for admission of students during the summer session who failed to qualify for admission during the regular session. This practice allowed students of all ethnic groups to gain admission to UT.

By early 1963 Volma was the recognized spokesman on Black issues involving discrimination and integration in Austin. After the successful picketing of the Austin Ice Palace and the steadily growing influence of the Austin branch NAACP, television and newspaper reporters frequently sought him out to get his feelings on issues close to the Black community.

Political leaders recognized Volma's reasoning. Newly elected Texas Congressman J. J. "Jake" Pickle saw that "Volma quietly came into leadership in the NAACP and he was always outspoken in his position . . . his approach was more to appeal to you what was right and wrong rather than saying 'If you don't vote this way, us Blacks are not going to forget it.' He never threatened."[23]

Volma found that he had to rely on the advice of two friends who became his mentors: Mrs. U. V. Christian, former president of the Austin branch NAACP, and Arthur DeWitty, community activist.

Christian, affectionately called "Madam" by Austinites who knew her well, operated Crescent Beauty School. Frequently she could be found sitting in on city council meetings. She brought information back to the branch about things that the city council planned for East Austin. She remained active in politics even though she was pushing eighty.

Volma stopped by her home on San Bernard Street four or five times a week. They spoke of the nagging problems of the branch, problems that Volma was often at a loss to solve. Christian often told him about things that happened during her presidency of the branch and what she used to do.

When Volma ruffled feathers on particularly sensitive issues, such as racial discrimination or the lack of participation by local Blacks in political issues that directly affected them, he found that Madam was right there by his side. "Don't stop, keep going!" she often told Volma.

Arthur DeWitty, an activist who helped organize the Travis County Voters League, an organization which helped defeat the white primary in Texas in 1944, also ran for a position on the Austin City Council in the early 1950s. He was also a journalist, writing the Austin section of the *Informer* for several years.

Christian and DeWitty were Volma's real inspiration.

When they encouraged him, Volma felt the sky was the limit and there was nothing he could not accomplish. But he also realized that there were many things that the national office of the NAACP could accomplish more efficiently from New York than the locals could do.

* * *

The summer of 1963 found Volma and the Austin branch taking part in the integration of a state park in a neighboring community, and participating in a landmark march on the nation's capital.

While Dr. Martin Luther King, Jr., led mass demonstrations to integrate public facilities in Birmingham, Alabama, and Eugene T. "Bull" Conner, Birmingham's commissioner of public safety, and his officers used cattle prods, fire hoses, sticks, and police dogs on non-violent demonstrators, the Austin branch accepted numerous complaints of discrimination. Many of the complaints involved business establishments or public facilities which refused to serve individuals because of their race.

The Austin branch often received complaints of discrimination from individuals in outlying communities. One such complaint detailed segregation at Bastrop State Park, a small community lying just thirty-two miles east of Austin.

Austin branch NAACP attorney J. Phillip Crawford forwarded a letter concerning the situation to Mr. Weldon Berry, attorney at law in Houston, informing him "of the desire of the Austin Branch to investigate, negotiate, and settle or litigate, if necessary, the right of Blacks to utilize the faculities [sic] of Bastrop State Park at Bastrop, Texas. This matter has been brought to our attention by several Black persons who have attempted, but were refused utilization of the golf course."[24]

Later that summer, Volma and several fellow golfers, including Walter McBride, Lonnie Jackson and James Sheard, drove members of his Boy Scout Troop #70 to Bastrop State Park. While the boys went swimming, Volma and his friends played nine holes of golf. Both groups made history. They became the first Blacks to successfully integrate Bastrop State Park facilities without being asked to leave because of their race.

Blacks' initial enchantment with the election of President John F. Kennedy in 1960 quickly gave way to disillusionment when they realized there would be no all-out push for civil rights from the White House.

However, Dr. Martin Luther King and the SCLC's crusade for integration of public accommodations in Birmingham and the resulting media coverage put the Kennedy administration's lack of a civil rights initiative in a bad light.

While Bull Connor bowed his head as non-violent protesters prayed when his men released tear gas, dogs, and water from fire hoses, King debated how the resulting bad publicity could best be used to get the Kennedy administration to move on civil rights.

On June 1, 1963, Kennedy went on nationwide television to ask for an end to segregation, stating that "he soon would propose to Congress a civil rights bill that would include a public accommodations title among its provisions."[25]

The next day, Mississippi NAACP Chairman Medgar Evers was viciously shot to death as he got out of his car at his home in Jackson, Mississippi.

The murder saddened the country.

True to his promise, President Kennedy saw to it that a major civil rights bill was introduced in Congress.

The next several months proved to be a waiting game for civil rights groups. Soon after the text of the proposed civil rights bill was released, opponents began to come out of the woodwork.

Chief among opponents to the proposed Civil Rights Act in Texas was Democratic Gov. John Connally. In a televised speech on July 19, 1963, Connally stated his opposition to parts of President Kennedy's civil rights program, including regulation of private business and widened enforcement powers of the U.S. Attorney General.

Governor Connally called the right to own and manage private property "one of our most cherished freedoms . . . I speak specifically of the proposed federal law which would deprive the owners of private businesses of the right to decide whom they would serve, and of the accompanying proposal to give broad powers of enforcement to the attorney general of the United States."[26]

Connally ticked off the progress already made "towards insuring equal civil rights for racial minorities . . . Sixteen of the twenty-one public senior colleges and universities are desegregated. Twenty-six of thirty-three public junior colleges are desegregated. Two hundred and twelve Texas public school districts have taken steps towards desegregation. Fifty-three percent of Black school children in Texas live in desegregated school districts. Seventy-five percent of restaurants serve everyone, regardless of race. Eighty percent of the hotels in Texas serve everyone, regardless of race."[27]

Connally also emphasized numerous appointments he made to responsible state and local government posts —people like Rev. C. A. Holliday, Dr. Joseph Chatman, Joe Scott, the Rev. Marvin Griffin and Dr. Vernon McDaniel. Connally stated he did not appoint these people because they were Black: "I appointed them because they were outstanding Texans who were qualified through education and experience to render service to the people of this state. I have not—and I will not—appoint any man to any position merely because he is a Negro."[28]

Volma read Connally's speech in the daily newspaper and was perturbed. Others were more demonstrative in their reactions to the Texas governor's negative stance on civil rights. Booker T. Bonner, described as a thirty-five-year-old Black waiter at a private club in Austin, staged a twenty-eight-hour sit-in in Governor Connally's office until he was given an appointment.

Bonner told the news media he was demonstrating against Governor Connally's civil rights stand. But his scheduled meeting with the governor was cancelled when

Bonner insisted that "a half-dozen other Black and Latin American integrationists accompany him."[29]

Bonner hailed from Waelder, Texas. Since he was not a member of the Austin branch NAACP and not a local, Austin's Black leadership saw him as an outsider, and therefore provided small support.

"Bonner is trying to create a sensation," J. J. Seabrook, president of East Austin's Huston-Tillotson College, said. "We don't want outside people coming in and telling us what must be done in Austin. They do not know how much has already been done in the city."[30] Bonner also received little support when he later ran for Travis County commissioner, a race which he handily lost. He was later fired from his waiter job for using the telephone too much.

In East Austin a conservative political group formed by a local businessman showed signs of overtaking the NAACP. The United Political Organization, known as UPO, was the brainchild of M. J. "Andy" Anderson and his wife Ada. Anderson moved to Austin as a young man. The industrious couple built a family real estate business that thrived during the 1970s.

In July 1963 UPO drew over 150 Blacks from all over Texas to its first general meeting in Austin. The organization hoped to draw over a million Blacks to form a powerful, cohesive political force in Texas. The Austin conference stressed political participation as a vehicle for better job opportunities. Gov. John Connally spoke at the UPO banquet.

Throughout the ensuing years, Anderson and Volma became friendly rivals in the political arena. Anderson espoused more conservative issues, while Volma's politics were to remain liberal.

Anderson drew some of the big names in politics to his cause and was known as the man to see for Blacks who contemplated running for political office in Austin.

Volma joined the Black Voter Action Project, or

B-VAP, a coalition of East Austin community activists who sought to get more Blacks into elected office.

MARCH ON WASHINGTON

In early July the branch received word that the March on Washington would take place on Wednesday, August 28, 1963. The news caught the Austin branch without adequate financial resources to send the many members who expressed a desire to go.

Eighty buses provided by the Congress of Racial Equality (CORE) drove in from Harlem; a fourteen-car train left Pennsylvania Station in New York; and two trains of thirty-seven cars each, one replete with a jazz combo, left Chicago. But the Austin branch could only provide funds of $200 for only two members to make the historic journey.

Volma and Rev. Lee Edwards found they were among many who came by car, rode bicycles, and even walked to Washington, D.C., for the march.

A local school teacher, a young man who taught at a Black school in Bartlett, was at first scheduled to go on the trip. But when the branch released the names of the representatives who would attend the march to the news media, the young man became concerned. He feared for his teaching position and later bowed out.

Volma and Reverend Edwards made the two-day journey from Texas to Washington, D.C., by car. With their protest signs neatly stacked in the back seat, Volma and Rev. Edwards took turns driving, giving the other one time for some much needed rest. While Volma napped in the back seat as they were driving through Alabama, they were subjected to the one thing most feared by Blacks driving through the South.

The flashing lights of a police car pulled them over.

"Boy, where y'all going?" the white cop asked, his eyes roaming over the back seat, and finally coming to rest on Volma's sleeping form.

"I'm taking my friend home, suh," Reverend Edwards said politely. "He live in South Carlina."

"He shore is sleeping," the cop said, all the while looking over the car.

But Volma wasn't really asleep. He was playing opossum. He listened to the cop's deep southern drawl, all the while wondering what would happen to them if the cop discovered the protest signs they planned to use at the march.

Black men heard stories of being stopped by white southern cops, being beaten and intimidated, landing in a southern jail, and drawing a stiff sentence for minor infractions of the law.

Both Volma and Reverend Edwards breathed a sigh of relief when the cop, apparently satisfied that nothing was amiss, returned to his patrol car and drove away. Volma would always wonder if he saw the protest signs.

Night had settled over Washington, D.C., when they drove across the Potomac Bridge. They spent the night in an apartment loaned by Volma's friend, Azie Taylor, who would marry and become Azie Taylor Morton, U.S. Treasurer in the Jimmy Carter administration. The next morning, after a light breakfast, they set out for the Washington Monument.

They knew over 100,000 people were expected to converge on Washington, D.C., for the march. But nothing could have prepared them for the enormity of the scene that greeted them. Over 200,000 people were thickly concentrated on the mall between the Washington Monument and the Lincoln Memorial. They were every color of the rainbow, all nationalities, and all ages. They were interspersed with volunteer members of the Washington, D.C., Police Department along with park rangers. The National Guard, standby military and even FBI agents were also in evidence.

But curiously absent were the very people whose lives the march hoped to dramatize. In his introduction to Haskins' *The March on Washington*, veteran civil rights activist James Farmer said: "The marchers were middle class people: well-paid labor union workers who had cars, middle-class whites and blacks. But the poor blacks were not there. They listened to the march on the radio or watched it on television and they were skeptical."[31]

Thanks to the organizing skills of Bayard Rustin, chief march organizer and A. Phillip Randolph's right-hand man, every conceivable amenity had been provided. Parking, extra blankets for the cool northern mornings and evenings, tons of drinking water, hot dogs, and sandwiches were all available on or near the grounds.

The march began with live entertainment at the Washington Monument by some of the most famous names in show business. Celebrities such as Marian Anderson, Lena Horne, Odetta, Joan Baez, Brook Benton, and Bobby Darin all came to share in what they termed a very special day.

When the entertainment was over, the ten leaders of the largest civil rights organizations almost missed leading the marchers from the Washington Monument to the Lincoln Memorial. They were in a meeting with Kennedy administration officials in the White House when they heard the marchers were leaving for the Lincoln Memorial without them!

Volma and the marchers heard stirring speeches by A. Phillip Randolph, organizer of the Black Sleeping Car Porters; John Lewis, national chairman of the Student Nonviolent Coordinating Committee; Walter Reuther, chairman, AFL-CIO; Whitney M. Young, executive director of the National Urban League; Matthew Ahmann, executive director of the National Catholic Conference for Interracial Justice; Roy Wilkins, executive secretary, NAACP; and Rabbi Joachim Prinz, president of the American Jewish Congress.

But it was the speech by a small Black man with the ancestry of Baptist preachers in his soul who stirred the crowd that day as no one else would. Volma was standing in the shade of the branches of a large tree when Martin Luther King, a minister from Montgomery, Alabama, took the stage. Volma knew of King's role in the

Montgomery Bus Boycott and his resulting popularity due to constant media coverage. While King garnered more publicity than the other civil rights organizations, Volma knew that he did not have a cohesive organization. His publicity drew countless marchers, as well as financial contributions, for the cause of civil rights. But King's Southern Christian Leadership Conference (SCLC) did not have the membership nor the organization to draw over a quarter of a million people to a one-day march to dramatize the civil rights cause.

As King began his speech, Volma noticed a stillness slowly descend on the crowd. The afternoon was growing late and the marchers were exhausted from all the speeches. But an electricity seemed to hang on the air as King spoke. His voice, powerful yet soothing, touched the hearts of everyone in the crowd. His dream became *their* dream. His wish for a worldwide peace, where children of all races would join hands, became their dream.[32]

A stillness hung over the crowd when King finished his speech. After a long moment, an eruption of wild cheering went up from the crowd to the heavens. People sang and wept, overjoyed at the events of the day and thrilled by King's speech.

As 5 P.M. drew near and the speeches came to an end, Volma and the rest of the marchers retraced their steps to their cars, buses, trains, and airplanes for the journey home.

The ten civil rights leaders travelled to the White House for a meeting. President Kennedy greeted Martin Luther King with the words "I have a dream."

Gone were the fears that the planned march would erupt into uncontrolled mob violence, setting back all of the civil rights gains of the past 100 years in one day.

Volma was pleased and filled with a heightened sense of commitment as he drove back to Texas. He experienced something that day that would stay with him forever. Throughout the years of his leadership of the Austin branch NAACP, he would always remember looking upon the faces of 200,000 people. They were ordinary people who would return to ordinary homes, jobs, families and friends. But it was the leaders, the individuals at the helm of the grass roots organizations who made civil rights a priority, who bore the burden of leadership.

For the first time since he became president of the Austin branch in 1962, Volma truly realized the enormity of his commitment. The president was the person that everyone else looked to for leadership. And if that leadership was not there, he was the person held responsible.

He would remember the March on Washington for a million reasons. But the foremost reason was that it showed him the depth of his responsibility.

They had only been home in Austin for a few weeks when a bomb exploded during a Bible class at Birmingham's Sixteenth Street Baptist Church. Four girls, ages eleven to fourteen, died in the blast on Sunday, September 16, 1963.

* * *

Volma found the presidency of the branch demanded more and more of his time. He worked the night shift at the post office so that he could devote the day to carrying on the work of the branch.

There were endless meetings, complaints of discrimination, and correspondence with the national office that demanded his full attention. Members of the media hunted him down for statements on the burgeoning civil rights movement. There was precious little time for Warneta and the children, who were growing like weeds.

In mid-November Volma awoke from a nap with a pain in his stomach that would not go away. When he tried to pull himself out of bed, his legs gave way and he landed heavily on the bedroom floor. When he had strength enough to pull himself upright, he was weak and spent. A telephone call to Warneta's job brought her home on the run. The next day, the doctors at Austin's Brackenridge Hospital diagnosed bleeding ulcers. They prescribed rest, a strict diet, and no stress.

Volma considered the many hours the NAACP required of him. He and the membership were beginning to see some progress. Meetings were well attended, more and more people joined the organization, and they were the Black community's representation on law enforcement, political, and legal issues.

Educational barriers were also slowly coming down. The University of Texas at Austin continued its slow climb towards eradicating the remaining racial barriers. On November 9, 1963, the UT Regents lifted the color bar on everything except housing.[33] Also, head football coach Darrell Royal said Negroes would be accepted for all the university's athletic programs.

As much as he hated the idea of having to leave the branch just as so much progress was being made and there remained so much more work to be done, Volma knew that for the sake of his health, he had no choice. "On the advice of my physician and for the sake of my family, I am submitting my resignation as president of the Austin branch NAACP as of this day November 21, 1963. May God be with you," Volma wrote just one day before a young and popular President Kennedy came to Texas. Kennedy, along with his wife, Jackie, Texas Gov. John Connally and Vice President Lyndon Johnson rode in a motorcade in Dallas that ended in tragedy.

Condolences for Volma poured in from everywhere. Friends flooded the house on Springdale Road. Most of all, the members of the branch wished him a speedy recovery, and begged him not to resign as branch president. They promised that if Volma stayed on as president, he would never want for help. Each active member promised Volma a new level of assistance. He would only have to give directions and the members would carry them out. By the time the December branch meeting rolled around, Volma had retracted his resignation and was again in charge. The members gave him as much help as they could, but before long Volma found himself again devoting more and more hours to the work of the branch, nursing his bleeding ulcers, and wondering what kind of president former Vice President Lyndon Johnson was going to make.

Volma's ties with Johnson went back to Johnson's days as a Texas senator. He wondered if Johnson would continue Kennedy's push for civil rights legislation, something many Blacks were convinced he would never do considering his past ties with the Southern Bloc. But the passing years had revealed a new side of the man who would become president. NAACP National President Roy Wilkins called Johnson "the old Br'er Fox of the Senate— and the most capable politician I've ever met."

Wilkins, president of the national NAACP between 1955 and 1977, knew that Blacks needed a powerful ally to champion their cause in Washington. He knew about Johnson's presidential aspirations and saw a change in Johnson's politics. "In those days, Johnson was just beginning to get religion on civil rights," Wilkins wrote in his autobiography. "The historical, irreversible impact of the Supreme Court's ruling in *Brown v. Board of Education* was not lost on him, and he had noticed the drift of Black voters away from the Democratic Party in the 1954 and 1956 elections. He dreamed of becoming president himself, but knew that so long as Jim Crow wrapped around him, the rest of the country would see him only as a Southerner, a cornpone Southerner at that, rather than a man of national stature. So around 1957 he began to change the course of civil rights."[34]

* * *

Television images traced the events of the summer of 1964. Intense heat combined with intercity pressures began what was to become a summer of violence in cities across America. Residents of many large cities in both the South and North were stifled under the smoke and fires that were a part of a summer of race riots.

Bottle-throwing crowds took to the streets in Harlem and Rochester, New York. Other disturbances broke out in Jersey City, Paterson and Elizabeth, New Jersey as well as Dixmoor, a suburb of Chicago. Philadelphia was also the site of a riot on August 28, 1964.

The Austin School Board also began to feel the fire on civil rights. During the 1964 school year, Austin school administrators began integrating teachers, an historic step and precursor to the wholesale "crossover" plan that would begin in earnest in 1969.

Three Black teachers, William Akin, B. T. Snell and Miss Narveline Drennan, transferred from Old Anderson High School and Kealing Junior High School to formerly white schools. The teachers all held master's degrees and were praised as being master teachers.[35]

Title VI of the Civil Rights Act of 1964, which applied to schools, was to change the face of education in the United States, especially in the South. Federal funds, vital to the operations of any school district, could be cut off in districts "that practice discrimination, principally by maintaining a dual system of schools for Negroes and whites."[36]

In Austin the waning months of 1964 saw Black students target segregation practices on The University of Texas campus. This time the students took issue with the Cowboys, a UT service group which held a popular charity show and parade each year. During the years that Hemann Sweatt sought entry to the university, the parade featured a caricature of Little Richard in blackface, madly knocking at a makeshift door on a rolling float. The figure was supposed to portray Sweatt knocking at the door of The University of Texas. Little Richard's hit song "Keep A Knocking But You Can't Come In" blared loudly over the public address system.

November 1964 saw members of the Students for a Democratic Society (SDS) picket the UT Student Union as the Cowboy Minstrels sold tickets for their annual show.

"Blackface perpetrates a false stereotype of the Negro," said Linda Talbert, secretary of SDS and the group's spokesperson. "This image is a carryover from the days of slavery."[37]

A response by the Cowboy Minstrels stated, "The show is not something the Cowboys cannot change. Our organization is not making fun when we put on blackface. This is tradition. We are providing entertainment and raising money for the Austin Council for Retarded Children."[38]

But an editorial in the UT student newspaper, *The Daily Texan*, called it something very different:

> The traditional Cowboy Minstrel Show—a painful reminder of the image of the Black formerly held by society. The picture and humor of the Black displayed in the minstrel show is a part of our culture. Removal of all references would remind us of the inferior treatment and status once rendered the Black would be impossible, and would falsely depict our history. But this does not provide the excuse to continue to bring forth this stereotype image which members of the race are working diligently to overcome.[39]

Amid the nationwide riots and local degradations, Rev. Martin Luther King, Jr. became the recognized leader of the Civil Rights Movement. Lauded for his non-violent stance in creating social change, King was awarded the 1964 Nobel Peace Prize in Oslo, Norway, on December 10, 1964.

A week later the Supreme Court upheld the constitutionality of the public accommodations section of the Civil Rights Act of 1964. The court also ruled that the act required reversal of convictions and dismissal of charges against sit-in demonstrators made prior to the act becoming law in July 1964, reversing about 3,000 cases left hanging in Southern courts.[40]

Volma was pleased at the progress made towards eradicating discrimination. He only wished the Austin branch could have made more headway in establishing a Human Relations Commission in Austin.

He spoke at the annual NAACP awards banquet traditionally held the first Friday evening in December. "Negroes are still on the merry-go-round of supposed freedom as the powers-that-be in Texas and Austin stay dedicated to the tokenism of leaving things as they are," he said.[41]

Volma cited two glaring segregation problems in Austin: a barber shop college, and business schools which still refused to admit Black students. He said that the Austin chapter, which led picketing and sit-ins against the city council over human rights in April, was today "better organized for action or demonstrations if needed than ever before."[42]

* * *

The issue of voting rights in the Deep South was the primary concern of many national and grass roots civil rights organizations, including the NAACP.

Although the Civil Rights Act of 1964 was the most far-reaching civil rights law the nation had ever seen, it lacked provisions in one important area. Throughout the South, Blacks could now eat in restaurants, stay at hotels, and see movies from the comfort of the lobby floor. However, a large segment of the Black population was still denied the right to vote.

The one thing that the Civil Rights Act of 1964 did not address was "a provision authorizing the assignment of federal registrars to aid southern Blacks who faced blatant discrimination when they attempted to register with local officials."[43]

Early 1965 brought renewed efforts to register Black voters in the South. Members of Dr. Martin Luther King's Southern Christian Leadership Conference walked Black neighborhoods, talked to residents who had never owned a voter registration card, and attempted to get them to register to vote. Many wanted to vote, but were held back by what they knew could be reprisals through their jobs, or threats to their families.

January and February brought the organization to Selma, Alabama, where a state judge had issued a ban on all gatherings after Blacks attempted to test the public accommodations section of the Civil Rights Act of 1964. Few Blacks, including many of the city's professionals, voted in Selma because they could not pass the stringent literacy tests or demonstrate a knowledge of the U.S. Constitution, which was required of them in order to obtain a voter registration card.

To Volma, the situation in Selma seemed far away. He heard accounts of King and demonstrators being arrested in Selma in groups of up to 3,000 people. He saw national news accounts of King's meetings with President Johnson, and knew that something would have to happen concerning voting rights in order for the country to heal itself and move forward.

The NAACP national office made voting rights a nationwide issue. In February, Roy Wilkins, executive secretary of the NAACP and Volma's "man," arrived in Austin at the invitation of the Austin branch and the Texas Union.

Volma was always pleased when Wilkins came through Austin, but was not always able to get off from the post office to meet with him. Sometimes Wilkins landed at Austin's Mueller Airport on his way to see President Lyndon Johnson at his ranch near Johnson City.

* * *

The 1960s push for civil rights brought back many of the fears prevalent in the country during the early part of the century. The early 1900s saw an increasing number of Black lynchings as well as riots in various parts of the country. Lynching became such a problem that NAACP leader Walter White often went undercover to learn the real facts. Light skinned enough to pass for a white man, White often spoke to the very people responsible for a lynching or starting a race riot.

The NAACP national office received word that *Birth of a Nation*, a film derogatory to Blacks, would be revived and shown again.

Volma wrote a letter, dated February 15, 1965, to Clarence Laws, southwest regional secretary in Dallas: "In regards to your memorandum concerning the showing of the film *Birth of a Nation,* no movie house in Austin has any plans for showing it."[44]

The following week, the fiery Black Muslim leader Malcolm X was shot to death at a rally at the Audubon Ballroom in New York City.

The Muslim leader's death ignited a controversy in the nation that was only overshadowed the following month by racial tensions in the small city of Selma, Alabama, where many Blacks were prevented from voting by the use of stringent qualification tests.

Rev. James Reeb, a Unitarian minister, died after he and two other white Unitarian ministers were beaten by white men while assisting in the Selma voting drive.

Volma and the branch issued a resolution condemning "the state of Alabama, its public officials, and its citizens who are in any way guilty of and are connected with the perpetration by omission or commission, which led to the violence, brutality and intimidation and injury on American citizens who seek full freedom of the American dream."[45]

The branch also stayed abreast of events at the local level, initiating a letter on March 12, 1965, to KHFI-TV in Austin to air two complaints. The first complaint protested the policy of the station allowing a tourist film about South Africa to be shown on television: "The South African government promotes the most vicious and evil policy of racial discrimination anywhere in the world today. We therefore feel it is far from fitting or proper that you engage in any form of promotion of South Africa. Civilized men who are concerned about human dignity must avoid furthering the cause of hate and violence, particularly as it is practiced in South Africa."[46]

The second complaint protested the actions of a photographer who filmed James Farmer's talk at St. Edward's University on March 5, 1965: "He intruded rudely during Mr. Farmer's speech, distracting and annoying the audience with his bright light and noisy camera. It was an incredibly rude action to both Mr. Farmer and the audience. Had your photographer wanted to have films of Mr. Farmer, he could have obtained them at the reception given for Mr. Farmer before the talk."[47]

On the national front, events in Selma, Alabama, escalated to gigantic proportions. Volma watched intermittent television footage and read newspaper accounts of Blacks as they attempted to gain the right to vote in the small town of Selma, Alabama.

The NAACP was in the midst of a nationwide voter registration campaign and Volma spearheaded the Austin drive. Dozens of volunteers converged on the Austin branch NAACP office on East 12th Street, listened to instructions, and took street maps of neighborhoods in East Austin for a full day of walking door to door.

Many East Austin Blacks were already registered to vote. But others were not aware that a poll tax was no longer necessary.

To Volma, the right to vote was as sacred a right as the ideals espoused in the Bill of Rights. To be able to vote meant you had a say in your own destiny and in the selection of those individuals who ultimately shaped the future of countries, states, cities, and towns. It was a right guaranteed by the Fourteenth Amendment. No one should be able to take that right away.

But for Blacks in some cities in the Deep South, voting had never been a right that segregationist whites let them enjoy. Some voting registrars in southern cities, towns, and rural backwaters insisted on qualifications from Blacks that bordered on the absurd.

Selma was a shining example of Southern bigotry gone awry. Although Blacks made up approximately half of the 28,000 people who lived in the town just fifty-seven miles from the capital city of Montgomery, by 1965 only 156 Blacks were registered to vote.

The early promise that the Civil Rights Act of 1964 would expand on provisions guaranteeing equal access to the polls, regardless of race, had given way to disillusionment. The final text of the act did not provide for assignment of federal registrars to hardcore southern areas where Blacks repeatedly experienced difficulty in registering to vote.

For Black leaders in Selma, the lack of federal guarantees involving voting rights meant they had to agitate the local citizenry for action in areas guaranteed under the Civil Rights Act of 1964, such as public accommodation and equal education. They would also have to keep the pressure on voting registrars to obtain their guaranteed Fourteenth Amendment right.

July 1964 brought an end to Black demonstrations for local compliance with the public accommodations section of the Civil Rights Act of 1964 in Selma. An injunction banning all such gatherings was issued by State Judge James Hare, an action which clearly showed that counting on judicial action to remedy ingrained attitudes was not an option.

The reputation for discrimination against Blacks in Alabama, Mississippi, and other states in the Deep South gained the attention of Martin Luther King's Southern Christian Leadership Conference (SCLC). King, fresh from a victory in the Montgomery bus boycott, and anxious to expand SCLC's operations beyond the bounds of Montgomery, set up shop in Selma.

The SCLC chose Selma because the city had "become a symbol of bitter end resistance to the Civil Rights Movement in the Deep South," King told an audience of 700 people in Brown's Chapel in Selma on New Year's Day.

The SCLC set up shop at Brown's Chapel Methodist Church in the heart of the Black community. They held organizational meetings with members of the Black community as well as representatives of the Student Non-Violent Coordinating Committee (SNCC).

King's SCLC and members of SNCC weathered basic differences in philosophy for the sake of the cause. While King's forces brought in their own leadership to work with members of the Black community on civil rights issues, SNCC preferred to have Black communities provide their own leaders. SNCC then provided assistance in areas of Black enfranchisement, political autonomy, and school desegregation.

Rev. F. D. Reese emerged as the leader of Selma's Blacks. With the assistance of King, his aides Hosea Williams and Andrew Young, Jim Bevel (director of the Alabama Project), and John Lewis (SNCC chairman who would later become a U.S. congressman), plans to stage marches to the Selma courthouse took shape.

But those marchers met resistance from Selma's Old Guard.

Volma saw a newspaper photo of what happened after Selma Sheriff Clark jabbed Mrs. Annie Lee Cooper with the heel of his hand as she stood in a line of several Blacks outside the Selma Courthouse waiting to register to vote. The fifty-three-year-old Mrs. Cooper reportedly shouted to Clark, "I wish you would have hit me, you scum." Sheriff Clark, known for his vile temper, then beaned her with a billy club. Volma saw the picture of the stout Mrs. Cooper being held down by three Selma police officers. In a later march to the courthouse, King, Abernathy, and about 100 protesters were jailed.

Selma's Black teachers also showed their support. On January 22, 1965, over 100 Black teachers marched to the courthouse to protest unfair voter registration practices. Many of them had been denied the right to vote. When they reached the courthouse, they were forced to turn around and march back to Brown Chapel after they were threatened by law officers brandishing billy clubs.

Later, in the small town of Marion, located about thirty miles from Selma, protesters headed for the courthouse after a rousing church rally. After troopers ordered them to turn around, the street lights were mysteriously doused. In the darkness that enveloped the scene, cameras could not record the incident that followed—state troopers flailing Black demonstrators with billy clubs as they fled. Seventeen-year-old Jimmy Lee Jackson was shot as he tried to protect his grandmother. Jackson later died.

Gov. George Wallace, calling marchers "professional agitators with pro-Communist affiliations," immediately issued an executive order banning night marches.

The attack on Marion demonstrators only fueled the desire of the civil rights leaders to do more. Consequently, they planned a march from Selma to the state capital at Montgomery to personally deliver their agenda to Governor Wallace.

Wallace, whose announced plans to run for president of the United States fizzled when Goldwater captured the 1964 nomination, still held aspirations to run again in the 1968 election. Instead of running on the Republican ticket, Wallace planned to organize a third party and run for the highest office in the land. An avowed segregationist, Wallace vowed to use "whatever measures are necessary to prevent a march" when plans for the march from Selma to Montgomery reached his ears.

Other atrocities surfaced. Sheriff Clark and lawmen reportedly drove 165 protesters into the countryside, using nightsticks and cattle prods all the way.

Newsmen photographed Sheriff Clark as he grabbed Mrs. Amelia Boynton by the collar. Boynton, who along with many others waited in line to be called into the courthouse to register to vote, was pushed about half a block to a police car after the Black protesters refused to move into an alley beside the courthouse as ordered by Sheriff Clark.

Even King, in addition to being jailed on several occasions, was not spared the growing indignities against the town's Blacks. He and two aides walked to the Prince Albert Hotel to register. Other establishments in Selma had given up the practice of not serving Blacks in the wake of mounting pressure by civil rights activists. Integrating the hotel would be another step in total integration for the entire city. As King stood before the counter, a strange man landed two hard blows to his temple. King's aides helped him to his feet and the man was subdued. He turned out to be a neo-Nazi, many of whom had dogged King's meetings and marches.

But King and the other protesters knew the struggle must continue. The planned march from Selma to Montgomery took place on Sunday, March 7th. During organizational meetings, marchers were drilled in non-violent techniques. They were also shown how to protect themselves from tear gas. The fifty-seven-mile march meant that they would have to camp out at least two nights. Consequently, many marchers wore comfortable shoes and carried bed rolls and backpacks. Four ambulances trailed the group of marchers.

King wanted to lead the marchers, but was persuaded against it by his aides. Consequently, when protesters left Brown's Chapel in the afternoon, they were led by Hosea Williams, King's aide.

What happened next would become a part of the shame of the Civil Rights Movement for all eternity.

* * *

Volma sat in his favorite chair in the living room of his home when the evening news panned to scenes shot in Selma, Alabama.

The scenes would remain etched forever in Volma's memory. What seemed like thousands of Blacks marched down the highway in sight of the Edmund Pettus Bridge in Selma. They actually numbered 525. They carried signs of protest—"Freedom Now" and "Down with Segregation." White law enforcement officers were strung out alongside the highway. Some sat erect on horses that pranced in the tall grass. Others stood with billy clubs in hand, revolvers strapped to their sides. They wore helmets and carried whips and gas mask pouches.

The television screen panned to law enforcement officers and others found to have been deputized by Sheriff Clark strictly for the occasion. They formed a wedge. When the marchers did not disperse as ordered by Major John Cloud, the wedge became a living organism, moving into the unarmed protesters with lightning speed.

The posseemen spurred their horses and rode roughshod into the demonstrators. Billy clubs flailed at Black heads, and whips cracked over the backs of hastily retreating demonstrators. Then a white cloud seemed to envelop the scene and lawmen could be seen donning gas masks.

The marchers had been warned to lie down if tear gas was used. But the flying billy clubs, whips, and ironclad hooves of advancing horses made lying down dangerous.

Four carloads of white onlookers who were parked on the bridge also charged after the retreating marchers, clubbing them as they ran away.

The troopers chased the retreating men, women, and children back to Selma's Black neighborhood, where residents of the homes near the church rained rocks and bottles on their heads.

Volma was stunned. With all the other violence he had witnessed in the fight for civil rights, this was the most cruel. He knew he had to do something. Anyone who espoused the tenets of freedom could not just sit back and wait for others to make the first move.

In the days that followed, Volma watched as Martin Luther King took charge. On Tuesday King personally led a march that was planned to culminate in Montgomery. At the Edmund Pettus Bridge, where marchers had been brutalized two days before, King and his marchers faced off with state troopers.

As if by some tacit signal, the troopers stepped back, leaving a clear path to Montgomery for the marchers. But King also turned back, leading the protesters back to the church, and not on the fifty-seven-mile march to Montgomery as planned.

SCLC leaders and Selma's white leaders had struck a deal. But unfortunately for King, the agreement not to proceed past the bridge had not been shared with others in his own camp. Charges of "selling out the movement" and "a classic example of trickery against the people" were flung at King by John Lewis and James Farmer.

Reporters obtained statements from various civil rights leaders, all critical of the turnaround at the bridge, stirring more criticism of King and his tactics.

But King had decided to work within the power structure to get needed support from locals as well as state and federal jurists. King played his cards pretty close to the vest in waiting for an injunction permitting a march to Montgomery. When Judge Johnson issued the injunction allowing the march to proceed, Governor Wallace branded the decision as coming from a "mock court."

Now King had his hole card—a sanctioned march where no law enforcement officers could interfere with the marchers. On March 21, 1965, two weeks after Bloody Sunday, King again amassed marchers for the fifty-seven-mile trip.

But this time the march took on national and international overtones. Supporters from all over the country converged on Selma and Montgomery to become part of the historic march. They were joined by the president of the Austin branch NAACP, an unassuming man with a serious demeanor and a passion for the rights of others.

And this time they also had the support of President Lyndon Johnson. When Governor Wallace fumed that Alabama didn't have enough troops to protect the marchers, Johnson called up the Alabama National Guard—1,863 military—to provide protection. But the cagy Johnson had also removed the National Guardsmen from Wallace's control.

Johnson also pressed 1,000 military policemen from Maxwell Air Force Base in Montgomery and Craig Field near Selma into service. He then placed 1,000 troops at Fort Benning, Georgia, on alert.

As Volma and two members of the Austin branch drove from Texas and entered Alabama, they kept a sharp eye out for lawmen and never exceeded the speed limit. They drove all night and arrived in Montgomery, the capital of Alabama. The city was crammed with locals as well as people from outside the state. As a final insult to the movement, Governor Wallace had given all white women employed by the state the day off.

Volma and his friends hitched a ride to the staging area where the marchers were waiting to make a triumphant entry into Montgomery. He saw them walking, some bone weary but happy, others jubilant that the march was seen as a victory for the movement. He saw the military vehicles and armed soldiers, and heard the sounds of military helicopters flying overhead.

He heard some of the marchers speak of the entertainment the night before in St. Jude's Complex. Entertainers from all over the country stopped what they were doing to become a part of the historic occasion. They included Harry Belafonte, Mahalia Jackson, Tony Bennett, Billy Eckstein, Pete Seeger, Odetta, Sammy Davis, Jr., Dick Gregory, Godfrey Cambridge, Leonard Bernstein, Alan King, Nipsy Russell, Bobby Darin, the Chad Mitchell Trio, George Kirby, Joan Baez, Peter, Paul and Mary, Ossie Davis, Ella Fitzgerald, Floyd Patterson, Ruby Dee, James Baldwin, Shelley Winters, John Kilins, and Nina Simone.

Thursday saw the 300 marchers who had made the entire trip converge on the capitol. They became a part of the 25,000 people who greeted them with wild cheers. Volma listened to stirring speeches by many of the leaders involved in the Civil Rights Movement.

But the most moving speech by far was made by a man short in stature, but with a big voice. He was the same man that Volma listened to three years before in 1962 while standing under the shade of a tree at the Washington Monument in Washington, D.C. Since the March on Washington, Martin Luther King had been presented the Nobel Prize for Peace and had become the foremost leader in civil rights that the country and the world had ever known.

Volma was so moved by the speeches that it hardly mattered when he heard later that the delegation which attempted to give Governor Wallace a petition had been told the governor had already left for the day.

They gained their car about sundown and immediately started on the long drive back to Austin. They had luck on their side. They were nowhere near a young white mother of five who had left Wayne State University in Detroit to participate in the march. She and a nineteen-year-old Black man provided rides back to Selma for several carloads of marchers. Because she was seen as a white woman riding with a Black man, the woman was harassed, insulted, rear-ended and practically forced from the roadway several times.

But Viola Liuzzo had not taken an incomplete in her courses at Wayne State University to run home at the first sign of trouble. When she and nineteen-year-old Leroy Motel headed back to Montgomery to get another load of marchers that evening, a car began passing them and three shots rang out. Liuzzo slumped forward while Motel managed to steer the car to an open field.

While he lay still on the floor of the car, covered with Liuzzo's blood, Motel heard the sound of a car coming to a stop and footsteps first approaching, then retreating from their car, and finally taking off.

Volma and his companions left Alabama and headed home for Texas. They read about Mrs. Liuzzo's murder in the newspaper.

* * *

The situation in Selma once again put President Johnson's feet to the fire on civil rights. On March 15, 1965, Johnson addressed a joint session of Congress while NAACP President Roy Wilkins listened from the gallery. Johnson's eloquent speech became part of civil rights lore:

> I speak tonight for the dignity of man and the destiny of democracy . . . The command of the Constitution is plain. There is no moral issue. It is wrong to deny any of your fellow Americans the right

to vote. What happened in Selma is part of a far larger movement that reaches into every section and state in America. It is the effort of American Negroes to secure for themselves the full blessings of American life. Their cause must be our cause, too. Because it is not just Negroes, but really it is all of us who must overcome the crippling legacy of bigotry and injustice . . . And we shall overcome.[48]

Congress passed the Voting Rights Act of 1965 and President Johnson signed it into law on August 6, 1965, in the same room where President Lincoln signed the bill freeing the slaves. "Let me now say to every Black in the country," Johnson said in a spirited speech at the signing, "You must register. You must vote. And you must learn, so your choice advances your interests and the interests of the nation."[49]

The Voting Rights Act of 1965 contained provisions which applied to state and federal elections. The provisions provided for suspension of the use of literacy tests and other such devices in the states of Alabama, Georgia, Louisiana, and the Carolinas. The law also authorized the appointment of federal voting examiners in those areas.[50]

The bill also required that state laws concerning voting passed by these states or counties must be approved by the U.S. attorney general or the U.S. District Court for the District of Columbia before becoming effective. It also declared state poll taxes to be discriminatory and directed the attorney general to start court proceedings against these requirements.[51]

* * *

With the passage of the Civil Rights Act of 1964, Volma and the Austin branch now had the ammunition to go after businesses which refused services to individuals on the basis of race.

Volma forwarded a complaint to the Department of Justice, Civil Rights Division, in Washington, D.C., from a young Black woman who was refused service at a local barbecue restaurant. According to reports, the restaurant owner told the young woman "he would not serve her unless a court ordered him to do so," and thus, "the Austin branch is unable to institute a suit at this time."[52]

The branch also sent a letter of protest to Sargent Shriver, director, Office of Economic Opportunity, to protest a proposal that the city of Austin and the Austin Independent School District pay Neighborhood Youth Corps (NYC) participants a rate of one dollar an hour: "It is dangerous in that it merely continues to support the present low level of salaries in this area . . . the danger in paying a dollar an hour is not that children will be earning more than their parents. It is that the children will not be taught that there is anything better to expect." Volma requested that a salary of $1.25 be extended to NYC participants in the Austin area and that "No program offering a lower rate of pay be approved for Austin."[53]

Volma also heard complaints of differences in patient care at some hospitals in Austin. Armed with this information, the branch acted upon it. Volma filed a federal civil rights complaint of racial discrimination against St. David's Hospital, bringing a three-million-dollar expansion to a halt, and freezing over a million dollars in federal money. The complaint accused St. David's Hospital of refusing to treat Black patients and refusing to hire Blacks for its professional staff, in violation of Title VI of the Civil Rights Act.

The suit ended in a hearing between NAACP officials, St. David's Hospital administrators, and federal representatives. During the hearing, St. David's Hospital administrators contended that they complied with all integration guidelines.

Volma was ultimately convinced that the suit and the resulting bad publicity had forced the hospital to take a long, hard look at its own policies. He felt the NAACP should accept the hospital's assurance of compliance, but continue to monitor the hospital in the future.

The Austin branch also initiated letters to Brackenridge Hospital and Holy Cross Hospital. However,

NAACP officials found no evidence of discrimination at these two hospitals.

As summer turned into fall, the Austin branch filed a complaint against a local barber college, accusing the owners of turning down three Blacks on grounds that there were no vacancies, but later the same day accepting a white student.

Several weeks later, the Veterans Administration wrote Volma a letter referencing Volma's initial letter of complaint against the business college. A. W. Stratton, chief benefits director, wrote that the business college ". . . has changed its policies voluntarily, has admitted Negroes and accepted the applications of others."[54]

The fall of 1965 found things at The University of Texas at Austin slowly changing for the better. The Cowboy Minstrels, a UT service organization known for performing in blackface at fundraisers, voted out the controversial practice. Earlier in March 1965, the Forty Acres Club, a segregated facility often used for UT functions, began accepting Black memberships.

In October 1965 the branch also filed complaints against a local business college and a large industrial facility, located about thirty miles from Austin, for discrimination in their treatment of Blacks.

Another complaint by the branch took on the city tax collector for not hiring Blacks, an accusation which he vehemently denied. W. C. Patton of Birmingham, the NAACP national associate director of voter registration, and Volma, charged, "some of our tax collectors have been dragging their feet in hiring Negroes" to collect poll taxes. "We have had our eyes on the tax collector in Travis County. The response we had from the tax collector here was not encouraging. Any time we can't get enough collectors deputized, we feel there's another motive—in a sense, it's a form of discrimination."[55]

However, the tax collector shot back, saying, "I've never denied anybody the right to sell poll taxes or the right to buy a poll tax or the right to vote. I've always felt that the colored people should have their own poll tax collectors."[56]

The bone of contention was the close proximity of two proposed poll tax collection stations on East 11th Street.

* * *

Although a federal lawsuit aimed at abolishing the poll tax in Texas was still pending in federal district court, the branch urged everyone to pay their poll tax anyway. The branch planned a "Poll Tax Sunday," to be conducted much like a political campaign, with speeches, committees, rallies, and publicity.

The state conference of branches set a goal to register 600,000 Black voters in Texas, and 8,000 to 9,000 in Austin and Travis counties.

Volma actively participated in NAACP state conference issues and could usually be seen with a knot of people discussing some burning civil rights question of the day. In his own quiet way, he made an impression on other members, and easily took the floor when there was a debate.

In October 1965 Volma threw his hat in the ring for the presidency of the Texas State Conference of Branches. He lost.

* * *

Bertha Means, a teacher at Allan Junior High School and longtime activist with the Austin branch NAACP, applied for membership in the Austin Teachers Federal Credit Union in early 1966. She was promptly turned down. The credit union accepted memberships from white applicants only.

Means was only one of many Black teachers who applied for loans at the Austin Teachers Federal Credit Union and was turned down solely because of race. Volma and members of the branch felt it was time that the organization moved into the twentieth century, especially in light of the passage of the Civil Rights Act of 1964.

Volma filed a complaint with the federal Civil Rights Commission citing the fact that Means' deposit was not accepted on the basis of race. However, the head of the credit union, A. J. Amundson, said that in 1949 there was a meeting between two formerly white credit unions which resulted in the creation of the Travis County Teachers Credit Union [TCTCU] for Negroes.

Amundson told the Austin daily that his group had "agreed not to give them [TCTCU] any competition. If we start taking Negroes, their credit union cannot exist. I would like to take them, but I don't feel like going back on our word. It would be doing them an injustice . . . We have been willing for several years to consolidate in the proper manner . . . They [the TCTCU] would have to liquidate and we take over its members, but the decisions are up to them."[57]

Volma later saw the TCTCU liquidated.

While the credit union situation hung in the balance, the Austin branch NAACP and Black Austin prepared for a visit from Roy Wilkins, executive secretary of the NAACP.

For Volma, Wilkins' visit was a great occasion. Wilkins spoke at the Mary E. Branch Auditorium on the campus of Huston-Tillotson College. A reception followed at the student union. As usual, Volma and the branch received the full cooperation of Dr. John T. King, president of Huston-Tillotson College. "We are delighted to share in this program and look forward to having Mr. Wilkins on campus. His being here will be a treat for the college," King wrote to Volma.[58]

The administrative council of the college supported the participation of Huston-Tillotson's students by paying half of the general admission fee.[59] Wilkins' visit came at the beginning of a year that held the promise of more civil rights gains for minorities. President Lyndon Johnson appointed a variety of minorities to government positions. His appointment of Robert Weaver as the head of the Department of Housing and Urban Development made Weaver the first Black to serve in a presidential cabinet.

* * *

The student protest groups still viewed the NAACP as too passive. Stokeley Carmichael was named the head of the Student National Coordinating Committee in May 1966, replacing John Lewis, who would later win election to Congress. The following month, Carmichael used the term Black Power for the first time during a march in support of James Meredith. The Congress of Racial Equality endorsed Black Power. Although more conservative leaders such as King and Wilkins condemned the term, it became popular nationwide.

Volma liked Black Power. He felt its use reflected racial pride, self-determination, and a desire for control of your own destiny.

In a move seen as racially biased, Black Georgia legislator Julian Bond was denied his seat on the grounds of disloyalty, due to his opposition to the Vietnam War and American policy towards Vietnam.

In Austin Volma and the Austin branch continued to keep the pressure on organizations and groups whose activities fell under the compliance provisions of the Civil Rights Act of 1964. Voting practices became highly suspect.

Following up on an NAACP complaint, the FBI visited Austin. FBI agents took a look at voter registration practices in Austin. Afterwards, Volma wrote to U.S. Attorney Nicholas Katzenbach at the U.S. Department of Justice in Washington, D.C.: "Sending the FBI to check Texas voter registration might have stirred the dander of Connally, Barnes, and Carr. Also, there might be areas where they are not needed, however, I considered this a worthwhile duty for the FBI. I welcomed them, and hope they return again."[60]

Later in the year the battle over the creation of a Human Relations Commission to process complaints of discrimination in Austin came to life once more. In June 1966 the Austin City Council established the Equal Citizenship Corporation, a non-profit corporation, to handle all human relations matters for the city on a contractual basis.

The action angered Volma. Memories of the NAACP's read-in and shut down of city council business for two weeks in April 1962 left him disappointed. The promise of a Human Relations Commission with real teeth still had not materialized. The Equal Citizenship Corporation was little more than an advisory committee with no real power to enforce its rulings. Volma stood firm in his opposition to the organization and urged minority groups to "refrain from using" it because "a private corporation presents absolutely no solution to the problems of human relations that exist today."[61]

Volma urged individuals having complaints of discrimination to continue to use the normal channels for filing complaints, such as the various federal agencies used in the past. Volma and the branch "spoke against it when it was created because we didn't think it was workable . . . it is not the type we needed . . . it could have been successful if the city had accepted it as an official arm of the city government."[62]

The branch spent the remainder of the year looking into complaints of discrimination throughout the city. In mid-summer, the branch looked into protesting against a University of Texas area dry cleaning company that "will accept Black cleaning, however, he has a tuxedo rental business in the same office and will not rent a tuxedo to a Black. The firm close to the University of Texas does lots of tuxedo rental rental business to students. This causes considerable trouble to Negroes because they have to go to another part of town for rentals."[63]

In mid-August, Volma sent a letter to the city of Austin Recreation Department concerning the poor lighting at Givens Park in East Austin. The branch received a promise that a new type of lighting fixture would be mounted approximately seventy feet off the ground, thereby providing greater security.[64] Later in August members of the Austin branch joined farm workers in their two-month-long march from the Rio Grande Valley to Austin to protest low wages.

The branch also protested the discriminatory referral policies of the local employment service, forwarding a complaint to the U.S. Department of Labor in Washington, D.C. They received assurance that the practice had been stopped. Arthur A. Chapin, special assistant to the secretary of labor, wrote, "We have since received a written report from the administrator which includes, for example, confirmation that occupational classification assignments will be made solely on the basis of qualification; that selection and referrals of applicants to job openings will be made solely on qualification and without regard to race."[65]

Later in September Volma attended a meeting of city garbage workers and listened to charges of discriminatory treatment. The group went on a four-day strike, resulting in thirty-nine garbage workers losing their jobs.[66] In late October the Rev. Dr. John Barclay, head of the Austin Equal Citizenship Corporation, scheduled a meeting with approximately forty Black employees of the city sanitation division, a meeting which none of them attended. Nonetheless, Barclay concluded that there was no discrimination in the sanitation division. Volma roundly criticized Barclay for basing his findings on talks with the sanitation superintendent, described as "the one man generally considered responsible for the appalling inequities in the sanitation department's personnel policies."[67]

Barclay responded, "Certainly we can't serve the community if people won't come to us . . . I don't want to get [into] a newspaper fight with Mr. Overton. We want to work with him."[68] Volma felt the garbagemen were getting a raw deal. He worked with both sides until a number of employees were reinstated.

*   *   *

In early November, Volma attempted another run for the presidency of the NAACP Texas State Conference of Branches. But even though he had the support of NAACP stalwarts such as Mrs. Juanita Craft, he again lost. Gillespie Wilson, the incumbent, won the election.

* * *

The branch took the Equal Employment Opportunity Commission (EEOC) to task for not hiring more Black clerical help in the regional director's office in Austin. Stephen N. Shulman, chairman of the EEOC in Washington, D.C., wrote Volma, "As you indicated, there are no Negroes filling the GS-3 and four clerical positions in our Austin office. However, of the office's six professional employees at GS-12 and above, one is Black, and we are about to hire another Black at a GS-13 level. You should also know that in our ten field offices we currently employ sixty-one whites and forty-seven Negroes."[69] Although some of the hiring struck Volma as tokenism, he felt the federal government did hire more Black applicants.

Just before Thanksgiving, Roy Wilkins, NAACP executive secretary, issued a "Distress Memorandum to all branches and youth councils," requesting contributions towards a judgment against the Savannah, Georgia, branch which lost an appeal to the Supreme Court.[70] The Savannah lawsuit had been filed because of the picketing of a neighborhood grocery store after its proprietor beat a Black boy. "Now we need every branch to help us dig up $75,000 on or before December 31, 1966," Wilkins wrote. The verdict was against the Savannah branch of the NAACP, the Georgia State Conference of Branches of the NAACP, and the national organization of the NAACP. "The honor of the NAACP is at stake," Wilkins wrote. "We cannot run out on our Georgia members."[71] The assessment of the Austin branch was $100.

The branch also found itself getting into the burgeoning urban renewal arena. They scheduled a meeting at Doris Miller Auditorium on Rosewood Avenue to discuss urban renewal and its impact on East Austin. "In the past, we have not concerned ourselves with urban renewal activities, however, we feel compelled to seek remedies, relief, and to inform the population of urban renewal," Volma wrote to Leon Lurie, acting director of the Urban Renewal Agency in Austin.[72]

The Austin branch did not have the manpower and finances to assist the numerous complainants whose homes were taken in the urban renewal movement. However, the branch acted as an intermediary between complainants and the Urban Renewal Agency.

In December 1966 the Austin branch initiated an annual dinner as a fundraiser. During his trips to NAACP national conventions, Volma attended formal dinners where the Spingarn Award, the most coveted civil rights award in the country, was presented. He thought the idea of a formal dinner and a civil rights award would be good press and help raise funds for the branch.

The Austin branch NAACP held its first DeWitty awards banquet at the Driskill Hotel in downtown Austin. The award was named for Arthur B. DeWitty, the journalist and tireless civil rights worker who was narrowly defeated for election to the Austin City Council in the early 1950s.

The first DeWitty Award, which became highly coveted, was presented to Mrs. Bertha Means, the school teacher and civil rights worker who instigated the suit against the Teachers Credit Union for their refusal to accept Black members.

4

CITY COUNCIL BID

In early 1967 Volma decided to run for a place on
the Austin City Council. There had never been a Black on
the Austin City Council. Since Arthur DeWitty's failed bid
for a council seat in 1951, council members were elected
by the place system. However, East Austin had yet to successfully field a candidate that was satisfactory to its various political factions.

To Volma, the reason was simple. The East Austin
community was too divided on the issues. Blacks could
not seem to agree on what was best for the community.
Consequently, they never gave their full support to any
one candidate. He felt that the present representation on
the Austin City Council sadly neglected the political,
social, and economic issues peculiar to East Austin citizens. Friends and acquaintances had often urged him to
run. There were many factors in his favor. The branch's
initial struggle for the creation of a Human Relations
Commission, picketing the downtown stores and restaurants for equal public accommodations, and public statements on television and radio, gave him the name recognition needed for success in politics.

Volma and other minorities who considered a run for
political office knew that there was a core group of political king-makers in Austin who decided which candidates
would receive funds vital to a successful campaign. Often
Black politicians could not wholly deliver the Black vote.

Consequently, they brought few cards to the table and were often turned away with no concrete promises of financial assistance.

After considering all the angles, Volma decided to throw his hat in the ring. However, he had not reckoned on the federal government's policy regarding government employees seeking political office. Volma found that he could run for political office as long as it did not interfere with his work schedule at the post office. He asked Richard Dockery, NAACP regional director, to check with the Civil Service Commission on restrictions imposed on running for political office. In February 1967 he also had the local president of the National Alliance of Postal Employees to write the association's national president concerning methods used to appeal the decision. He received a letter from Austin Postmaster O. N. Bruck, "stating the decision of Assistant Postmaster General disapproving his request to run for the position of city council member."[1] Volma continued to have dealings with Postmaster Bruck and enjoyed a relationship that was cordial yet strained.

Many individuals who supported Volma throughout his years with the Austin branch NAACP were disappointed that he was not going to run for a place on the Austin City Council. One of those individuals was Mrs. U. V. Christian, his friend and mentor. Time and again, Christian came to Volma's defense on some community matter that he had jumped into with both feet. In 1967 an incident occurred that allowed Volma to come to Christian's defense.

Although the small woman who had done so much towards schooling Volma on the needs of East Austin, and politics in general, was much loved by the Black community, she was just another employer to the city of Austin administration.

The seventy-three-year-old Christian was jailed for failing to comply with a city zoning ordinance that required businesses to have off-street parking. Crescent

Beauty School, Christian's beauty college, was situated on East 11th Street in the heart of "the cuts." Christian's business did not have off-street parking, which was a real financial burden for a small business.

"The NAACP is concerned about the jailing of a seventy-three-year-old widow because of a so-called zoning order," Volma wrote city officials. "We are extremely concerned with the procedure in which the matter was handled and will make such inquiries and investigation as necessary."[2]

* * *

In March 1967 a federal court ordered Alabama to desegregate all public schools, something Alabama and the South would not take lying down. The federal court ruling preceded what was to become a sweltering summer of race riots and anti-war demonstrations. Students on college campuses throughout the nation continued to protest the United States' role in the Vietnam War.

Martin Luther King came out against the war in Vietnam. On March 25, 1967, he led a march of 5,000 white and Black anti-war demonstrators in Chicago.

Although King's anti-war stance was unpopular with NAACP leaders and others, many Americans agreed with him. In the White House, a weary President Johnson paced back and forth in the oval office, as hundreds of anti-war demonstrators marched and chanted "Hey, hey LBJ. How many babies have you killed today?" President Johnson's approval rating by the American public took a nosedive.

In Austin many establishments formerly unfriendly to Black business now found that they faced the possibility of public censure if they did not change with the times. Lonnie Fogle and Ezell Green, two veteran NAACP members, reported to a branch meeting held in late April that they had eaten in a restaurant in Smithville "and that it is now integrated!"[3]

But progress in acquiring full integration in all Austin public facilities sometimes took one step forward and two steps backwards. In early May 1967 a Black legislator was denied service at the Austin Club in downtown Austin. "It's against our rules, you know, to have a Negro guest in the club," the club's manager was quoted as saying in the Austin daily. "I don't make the rules, I just enforce them."[4] For Volma, the incident only highlighted how far Austin had to go to attain full civil rights for all citizens.

In mid-May 1967 a sparse crowd descended on Kealing Jr. High School in East Austin to hear a giant of the civil rights movement. It was the NAACP's annual Freedom Day program. Daisy Bates accepted the Austin branch's invitation to speak after Robert Kennedy sent his regrets. "Although I would very much like to be with you for this event, my schedule is such that I will be unable to attend," Kennedy wrote to Volma.[5]

A stalwart of the American Civil Rights Movement, Bates detailed the struggle of the Little Rock Nine during the attempt to integrate Central High School in Little Rock, Arkansas in 1957. She spoke of the role all citizens concerned with morality and the advancement of the nation must play to eradicate discrimination.

Volma was disappointed at the small size of the crowd, but warmed by Bates' speech. "Our crowd was not as expected, however, the coverage has been wonderful from the people that attended," Volma wrote Bates.[6]

Later in May 1967 Volma and the branch initiated a letter to Gov. John Connally which took issue with the use of Texas Rangers during the Rio Grande Valley strike. "We feel that such use of Rangers serves to intimidate and harass these citizens who are working to better their living standards," Volma wrote. "As Governor, we believe you should have sent a conciliatory team in rather than one to arrest, intimidate and harass citizens."[7]

The branch got little in the way of a concrete response, except for a letter from Connally stating, "I appreciate your letter and your comments concerning the Texas Rangers in Starr County. Thanks for contacting me . . ."[8]

A week later Volma sent another letter of protest. This time, it was directed to Louie Welch, mayor of Houston, after student demonstrations at Texas Southern University:

> The students were not criminals, but the methods used would indicate otherwise . . . I understood the seriousness of the situation that existed, however, at times like this it would seem that it is incumbent upon the law enforcement agencies to utilize an acquired skill rather than Gestapo tactics. Also, they should have taken into consideration the safety of hundreds of innocent students that had no advance knowledge of the events that occurred that night. Further, there was no excuse for the unnecessary destruction of the students' personal property.[9]

But Welch fired back in a letter dated June 6, 1967: "I can only conclude from your letter that you have been exposed to some of the unfounded rumors that cropped up after the incident. The fact is that the Police Department exercised considerable restraint in handling the students, considering that they were being fired upon from the dorms."[10]

The confrontation at Texas Southern University in Houston was only the beginning of what was to be a summer of rioting, burning, looting, and discord in a substantial portion of America. Black students rioted at Jackson State College, a historically Black college in Mississippi, on May 10 and 11, 1967, followed in June by the first large-scale riot in Boston in several years. Riots also occurred in Tampa, Florida, and Cincinnati, Ohio, in June. In mid-June Stokeley Carmichael provoked police and was arrested.

In July twenty-three persons died, 725 were injured, and over a thousand people were arrested in riots in Newark. The monetary damage was estimated to be in the millions.

A white policeman was shot and beaten to death by

a mob in Plainfield, New Jersey, on July 16, 1967, followed by violence in Cambridge, Maryland, on July 26.

The escalation of rioting worried Black leaders. On July 26, 1967, the leaders of four of the nation's largest civil rights organizations issued a joint statement waging calm.

Martin Luther King, Jr., of SCLC, A. Philip Randolph of the Sleeping Car Porters, Roy Wilkins of the NAACP, and Whitney Young of the Urban League condemned the riots and those who participated in them.

President Johnson appointed a riot commission to conduct an investigation. While the entire country seemed to be breathing the smoke of some riot or near riot, Austin was amazingly calm.

* * *

Bergstrom Air Force Base had long been a mainstay of the Austin community. Activated on September 19, 1942, it was first named Del Valle Air Base. On November 11, 1943, during the height of World War II, it became Bergstrom Army Air Field at the suggestion of a young Texas congressman by the name of Lyndon Johnson. The base was named for Captain John August Earl Bergstrom, who may have been the first Austinite killed in World War II. He died when Japanese bombers attacked the Philippines.[11]

But Volma and an assortment of Black enlisted men and women saw the air force base in a different light. On August 3, 1967, Volma wrote Secretary of Defense Robert McNamara: "The Austin Branch NAACP has found discrimination in housing in the Bergstrom AFB community and the Austin, Texas, area . . . We request that the government impose off-limits housing sanctions on this area. Also, we request that further federal spending on construction at Bergstrom AFB be suspended until the Austin community takes steps to stop subjecting military personnel to discrimination in housing."[12]

But instead of concrete action, an Air Force representative came by to inquire if the NAACP had been talking about base housing. Volma told him "no," and that was the last that they heard about the matter.[13]

* * *

In the summer of 1967 the Deacons Nominating Committee at Austin's First Baptist Church nominated Volma and about ten others for deaconships. The entire congregation voted by secret ballot on who would become a deacon. Despite being one of the few active Blacks at the church, Volma did not feel his nomination would pose a serious problem. He knew some members would be for him and others against him. After the votes were counted, Volma found himself as the first Black deacon in First Baptist Church's history. If there was controversy over his nomination, no one told him. No one discussed the proceedings or the results. He was now a part of the church deaconate.

But Volma found that his membership in a predominantly white church was a source of irritation to some Blacks in the community. Several times NAACP members who sold memberships were turned away by Blacks who questioned Volma's choice of church membership. They understood why he left his church in East Austin. In a time when the Black church was growing, expanding its horizons and finding its way, it was not unusual for members to change their membership to better meet their own needs. But they questioned why he had to join a white church. To their way of thinking, he could just as easily have joined another Black church.

Members of his former congregation often asked, "Are you coming back?" But Volma had become too involved in the First Baptist Church Bible study, the social ministry, the deaconate, teaching, and other church activities to even consider changing churches. Much later, a white friend asked Volma if he thought Blacks felt he had sold them out. Volma almost laughed. Considering that all of his civil rights activities—the read-in at city council chambers, his participation in the various marches in Washington, Montgomery, and

Boston, the school desegregation lawsuit, and the struggle for single member districting—occurred after he
joined First Baptist Church, Volma didn't really feel that
it was an issue.

For the next thirty years Volma was so busy with
church business and activities that he hardly had time to
wonder if someone in the congregation did not want him
as a deacon. He served as both an active and inactive deacon; he was a member of the Social Ministries
Committee, the Mission Committee, and he worked as a
teacher for the pre-school and teenage classes. He was
also a public greeter, taking up offerings and passing out
visitor cards. He also worked with the Worship Care
Committee, visiting church members in the city's hospitals and nursing homes.

* * *

In August 1967 Volma wrote a letter to the Office of
Economic Opportunity in Washington, D.C., concerning
"a number of complaints of unequal distribution of
employment in the administrative staff of the Gary Job
Corp Training Center, San Marcos, Texas, with respect to
Negroes." The letter also pointed out the disparity
between whites and Blacks in policy-making and administrative positions: "The opinion of the Austin NAACP is
that more Negroes should be employed in the administrative positions and that these corrections be made
immediately . . ."[14] As a result of the NAACP's complaint,
John P. Crawford was appointed center director.

The Austin daily had always been conservative when
it came to publishing positive stories about Blacks in
Austin. Volma found that unless they were running stories about "who shot John?" the pages were usually quiet
concerning accomplishments of Blacks.

The newspaper also had a policy of not placing pho-
tographs of Black brides in with other brides. Black
brides were placed on another page. But in late August
1967 Volma wrote a letter to Richard F. Brown, publisher, saying, "I have received many favorable comments

regarding the Negro bride's picture in Sunday's newspaper. As per our conversation, I do hope this will be a policy of the paper and not merely an accident."[15]

Good news about the Bergstrom Air Force Base housing situation came in September 1967, when McNamara announced that the Pentagon would extend the campaign to end housing discrimination against Black servicemen: "Bergstrom Air Force Base, like every other major military installation in the continental United States, is participating in this program."[16]

In August of the following year Bergstrom Air Force Base followed through on McNamara's lead by surveying apartments and trailer courts around Austin. Twenty-nine properties which failed to meet the Defense Department's directive on non-discrimination in housing were listed as off limits to military personnel. Single-family dwellings were not included.

* * *

October 1967 was an important time for both Volma and the city of Austin. Volma finally saw the fruit of the "read-in" which the Austin branch NAACP and others held in April 1964 to get the approval of the Austin City Council to create a Human Relations Commission. The issue had been on the back burner for over three years.

City Ordinance Number 671005-B amended the city code to create a city of Austin Human Relations Commission (HRC).[17] Volma and others who agitated for passage of the ordinance were disappointed that the commission was little more than an advisory board. The ordinance did not contain a penalty clause, which would have given the HRC authority to go after individuals and businesses who practiced discrimination. But they were forced to take what they could get. Volma was well aware of the climate of the city and the political atmosphere which produced the ordinance. The ordinance provided that the HRC "shall advise and consult with the city council on all matters involving racial, religious and ethnic discrimination, and devise practices for equal opportunity."[18]

He found that working with the twenty-four other members of the HRC was a lesson in cultural diversity. There was a CPA, a bank executive, a union president, a president of a furniture manufacturing company, a public relations and journalism professional, the president of the Better Business Bureau, a protestant minister, a Catholic priest, two University of Texas students, a bookkeeper-secretary, a home builder, two UT professors, two school teachers, a newspaper publisher, a media executive, and two housewives, as well as community workers.[19]

The annual DeWitty Awards Banquet was held in early December. Volma received a standing ovation as he was presented the Arthur B. DeWitty Award for excellence in civil rights gains. The award almost made up for the city council campaign that never happened.

* * *

In 1968 the Austin branch was still struggling to obtain local compliance with the public accommodations provision of the Civil Rights Act of 1964. Major obstacles facing the branch was the quest for an open housing ordinance, fair treatment, and trying to get Black achievements into history books.

In January 1968 Lonnie Fogel reported on the worsening situation at Camp Gary Job Corps. "If no improvement, will report to Washington," a membership committee report stated.[20]

In early March the Texas Conference of Branches sent out an announcement urging all branches "to send chairs of their Branch Education Committee to a state meeting," where, "our immediate objective is to seek to get Negro History integrated into the American history classes of the schools in Texas."[21]

It would be later in October 1968 that The University of Texas offered its first course in Black history. It was taught by George Washington, a member of the first integrated class of the UT Law School in 1950.[22]

The members of the Austin branch were also elated when a Black candidate filed for election to the school board. Wilhelmina Delco, a housewife and Parent Teacher Association worker, ran for a seat on the Austin school board. Volma was particularly proud of Delco, a longtime acquaintance and good friend. He, along with many others, urged Delco to run for the position.

* * *

The Austin branch took the lead in educating the public in matters that directly affected the Black community. On March 24, 1968, the branch sponsored a mass meeting at Doris Miller Auditorium in East Austin to hear about the model cities proposal.

Later in the month the branch sponsored interviews with political candidates in a program to educate the public. James Means, an educator at Huston-Tillotson College and an NAACP veteran, chaired the Political Action Committee during the NAACP's initiation of the first interviews with political candidates in the Democratic Primary.

On the national scene, Martin Luther King took time out from planning a Poor Peoples' Campaign and building a shanty town in Washington, D.C., to highlight the living conditions of the poor. King journeyed to Memphis to give his support to a sanitation workers' strike. But as he stood on the second floor balcony of the Lorraine Hotel, an assassin's bullet caught him in the right jaw.

King's death resulted in massive demonstrations and riots in more than 100 cities across America. Many people who believed in King's dream, both Black and white, felt the Civil Rights Movement would die.

However, some good came of King's death. President Lyndon Johnson shepherded the Fair Housing Act of 1968 (Title VIII of the 1968 Civil Rights Act) through Congress. The new measure contained provisions that outlawed discrimination in the sale or rental of housing.

On the local front the most pressing issue of the year was the housing ordinance. The Austin City Council voted to initiate a Fair Housing Ordinance for all of Austin. But the issue became a political hot potato when opponents

obtained enough signatures on petitions to submit the
matter to the voters in a referendum.

Perhaps the biggest critic of the Fair Housing
Ordinance was the Austin Board of Realtors. In a full
page advertisement in the *Austin American-Statesman*,
the board warned property owners that "a drastic federal forced housing bill now pending in the U.S. House of
Representatives will—if passed—strip you of your basic
right to sell or rent your home to whom you choose!"[23]

* * *

The Federal Fair Housing Bill passed Congress and
became law on April 11, 1968. Lyndon Johnson had given
Blacks a parting shot before leaving the presidency, never
to return. The escalation of the war in Vietnam, together
with his increasing unpopularity as a wartime president,
had convinced the boy from the Texas Hill Country that he
should withdraw from political life. He did so with a minimum of fanfare, but he would be looked upon throughout
history as a friend of America's minorities.

The Fair Housing Ordinance in Austin also passed
the Austin City Council thanks to the votes of council
members Harry Akin, Emma Long, and Dick Nichols.
Volma sent a letter to each one thanking them for what
amounted to "an act of political courage, humanitarian
understanding and justice. Even though others may not
agree, we feel very strongly that this was a significant
step in the right direction for Austin."[24]

But Volma had not reckoned on the groundswell of
public sentiment that resulted from the city council's passage of the Fair Housing Ordinance. Opponents of the
measure organized and collected petitions containing over
29,000 signatures, more than enough to bring the measure to a public vote.

Volma was against submitting the Fair Housing
Ordinance to a public vote. He felt that the public would
always vote against any such measure, and the white
majority would be able to control the election.

In early July Volma told a meeting of the Austin

branch executive committee that since a referendum had been called on the ordinance, the city council had a choice of either rescinding the ordinance or calling an election on it. After conferring with the NAACP legal division, Volma recommended that the branch seek an injunction against the referendum. The only problem was that it would cost the branch approximately $2,000, money that they did not have.

The branch would also require legal representation. After a discussion of his qualifications, the executive committee voted to give attorney Sam Houston Clinton power to prepare an injunction against the referendum.[25]

In November Americans elected another president. Richard M. Nixon, former vice president during the Eisenhower administration, defeated Hubert Humphrey. But the Nixon administration's policies on integration proved disheartening to the country's Blacks. "The Nixon Administration did all it could to turn back the clock on the progress we had made under Presidents Kennedy and Johnson," NAACP Executive Director Roy Wilkins wrote in his biography. "He told us his goal was to walk between those who sought 'instant integration' and those after 'segregation forever.' He also said he was going to allow Southern schools more time to comply with school desegregation deadlines."[26]

The branch geared up for another voter registration drive. Milton Gooden and Bertha Means, two NAACP stalwarts, led the voter registration drive. The branch recruited volunteers from all over Austin to walk door-to-door in East Austin, informing residents that a poll tax was no longer necessary to vote. One of those volunteers, a University of Texas student from west Austin named Peck Young, would later become indispensable to the NAACP in organizing the student vote.

Young found the experience of working with Means and Volma very interesting, but different: "Bertha was what she appeared to be which was a school teacher. She treated you like what you were which you'd always been all your life at that point, which was school kids. Volma treated us a lot more like adults. There was a presence about him and a reserve, but he wasn't unfriendly. We called him the Colonel."[27]

Young became one of Means' regular team leaders. He organized young people on The University of Texas campus to participate in elections and worked hard to get out the vote.

Throughout his tenure as president of the Austin branch, Volma saw many Blacks, both young and old, whose ideas did not quite gel with the NAACP's philosophy of gradual change through the legal system. Volma knew they were just as vitally interested in social change and more freedoms for Blacks as any dedicated NAACP member. He saw them attend a few of the branch meetings, then gradually fade into the more radical groups that began to make their presence felt in Austin during the 1960s.

A group of Black Panthers formed in East Austin. Stokeley Carmichael was busy throughout the country organizing the student movement into the Student Non-violent Coordinating Committee, also known as SNCC, or Snick. Carmichael came through Austin on a speaking and organizing tour in 1967.

Larry Jackson, a young Black activist from Hearne, Texas, came with him. Jackson became a student at The University of Texas at Austin in January 1968, but quit after three and a half years to become a leader in the student movement. Jackson became one of the growing cadre of young Blacks who were disillusioned with the NAACP's methods of gradualism to obtain social change and more freedoms for Blacks. He found the Black community in Austin to be "the next step above comatose." But Jackson's activism was more akin to radicalism to a number of people in Austin who observed his tactics.

However, Jackson's recognition of serious social problems often brought concrete results. In August 1968 the Austin daily ran a story about the seriousness of the rat infestation problem in East Austin. The six to seven daily

rat complaints seemed to be increasing, the chief sanitar-
ian for the Austin-Travis County Health Department said.
With no rat control program, the city could soon face a
problem of gigantic proportions, all in East Austin.[28]

Jackson's off-campus organization, Community
United Front, Inc., established a free breakfast program
in the public schools, and brought a rodent control program and infant child care to the city. But Jackson
remained firm in his views. Despite President Lyndon
Johnson's Great Society program, and the passage of the
Civil Rights Act of 1964, Jackson's group had differences
with the NAACP's support for him and "all the
hand-picked Uncle Toms that were around him."

Jackson and his followers were also actively involved
in protesting a university area service station which rou-
tinely refused service to minorities. Don Weedon's service
station, located on Guadalupe Street near The University
of Texas campus, was the scene of an altercation between
police and protesters. The protest landed Jackson and a
number of followers in jail and on the front page of the
newspaper.

Jackson placed a billboard at the corner of Martin
Luther King, Jr. Boulevard and Interstate Highway 35
that read, "Welcome to East Austin. You are now leaving
the American dream. Beware of rats, roaches and people
with a lack of food, clothing, jobs and the American
Dream. Support Community United Front." However,
Jackson respected Volma and his initiative in the civil
rights struggle more than Volma ever knew:

> I know I really made Mr. Overton mad. A lot of
> things I did I know he didn't see the rationalization of
> . . . I talked about going up side somebody's head in
> some of those meetings . . . We would antagonize folks.
> End up calling them names—crackers, pecker-woods.
> We would call the police pigs and things like that.
>
> I think a lot of people misunderstood Volma
> Overton. I think given the environment and the climate
> and the kinds of things that he was out here trying to

accomplish, he probably got as close to what he could
do with the resources he had at hand . . . He ended up
being the glue that held the Black community together.

We would go out here and do these things and he
would have to bail us out . . . Mr. Overton was always
there if you needed him. Always. Never, ever betrayed
me.[29]

Volma and his followers, whom some student radi-
cals often referred to as the "Uncle Toms down at the
NAACP," eventually earned the respect of student
activists. Although the two groups never saw eye to eye
on a remedy for the lack of Black progress, each learned
to respect the other's position.

* * *

The Austin branch NAACP's application for a credit
union for East Austin was making headway. Blacks in
Austin sorely needed a place where they could get a small
loan that would tide them over until their next payday.
The banks and savings and loan institutions required col-
lateral, something that most Blacks did not possess.

Blacks who traditionally could not obtain loans from
the financial institutions downtown had one last resort.
They usually ended up at one of the nondescript buildings
sandwiched between the department stores, drug stores,
beer joints, and fruit stands along East Sixth Street. They
were buildings that the average working person would
not notice. But the poor Blacks who came from their
farms into Austin on Saturdays to "trade" at the Piggly
Wiggly, look through the cheap merchandise in the
department stores, and stand around East Sixth Street all
day, knew those buildings only too well. Blacks who
labored all week in the private homes of wealthy whites,
or poured foundations and nailed boards at the construction projects in a growing Austin, frequently went into
those buildings when there was too much month left at
the end of the money. The buildings held loan companies,
or "loan sharks," as most people called them. Sometimes
their interest rates were as high as fifty to seventy-five

percent. Volma and many others, such as Dr. James Means, Mrs. U. V. Christian, and Milton Gooden, thought it was a good idea to have their own institution in East Austin where individuals could borrow money.

In 1969 the Department of Health, Education and Welfare, the federal agency which then regulated federal credit unions, approved the NAACP's charter for the NAACP Credit Union. The credit union was housed in the Mt. Carmel Grand Lodge building on East 12th Street, in the same office with the Austin branch NAACP.

* * *

The branch conducted a telephone survey to determine if a credit union was needed and would be used by people living in East Austin. The survey posed three questions: If the local branch of the NAACP organized a Federal Credit Union, would you become a member? Are you eligible to join another credit union? Would you actively work in the credit union?

The responses were overwhelmingly positive, and prompted the branch to continue with plans to establish a credit union. But getting the interest of the Black community proved to be more difficult than they first imagined. The community did not show a great deal of interest. The organization began with fifty members. They did not do a lot of advertising and money was a continuous problem.

In 1969 the maximum loan amount was $200. A downtown bank would not make a loan for $100. The credit union would. A $100 loan to a poor person could pull him through hard times, something many individuals in the community came to appreciate. Also the credit union was not a cash handling institution and did not offer checking accounts.

The first audit by bank examiners found the small credit union barely surviving. The audit indicated a lack of knowledge of credit union operations. There were no scheduled hours of operation. The audit also indicated a lack of financial activity. Members made donations just to keep the credit union afloat. Volma donated $38.50. But he knew the money was only a small hedge against a mountain of indifference by his own people. Their chief problem was that the credit union was not attracting members. Volma found that Black people were not accustomed to Black entrepreneurs. Consequently, they often had the feeling that Black institutions were not sound. But patience paid off. People would get a loan and tell others. Also, other local credit unions deposited money to help out the lone credit union in East Austin.

In 1994 the credit union changed its name and focus in order to attract a larger clientele. Membership in the NAACP was no longer a prerequisite to join. But members were required to reside in one of four east and northeast Austin zip codes to qualify for membership.

Volma and the early organizers of the NAACP's credit union found that persistence paid off, a trait that served them well in many other endeavors.

The following month Volma found he had been elected to the committee on convention procedure as a result of his activities at the national NAACP convention. The committee was one of the two he served on at the national level.

When he went to New York to meet with the committee, the members decided to offer Volma the chairmanship, a post which he readily accepted. The chairmanship of a national committee would give him excellent credentials for future endeavors with the state conference of branches.

But Volma found he was a novice in national NAACP politics. When the crucial vote on an issue was placed on the table, Volma found that, as chairman, he could not cast a vote. The meeting was over before he could even express his opinion. He chalked the matter up to experience, and went out and enjoyed New York City.

The Austin branch sponsored a 21D3 low-rent housing program for the community's poor. Volma spearheaded the drive to name the apartments the Arthur B. DeWitty Apartments. He wrote DeWitty's widow, who responded, "I can't find words to express my grateful appreciation for the branch desiring to name the apartment after him. Arthur gave of himself in a big way helping to implement those ideals for which the NAACP works so hard. I consider it a singular honor to have the apartments named for him." But the program never got off the ground. The NAACP national office refused to approve it because the Austin branch did not have the funds to keep it going.

Volma found his first year as a member of the Austin Human Relations Commission full of issues that affected both the Black and white communities. He and his friend Charles Miles collaborated on a number of issues which impacted the Black and Hispanic communities.

The branch initiated a complaint of discrimination against the Camp Gary Job Corps Center in San Marcos, Texas, alleging discrimination in both salary and working conditions, and requesting a full investigation.

In preparation for the annual banquet, Volma wrote a letter to former President Lyndon Johnson informing him that, "The guest speaker for the evening will be Mr. Clarence Mitchell . . . we should be most gratified to have you and Mrs. Johnson as our most esteemed guests . . ."[30]

In November Volma initiated a letter to O. N. Bruck, postmaster, requesting sensitivity training: "Negro employees sense the inability of those who are attempting to teach by the human relations exhibited by new supervisors toward them . . . We feel that a better caliber of instruction in human relations will upgrade the total postal service, and that qualified personnel should be given this vital area of responsibility."[31]

Bruck wrote back, "I was not aware that 'Race Relations' in the Austin Post Office are below par . . . We are not authorized to include 'Race Relations' in the training of new supervisors . . . In sensitivity sessions, emphasis is placed upon awareness of oneself; therefore, sensitivity sessions, if they were authorized may not be as valuable to a new supervisor as orientation in the entire realm of human relations."[32]

Volma felt that Bruck simply did not understand Black people, especially in terms of how they felt about their supervisors.

* * *

The first Saturday night in December saw Black Austin come out in its finest for the annual Arthur B. DeWitty Awards Banquet. Clarence Mitchell, a well-known NAACP lobbyist (often referred to as the 101st senator) gave a stirring speech. He praised former President Lyndon B. Johnson for using "his vast power to chart a course for the nation that was designed to eliminate second-class citizenship, feed the hungry, provide decent housing for all Americans and give all Americans a chance to work on jobs that provided both fair working conditions and adequate wages."[33]

Mitchell also criticized the Nixon administration for appointing Clement Haynsworth to the Supreme Court: "Unfortunately, under the Nixon Administration, the executive branch of government is not committed to the principal of desegregation now . . ."[34]

The DeWitty Award was presented to Charles Miles, former executive director of the HRC and the first Black city of Austin department head.

The composition of the grand jury was another area that concerned Volma. He was usually asked to forward names of citizens for consideration for serving on the grand jury. Late in December, Volma forwarded a list of names to Judge Mace B. Thurman, Jr., saying, "I would like for you to add to your present list of names used for selection of the Grand Jurors Commissioner's Panel."

The names included Mrs. Geneva Connally, school teacher; Mrs. James H. Means, supervisor, Headstart; Mr. Lamar Kirvin, teacher, Huston-Tillotson College; Mr. Timothy Johns, Grandmaster, Mt. Carmel Grand Lodge; Mr. Milton Gooden, city of Austin employee; Mrs. Ada Simond, Texas Tuberculosis Association; Mrs. Morene Douglas, Austin Housing Authority; Rev. Frank Walker, counselor, public schools; and Dr. June Harden Brewer, teacher, Huston-Tillotson College.[35]

* * *

Although the Civil Rights Act of 1964 provided many new privileges for America's minorities, it also created problems in the educational system. Many parents chose homes in neighborhoods because of their close proximity to schools. But with the passage of the Civil Rights Act of 1964, Department of Health, Education and Welfare (HEW) officials said that "desegregation within the meaning of the Civil Rights Act could be accomplished only by removing the racial identity of Negro schools, thus clearing away the remnants of the now outlawed dual school system."[36] There remained some forty-four schools that had students of one race. HEW officials requested that the Austin School Board submit a satisfactory desegregation plan or risk the loss of up to $2.3 million in school funds. School board president Roy Butler voiced the sentiments of many concerned Austinites when he said some board members felt HEW should be told it can keep its educational funds.[37]

But Volma saw the situation differently. In a statement released by the Austin branch NAACP, Volma said, "The school board should try to comply with the HEW guidelines because Texas schools rank 30th (in the nation) in total expenditures on education, and we do not want to fall lower."[38] Many of Austin's Blacks felt there was a viable alternative to closing the city's all-Black schools. However, despite ideas for changing grades around and changing the focus to vocational training, none of the plans drawn up by the Austin School Board and HEW officials were acceptable to the other side.

At the beginning of the 1969-1970 school year, seventeen non-Black students registered at Old Anderson High School. Anderson High School Student Council President Larry Houston said, "We understand how it feels to be a minority group, so we want to make these students feel at home—but not like exceptions."[39] By January 1970 thirty-five non-Black students had transferred to formerly Black schools.[40]

By May 1969 HEW had rejected the Austin district's desegregation plan two times. But the Austin School Board refused HEW's desegregation plan in favor of creating one of its own. However, the Austin School Board was back to square one when HEW again rejected its plan, and gave the board a June 1969 deadline to submit another plan.

Later in February 1969, Gillespie C. Wilson of Amarillo, the newly elected state president of the NAACP, attended an NAACP meeting in Austin for leadership training for the organization's officers. He severely criticized Austin for trying to maintain its Black schools. He also criticized the quality of multi-ethnic textbooks. "So you believe in law and order," Wilson said. "Then what about Anderson High School [an all-Negro school] which evidently you, as citizens of this city, fully intend to maintain until someone outside the state solves your integration problems for you?" Wilson also stated that if Austin did not comply with recent Supreme Court decisions, the NAACP would ask the Justice Department to step in.[41]

Concerning school textbooks, Wilson said, "There has been a tendency for our people to be stereotyped in texts or entirely left out. We demand the inclusion of integrated material in all educational levels—from elementaries to universities. We also want specialized courses in Negro history."[42]

* * *

In early May 1969 school board officials flew to Washington, D.C., to confer with HEW officials where, after a three-hour meeting, both agreed to "an eleventh hour try to find a desegregation plan that both can buy."[43]

A hearing set for Dallas on November 12, 1969 (which had to be postponed two times), meant that possible funding loss would be delayed for at least another school year.[44]

Meanwhile, Old Anderson High School opened for classes in the fall of 1969 with a mixed faculty. Twenty-five white teachers stood in the hallways as students hurried to their first day of classes. At Kealing Jr. High, twenty white teachers were on hand for classes. Predominantly white schools also received Black teachers—three at Austin High School; three at Crockett High School; eight at Johnston High School; five at Lanier High School; five at Reagan High School.[45]

* * *

With the possibility of a loss in funding and two plans already nixed, the Austin School Board took a drastic step. In June 1969 the board presented a plan dubbed the "seven school plan." The plan called for closing Anderson High School, Kealing Jr. High, and St. John's Elementary (three all-Black East Austin schools), and busing students to predominantly white schools. The plan would also redraw boundary lines of seven schools in East Austin "to remove the racial identity of four of them as all-Negro schools."[46]

Meanwhile, various groups in the community sought to devise their own desegregation plan. The East Austin Plan was drawn up by a committee co-sponsored by Rev. I. J. Fontaine and Miss Elaine Doherty. It sought to force two-way busing, as well as keep Old Anderson High School, Kealing Jr. High, and St. Johns Elementary School open.

However, some board members knew that white families would never accept two-way busing. Board President Roy Butler, acknowledging two-way busing would "just inconvenience twice as many students as our plan does," also said, "The pattern over the country has been that blocks of white families selected to send their children to Negro schools move out of the area."[47]

The lone Black school board member, Mrs. Wilhelmina Delco, said, "If they [East Austin residents] can come up with a workable plan without running the risk of having the people abandon the communities or gravitate to all private schools, then I am certainly willing to listen."[48]

But Volma had dire reservations about the East

Austin Plan: "There are too many ways it can be manip-
ulated. If I found out that I was the guy picked by the
computer, I could move next door." And although Volma
felt, "The only integration plan that would be fair to all
races would be one that provides for transporting students in both directions," he and the branch supported
the school board's plan. The local branch's newsletter
stated the school board's plan "goes only halfway
towards solving the problem of racial imbalance and
unequal educational opportunity in our schools." Volma
told the news media he was not able to come up with a
better approach.[49]

But in late June 1969 the school board, "after a few
moments of high drama decided unanimously to scrap
plans for closing three East Austin schools and busing the
students in those schools to other schools throughout the
city."[50]

The East Austin Plan was also rejected. The board
issued a statement saying, "It has now become quite apparent that this plan is not acceptable to either the Negro or
white communities."[51] The school board decided to extend
freedom of choice "to all white high school students and to
Black and white junior high school students . . ." The plan
also involved broadening Old Anderson High's curricula,
integrating the faculty, installing air conditioning, and
building a new gymnasium. The board also hoped that
white students would voluntarily integrate Old Anderson
High School.[52]

The $2.3 million in school funding was safe until
June 1970, but school board members knew they could
lose the funds if their plan was unsatisfactory to HEW.
Since the plan had been rejected by HEW two times
before, the outcome this time was a gamble.

Board member Mrs. Wilhelmina Delco's statement
was almost prophetic: "The success of our plan depends
upon the degree to which whites will volunteer to integrate. If they do not come forward to be counted, it's just

a matter of time before HEW and the court do what we haven't been willing to do."[53]

The Nixon administration dropped a bombshell on civil rights proponents in July. A press conference held by Nixon administration officials Secretary Robert H. Finch of HEW, and Attorney General John N. Mitchell said, "their departments were dropping arbitrary deadlines for school desegregation, and would give school districts additional time for compliance, if they have bona fide educational and administrative reasons for delay."[54]

But any hope that the relaxed deadline might apply to Austin's school problems was dashed. A July editorial in the Austin daily stated: "Austin had already been singled out by the Justice Department as a 'hard core case of non-compliance.'" The editorial also said, "a spokesman for Panetta relayed to Austin the information that the letter meant what it says."

National NAACP leader Roy Wilkins was furious. He expressed disappointment concerning "the administration's position that a deadline set fifteen years after the Supreme Court ruled out segregation was 'too rigid.'" Also, Wilkins added, "If that is the level of political accuracy we are to expect from the Nixon administration then we all ought to declare some sort of moratorium on political action."[55]

The Austin School Board decided to appeal HEW's ruling, a process that could take up to ten months. All students in grades 1-12 could now take advantage of freedom of choice, something previously available to junior high and high school students only.

In mid-July 1969 HEW again rejected the Austin district's desegregation plan. HEW Director of the office of Civil Rights Leon Panetta wrote: "The plan . . . is not adequate to accomplish the purposes of Title VI of the Civil Rights Act of 1964 . . . the amendments to the plan do not fulfill the Board's affirmative legal duty to desegregate those schools which constitute visible vestiges of the dual school structure . . . Accordingly, I am referring this matter to the Office of the General Counsel of this Department with a request that administrative enforcement proceedings be initiated." The HEW letter also curtailed federal funds for new programs and activities.[56]

* * *

By January 1970 the hoped-for influx of white students into revamped programs at Old Anderson High School had not happened. Thirty-five students transferred into Old Anderson High and Kealing Jr. High.

In late January 1970 members of the Austin School Board attended the HEW desegregation hearing held in Dallas. Board members contended school discrimination in Austin was the result of housing patterns, and not actions taken by the board.[57] In July 1970 the HEW examiner ruled "that the school district is in noncompliance with the 1964 Civil Rights Act and that federal funds will be withheld until the district designs an integration plan acceptable to the U.S. Department of Health, Education, and Welfare."[58]

In early August 1970, the federal government filed suit against AISD in U.S. district court for ". . . failure to comply with desegregation guidelines."[59] The suit, expected by AISD board members, set the tone for what proved to be ten more years of controversy in attempting to find a satisfactory method to desegregate Austin's public schools.

* * *

In July 1970 Volma made his feelings public on the busing issue. "Busing should not be ruled out as a way to achieve integration," Volma said. "It is not the only means, but it is one way."[60]

Volma wrote a letter to school board president Roy Butler: "We strongly condemn opposition to school busing as an excuse for segregated schools. The use of school busing is not a new phenomenon for public schools. As you know, it has been used in Austin for decades to take children to segregated schools in order to maintain segregation. We therefore reaffirm our position that if integration is to be achieved, then busing may be the means of achieving it."[61] Volma felt the NAACP had to support busing to achieve school desegregation, or face the possibility of having only Black children bused one way. He faced the future with optimism that fairness would prevail.

5

NIXON

In early August 1971 President Nixon released a statement announcing the administration's decision to appeal on ". . . limited constitutional grounds in the case of the *United States v. Austin Independent School District*, involving school desegregation . . ." Nixon was straightforward in his criticism of busing to achieve desegregation: ". . . I am against busing as that term is commonly used in school desegregation cases. I have consistently opposed the busing of our nation's school children to achieve a racial balance, and I am opposed to the busing of children simply for the sake of busing . . ."[1]

The school desegregation plan which HEW submitted to the Austin School Board in mid-May was the first such plan initiated by the administration since the Supreme Court's 1971 approval of busing as a desegregation tool in southern cities. The Supreme Court voted unanimously in favor of busing.[2]

Nixon faced several problems with the busing situation. He was up for re-election the following year, and did not want to be connected with any sort of real or perceived effort in favor of the busing issue. A $1.5 billion school desegregation bill, which would help finance desegregation efforts, was set for a vote in Congress. If it passed both houses of Congress, it might appear as if Nixon supported it. In an attempt to disassociate itself from the bill, the administration circulated a memorandum stating that busing would have "low priority" when funds for desegregation were handed out.[3]

In late August 1971 the Fifth U.S. Circuit Court of Appeals voted approval for two intervenors to enter the Austin school desegregation case. Volma knew that it was important for the views of the minority community in Austin to be heard during the school desegregation case. His youngest daughter, DeDra Estell, was a nine-year-old sixth grader. On August 25, 1971, "a motion to intervene in this case was granted to DeDra Estell Overton, et al., a group of parents and students representing both Blacks and Mexican Americans in Austin."[4]

The NAACP and the Mexican-American Legal Defense Fund were granted permission to enter the case as intervenors, prompting school board president Will Davis to say, "I would have thought that the court would have at least given the parties in the suit a chance to oppose application to intervene before making a ruling. However, it appears that the notice of appeal filed by the federal government has opened the door for all sorts of parties to appear before the Fifth Circuit Court and complicate the hearing in the Austin case."[5]

But Volma disagreed. He said he was "glad to know we are a part of the case . . . the only way the Black people will be heard" is to allow them to be a part of the court case. "The court is the place where all parties should be heard—otherwise we really would be in bad shape."[6]

On August 3, 1971, the federal government filed a notice to appeal the decision handed down on July 19, 1971, by U.S. Judge Jack Roberts. Roberts' decision rejected the HEW plan and approved the Austin School Board's plan.[7]

The opening day of the school year saw few problems beyond the normal logistical headaches—one bus carried students to the wrong school. There were also schedule mix-ups, and about seventy-five people gathered at Old Anderson High School to protest the school's closing and the one-way busing of former students across town.[8]

Hot pants and Afro hair styles were the order of the day as 52,166 students made their way to schools all over Austin. But a few days later, school officials and the local police force had decidedly more excitement.

The local daily reported a Black student and his mother were arrested for disorderly conduct. The son had also been arrested the previous day. A sixteen-year-old white girl was arrested for loitering at Crockett High School. A seventeen-year-old Black girl was also arrested for loitering and abusive language. At Reagan High School, a seventeen-year-old Black student was arrested for abusive language, "after reportedly making an obscene suggestion to a faculty member."[9]

Board president Dr. Davidson beefed up security at the schools. "We are having school to provide an atmosphere for good education," he said. "Any student who comes for any other reason will not be welcomed and will not be allowed to stay."[10]

Eighteen officers were assigned to a security detail at the seven high schools. Plainclothes officers were assigned to McCallum and Crockett high schools, where fourteen students and one parent were arrested.[11]

Hobart Gaines, the former principal of Anderson, and now assigned to AISD administration, and Leon Cashaw, director of human resources, organized parent discussion groups.[12]

The school administration also took steps to insure safety on the school buses. Bus passes were issued to students riding school buses. Emergency bus cards were issued to students at Reagan High School, which they could only show to either the driver or the monitor. Some students riding the school bus to Crockett High School were seen throwing rocks out of the bus windows.[13]

On the national front, the chief justice of the Supreme Court began to back away from the landmark decision he wrote. In a statement made during the Supreme Court's recess, Chief Justice Warren E. Burger said that the Court's unanimous decision did not require a fixed racial balance—the same racial percentages were required in each school, as in the school system as a whole. Burger felt some federal judges might be "misreading" the Court's April busing decision and "ordering more school desegregation in Southern cities than the law requires." Burger's opinion shadowed President Nixon's statement a month earlier that he would seek to hold busing henceforth to the minimum required by law.[14]

In the four months since the Supreme Court issued its decision, about twenty of the forty largest school districts in the South came under busing orders by federal judges. The forty affected districts had about a third of the South's African-American school children.[15]

The new school year began with numerous confrontations throughout the city. What school officials and many onlookers hoped would be a peaceful entry into the school term turned into a scene out of *West Side Story*. The incidents occurred during lunch at McCallum High School in north Austin. Witnesses blamed the confrontations alternately on African-American students and white students. When it ended, principal W. A. Sloan issued an order for McCallum to close for the remainder of the day, an order that resulted in several students loitering near the campus, causing the AISD and city police headaches for days afterwards.

A sixteen-year-old girl reported she was slashed across the forearm by what might have been a razor when several Black girls entered the girls restroom and asked her for money. Another seventeen-year-old boy underwent X-rays at a local hospital when he reported he was struck on the back with a chair while leaving the cafeteria during a confrontation between Black and white students.

One account of the cafeteria fracas had five or six Black students surrounding a white football player and following him into the school cafeteria. Another white football player joined the first student. The whole scene erupted when a Black youth broke a bottle against a wall and waved it. Chairs and bottles were thrown and tables overturned as Black and white students fought.

Fighting spread through the school. A "roving bunch" of youths, which the newspaper reported were not students at either McCallum or Anderson High School, roamed the hallways and grounds. At one point, an unidentified student struck football coach Jim Tolbert when he ordered the group to leave the gym.

Six patrol cars, plainclothes detectives, and a paddy wagon were routed to McCallum. The paddy wagon wasn't used, even though a crowd of about 100 African-American youths gathered in front of the school chanting, "We don't want your school! Call the bus! Where's the bus?!"[16]

A group of about sixty to eighty white students, many carrying two-by-fours, gathered on the west side of the building, only to be dispersed by law officers. Another group of white students formed on the north side of the school. A patrolman reported that many carried tire tools and belts.

Former Old Anderson High School principal Hobart Gaines rushed to the school and attempted to calm the students, many of whom he knew by name. Principal Sloan told the students over the public address system that fifth period classes were being extended because, "There have been a number of little get-togethers and fracasses, but no serious injuries. There are a lot of hurt feelings and some excitement, but we will get over it. Remain calm and our problems can be settled peacefully."[17]

School was dismissed a little after 2 P.M., but Supt. Jack Davidson emphasized Wednesday night that classes would be held at McCallum the next day. He also said protection would be provided students and faculty at McCallum.[18]

The following day brought a different atmosphere to McCallum High School. Tensions dissipated, and "groups of Blacks and whites were seen standing in corridors laughing and joking."[19]

A pep rally at Veterans Field that night brought 800

students, both Black and white, to shout football cheers. Five African-American players were a part of the football team, and were introduced at the pep rally.[20]

Later, school officials found a unique method to open lines of communication and air student ideas about the integration of Austin schools—"rap" sessions. Students from white, Mexican-American and African-American backgrounds sat down and discussed problems related to the closing of Kealing Junior High and Old Anderson High School.

More criticism of Judge Roberts' decision to bus only African-American students surfaced. The AISD brief was only one of a number of briefs filed in reply to the Justice Department's appeal of the school desegregation order.

In early September 1971 the Central Texas chapter of the American Civil Liberties Union filed a friend of the court brief. The organization hoped to gain permission to file in the Fifth Circuit Court of Appeals in New Orleans. The brief maintained that the "closing of the schools of one race only and busing only that race is a denial of equal protection of the law guaranteed by the Fourteenth Amendment to the Constitution."[21]

The Texas Education Agency filed a brief on September 23, 1971. The NAACP's brief was filed on September 25, 1971.

* * *

Black teachers saw it happen over and over again. They had either voluntarily or mandatorily "crossed over" to teach at formerly white schools in Austin. Regardless of their lofty moral desires to uplift their own race by teaching in Black schools, they were often forced by circumstances to "cross over." If they didn't volunteer to "cross over," they might be selected to go to another school on the other side of town anyway. They could refuse to go. But such a refusal was not seen as a smart career move. Ultimately, many Black teachers crossed over. Where once they were greeted by the raucous laughter of their own kind, now there were forced smiles, guarded whispers, and polite notes on lesson plans that had to be returned for "revision."

But the Black teachers forgot their own plight when they saw the big yellow school buses pull up to the campus and discharge students bused in from Austin's east side.

In some instances, the students were spat on and called "nigger." When they fought back the only way they knew how—with curses, shoves, kicks, and all out fighting—the Black students were usually expelled for fighting, while white students were sent back to class. Even when it came to placing Black students in classes at their assigned grade level, many were reassigned to remedial and special education classes.

A report released in early October 1973 only confirmed what Volma and many Black parents and teachers knew all along. Minority students received the lion's share of discipline meted out in the Austin public schools.[22]

The continuing report done by the student development department of the Austin school district showed that Black students were often spanked, making it "the second most frequent discipline for Blacks the second semester last year."[23] Consequently, the fights which broke out when Black students were bused one way into formerly white schools seemed to be an indication of things to come for the remainder of the school year.

Volma made sure parents of students expelled from school knew the NAACP's door was open to help them. He invited them at every opportunity to use the organization as a buffer when approaching school officials about disciplinary problems.

Many did. When fighting broke out at Reagan High School in northeast Austin, Volma petitioned the office of Civil Rights in Dallas to initiate a federal investigation of the subsequent handling of the affair.

When federal officials wrote Volma that no investigation could be considered because the Austin school district was under a federal court desegregation order, he released a statement to the press: "The NAACP and the citizenry of Austin are tired of listening to those officials, local, state and federal, using the excuse of Austin being under court order to justify their failure to deal with the problems in the Austin schools . . . Court order or not, we have problems in the schools which must be resolved. It is pointed out in the letter from the Office of Civil Rights that Austin has not begun to implement the program for which it received an Emergency School Assistance Program Grant. Why?"[24]

The Austin branch NAACP also asked to meet with Texas Education Agency officials concerning recurring racial incidents. In another press release concerning the Reagan High School incidents, Volma said the NAACP "is concerned about recent outbreaks of violence at Reagan . . . as well as tension and racial incidents in numerous other high schools and junior high schools in the Austin Independent School District." Volma added, "We feel that the school district's inability to deal with the situation is caused by the inability to objectively investigate and evaluate the real cause of the problems. And until the real causes . . . are established and admitted, and subsequently dealt with by school officials, violence will probably be a way of life in the halls of the schools. The NAACP chapter feels the Austin school board cannot and will not deal with the situation until the incidents are investigated by a party outside the school district."[25]

The letter stated the organization wanted certain areas looked into, such as: the extent of racism among teachers and administrators in schools with black students; misuse of federal funds designed to aid desegregation and help minority students; availability of counseling for black students; decline of free lunch and free breakfast programs; differences in punishments administered to black and white students for the same offenses; the availability of black cultural programs and activities in the school.[26]

* * *

Despite the efforts of school administrators, racial fighting among students flared up again in late April. This time, fighting broke out at Murchison Junior High, McCallum High School, and Martin Junior High. At Murchison Junior High, thirteen girls, seven of whom were Black, were suspended for fighting. About eight Black boys were suspended from McCallum for fighting with weapons. Martin Junior High, whose student body was half Mexican American and half Black, locked its doors after a fourteen-year-old Black student allegedly assaulted an industrial arts teacher. That student, as well as two other Black students who were arrested for loitering, were taken into police custody. Other students returning home from school were also involved in altercations.[27]

The following day (Thursday, April 20, 1994), the tense situation was cited as the cause of over half of the students at Martin Junior High School staying home from classes.

Superintendent Davidson recognized the increased amount of student altercations during early April 1972. He said the closing of Old Anderson High School was hard on those Black students displaced, and that it was something that was "not easily understood."[28] Davidson blamed an incident at Lamar Junior High School on Black students, and said that an incident at McCallum was "obviously planned by whites."[29] McCallum principal William A. Sloan held students overtime in discussion groups, in an attempt to outline suggestions, and stem mounting problems.[30]

But administrative action was not enough to turn the tide of rumors which blanketed the entire school system for the following month. The rumors of expected violence in junior and senior high schools might have been commonplace in the large urban cities of the north, but this was Austin, Texas, a small backwater by the standards of some urbanites.

* * *

The rumors that blanketed the schools and caused panic among students, teachers, and parents alike were strong, focused, and specific. May 1, 1972, would bring riots in junior high and high schools in Austin. Four students at each school would be killed.

Superintendent Davidson and school administrators took extraordinary measures, saying that the system "cannot afford to ignore the possibility" that the rumors were true.[31]

A special task force of central office administrators was assigned to each junior and senior high school. Additional monitors and community liaison workers were assigned to certain schools. The chief of police and the director of the Department of Public Safety also cooperated in the effort. Each school was given special instructions for dealing with conflict. Students who were found to be part of altercations faced suspension for the remainder of the school year.[32]

But May 1, 1972, brought little more than forty percent of the regular student body to classes, prompting one radio announcer to quip, "There weren't many at school to be disturbed." There were reports of some shoving and fighting at several schools, and strained tensions, but little all out fighting.

* * *

Mexican Americans were considered a minority by the government, but not by the Austin school district.[33]

The brief filed by the AISD backed up Judge Roberts' finding that "there was no discrimination against Mexican-American students. The evidence reflected that Mexican-American students traditionally attended schools throughout the city without regard to race or national origin . . ."[34]

Three U.S. Fifth Circuit of Appeals judges studied the briefs to decide whether to rule on the appeal without a hearing, or to set a hearing date. The judges involved were John Minor Wisdom of New Orleans, James P. Coleman of Ackerman, Mississippi, and Brian Simpson of Jacksonville, Florida.[35]

The NAACP filed a brief as an intervenor, which supported the government plan for mixing students. The organization felt the AISD plan was inadequate as a means of desegregating the schools.[36] The brief filed by the Travis County Legal Aid and Defenders Society was withdrawn when they found that it violated the organization's charter and by-laws.[37]

* * *

The trial in Judge Roberts' court lasted six days. The government's strongest point was that discrimination existed against Mexican-American students. But Judge Roberts commended the AISD for special programs aimed at meeting the needs of Mexican-American students. Roberts said the district's policy did not discriminate against Mexican-American students. The government's appeal criticized the proposed mixing of elementary school students on a part-time basis.

When Roberts ordered an AISD and HEW joint plan, it seemed the parties involved could never find a time or place to get together for discussions. It became, in the words of Supt. Jack Davidson, a "game of hide and seek."[38]

Judge Roberts said, "the AISD was not given the benefit of HEW recommendations in drawing its plan, despite repeated efforts to obtain such recommendations until approximately thirty days prior to the trial."

Roberts further stated, "This inflexibility on the part of HEW is inconsistent with this court's understanding of the role to be played by HEW in the complex, difficult task of urban school desegregation, and it is further inconsistent with the clear and obvious purpose of this court's order of September 4, 1970, directing the parties to attempt agreement on a common desegregation plan . . . This case appears to depart substantially from the usual run of school cases in that here the uncommunicative, uncooperative and recalcitrant party has been not the local school board, but the department of Health, Education and Welfare."[39]

Roberts also called the elementary plan "unique" and "innovative," while the government called it "part-time desegregation."[40]

In late October 1971 HEW forwarded the Austin

school board a letter saying the district would receive $203,100 in grant money instead of the $2.1 million requested.[41]

The *Swann* decision had a prominent bearing on the AISD desegregation case. The *Swann* decision (Charlotte-Mecklenburg) was a case which determined that a plan had to be filed in federal court by a school district and the Department of Health, Education, and Welfare. The *Swann* case was important because it found that busing was a legal, viable tool to use in desegregation.[42] Superintendent Davidson said it became "more apparent to the full board and the media that Austin was the first case in the entire United States after the Swann decision where a plan had to be filed in federal court by a school district and the Department of Health, Education and Welfare as well."

This decision resulted in the Austin case garnering the national spotlight, as well as the attention of politicians and minority groups. "It was obvious the case would have political impact and everybody interested in the national scene focused their attention to the Austin scene to see what position the Nixon administration would be," Davidson said.

* * *

In early November the U.S. House of Representatives approved actions opposing busing of school students to achieve a racial balance. This measure would "prohibit use of federal and state funds for busing of students and delay effective dates of court ordered busing plans."[43]

School board member Mrs. Wilhelmina Delco objected to the House action, saying it was "just another smoke screen thrown up to circumvent the law of the land." She said the House action would only delay integration, if the Senate concurred: "It will not go away, it will just be delayed and make the matter more difficult and anxiety greater for future generations."[44]

6

POLICE BRUTALITY AND OTHER ISSUES

When the school bell rang for the last time at Old L. C. Anderson High School, Blacks in East Austin felt they were losing part of their family. The feeling of Black pride in their only high school could never be replaced. However, the school's name could live on. Three new public schools scheduled to open in 1973 had not been named. On several occasions citizens of East Austin went before the school board to request that the name L. C. Anderson be given to one of the schools. When the school board convened on April 16, 1973, to select names for the three newly constructed schools, the Black community was ready to make its request a reality. They wanted the new Northwest High School to bear the name L. C. Anderson High School.

The school was located on Mesa Drive in far northwest Austin where only a sprinkling of upper income Blacks lived. Blacks in favor of the issue expected some resistance from northwest Austin, so they were not shocked when several residents of the northwest Austin community spoke in protest of the proposed name change. One resident called the proposal "mere tokenism."[1]

A future student of the school wrote a letter to the editor of the Austin daily saying, "We do not object to attending a school named after a black person. What we do object to is the use of our school name to appease the desires of certain citizens who will have no active role in the school whatsoever."[2]

But the East Austin community was ready. Dr. John T. King, then president of Huston-Tillotson College and a former East Austin precinct chairman, spoke on behalf of naming the school for L. C. Anderson. He said Anderson was a great educator and "hearing this noble person flaunted about tonight is an insult to his memory and to those of us who love him. Regardless of the name, the school will belong to the community and we will have to support it."[3] Board member Mrs. Wilhelmina Delco made the motion that the school be named for Anderson; Gus Garcia seconded the motion.

The new L. C. Anderson High School opened its doors to students August 27, 1973. The school district named Charles Akins, a seasoned Black educator, as principal.[4] Akins started with the school system as a coach in 1959. His appointment made him the district's sole Black principal.

The controversy marking the naming of the school was nowhere to be found when the new school held an open house on Thursday, August 16, 1973. Principal Akins was surprised when the 100 parents expected for the occasion swelled to over 600.[5] East Austinites were thrilled that the name of the sole Black high school in the community would live on.

* * *

The Human Relations Commission, although limited in authority to the role of an advisory board for the Austin City Council, heard many kinds of citizen complaints.

In late September 1973 an East Austin citizens group calling itself "We The People" appeared before the commission to air complaints of police brutality.

A spokesman for the group, evidently skeptical of the HRC, said they came to the meeting to "see if y'all are really planning to accomplish anything or if you are just going to keep trying to fool us about your intentions."[6]

HRC commissioners could only sympathize. The commission had no real authority to look into police matters.

They could simply refer the complaints to the police department, which was small comfort to the complainant.

Despite the lack of headway by the HRC, the problem of the minority community's relationship with the Austin Police Department remained a thorny one.

In late October, the police department announced a "concentrated effort to recruit Black and Mexican-American patrolmen."[7] Representatives of the police department touted their new posters and bumper stickers, as well as their plans for contacting churches, civic groups, and clubs in the Black and Mexican-American neighborhoods to augment their numbers of one Black lieutenant, two Black sergeants, and twenty-eight Black patrolmen and cadets. Mexican Americans on the force included eight patrolmen and cadets, six sergeants, and one lieutenant.[8]

The change in focus to concentrated minority hiring was due in part to Police Chief Bob Miles, who led the Austin Police Department for fifteen years. A staunch believer in the professionalism of the people who made up the police department, Miles' conservatism sometimes brought him more than his share of criticism. He refused to hire women police officers, believing them incapable of performing on the same level as male officers. "Maybe I am a male chauvinist pig, but there are just some jobs women can't do," Miles said in an *American Statesman* article. "Not too many are qualified to arrest a fighting drunk. I fought my share of drunks. I don't think you can afford to hire women as policemen unless they are prepared to do the same job a man can do."[9]

He was roundly criticized by city councilman Jeff Friedman, who said Miles "overlooked the problems of the individual police officers, had no feel for community racial conflicts, was not innovative, could not communicate with the press or the public, and had lost the ability to keep up with his job."[10]

Miles admitted some people were simply not comfortable around him. He claimed no personal animosity

Austin City Council chambers in April 1964. NAACP member Mary Wadley reacts with dismay at the turn of events. Photo courtesy of the Austin History Center.

Rev. Wesley Sims is proclaimed mayor of Austin by civil rights demonstrators after city council members leave the chamber during demonstrations in April 1964. Photo courtesy of the Austin History Center.

Read-in at Austin City Council chambers in April 1964. Volma Overton, president of the Austin branch NAACP, reads from Black Like Me *as Warneta Overton (left) and Mrs. Hattie Pinkston listen and baby DeDra slumbers.*

B. T. Bonner, an activist who participated in civil rights demonstrations in Texas as well as other states, defies police officers at Austin City Council chambers. Photo courtesy of the Austin History Center.

Civil rights activist B. T. Bonner is bodily carried from Austin City Council chambers when he refused to sit down. April 1964. Photo courtesy of the Austin History Center.

Activist B. T. Bonner draws a crowd of young people during the civil rights demonstrations in April 1964 at Austin City Council chambers. Photo courtesy of the Austin History Center.

Folk singer Joan Baez lends her support to the demonstrations as she sings folk songs on the steps of city council chambers. April 1964. Photo courtesy of the Austin History Center.

Rev. Wesley Sims, accompanied by an unknown companion, tests the Piccadilly Cafeteria's response to the public accommodations section of the Civil Rights Act of 1964, which removed racial barriers. Photo courtesy of the Austin History Center.

The late city councilman Jimmy Snell presides at renaming Congress Avenue to Volma Overton Avenue for a day. The street name change was part of Volma Overton Appreciation Day in 1976. Photo courtesy of the Overton Family Collection.

NAACP Read-in in Austin City Council chambers in April 1964. Warneta Overton (in foreground) was a frequent participant in civil rights demonstrations during the early 1960s. Standing beside her are Mary Wadley and Florence Bonner. Photo courtesy of the Austin History Center.

An NAACP awards ceremony during the mid-1970s. (left to right) Ezell Green, Volma Overton, Fay Willis, Ethel Barrow, and Ada Simond.

Golfing in San Francisco, California. Volma (third from left), Gerald Baxter, Woody Andrews, and Luis F. Gomez. Photo courtesy of the Overton Family Collection.

Birdie Mackey-Caldwell, former life membership chairman, Austin branch NAACP. Photo courtesy of the Mackey-Caldwell Family Collection.

Milton Gooden, former chair of the Labor and Industry Committee. Photo courtesy of the Gooden Family Collection.

James Sheard, former second vice president, Austin branch NAACP. Photo courtesy of the Sheard Family Collection.

Fay Willis, former Austin branch NAACP Youth Advisor. Photo courtesy of the Willis Family Collection.

Willie Mae Kirk, former chair of Volma Overton Day Committee in 1976. Photo courtesy of the Kirk Family Collection.

Morris X. Winn, former vice president of Austin branch NAACP.

DeDra Estell Overton as a child. She would later be named lead plaintiff in the Austin Independent School District's desegregation case which dragged on for nine years. Photo courtesy of the Overton Family Collection.

Veteran NAACP worker Ed Hill addresses Volma Overton's appreciation banquet in 1976. Photo courtesy of the Overton Family Collection.

towards Friedman, but said Friedman had "his own ideas.
I happened not to agree with his ideas . . ."[11]

The Austin Police Department was as free of corrup-
tion as Miles could make it. He was known for firing or
accepting the resignation of officers who even remotely
compromised their positions. Miles attributed the spate
of police brutality charges during 1973 to "a tavern on
the East Side [Soul Factory] who felt we were checking
them too frequently."[12]

Volma respected Chief Miles. He found that Miles
would hear you out, although he often did not act on matters concerning minorities that Volma brought to him.
Miles' officers also gave him credit for hearing them out.

In late November 1975 Miles spoke to a group of
ninety-two high ranking officers at the Thompson
Conference Center in Austin in what some referred to as
a farewell address before his retirement. Miles told the
group that several minority officers had complained that
white officers were using racial slang terms for Blacks and
Mexican Americans. Miles told the group of officers to
"be careful of what you say and how you treat your fellow officer."[13]

Later in October, Roy Wilkins, executive director of
the NAACP, journeyed to Austin to accept the prestigious
Zale Foundation Award. Wilkins was the first person to
receive the award.

Mrs. Lyndon Baines Johnson presented the award to
Wilkins, and said the foundation committee wished to
"identify and honor a true hero."[14] Wilkins said the nation
must hold on to the traditions that made it great, despite
doubts and a "whom shall I trust?" attitude in the wake
of 1972 campaign activities.[15] Wilkins also said govern-
mental integrity was only one of the nation's problems:
"Until we do something about housing, employment, and
schools, we cannot hope to do anything constructively cor-
rective about crime."[16]

* * *

The annual DeWitty Awards Banquet was held

Saturday, December 8, 1973, at the Stephen F. Austin Hotel. The DeWitty Award was presented to Milton Gooden, veteran NAACP worker and chairman of the local branch's employment committee. Gooden, a native Austinite and activist in the labor union movement in Austin, was a fixture at meetings and often represented disgruntled employees in grievance hearings with their employers. The branch lauded Gooden as a person who "has distinguished himself in the labor movement and in civil rights."[17]

Ed Hill, also a veteran NAACP worker, received a special award for his work with the organization. A housing development executive, Hill was presented an award for "outstanding accomplishments in his own endeavor."[18]

C. Delores Tucker was the featured speaker for the annual banquet. As the secretary of state of Pennsylvania, Tucker was the highest ranking Black woman in state government. Tucker warned the audience of the danger of becoming complacent. Blacks have come a long way with many nice homes, with nice cars and nice clothes, she said, adding, "Maybe these are the best of times—for you. But no man is an island. Never forget that most of your brothers and sisters are still back there at the starting post."[19]

* * *

In early 1974 The University of Texas at Austin was still under pressure to increase minority enrollment and employment. UT had made efforts to erase its image as a segregationist institution, which still lingered from the Heman Sweatt case filed in 1946. But in January 1974, the Austin daily ran an article giving UT's employment figures broken down according to ethnic groups. UT faculty was less than one percent Black in January. The numbers included 1,565 Caucasians, thirteen African Americans, and twenty-one with Spanish surnames. Women fared little better. Of 1,482 faculty, 538 men were professors, while only thirty-one women held the same position.[20]

* * *

An East Austin landmark burned to the ground in late January 1974.[21] When Volma was a student at old L. C. Anderson High School, and later a working man, he and his friends often went to midnight shows at the Harlem Theater. Prior to integration, the Harlem was one of only a few movie houses where Blacks were welcomed. The Harlem's midnight shows were frequently top-rated movies. Because Blacks could not go to the other side of town for entertainment, the Harlem's midnight shows were popular with people in East Austin, and frequently drew large audiences.

* * *

In late March 1974 protesters again took to the pavement to protest against Police Chief Miles and alleged police brutality. The twenty to thirty protesters first marched around the police station and then descended on city council chambers. This time they had the support of Councilman Jeff Friedman, who proposed funding the position of public safety director. But many agreed with Councilman Dan Love that Friedman's proposal was a "transparent move to move police chief Bob Miles up and out."[22]

Two protest groups, including the East Austin Committee for Justice, and the Brown Berets, a Mexican-American protest group, crowded city council chambers to support Miles' ouster. Nine residents of East Austin took over two hours to complain of harassment by police. Ernsta Frago told the audience that the groups were not complaining about every officer. "We are concerned about people being beaten and killed," Frago said, adding that twenty complaints of police brutality had been filed since the beginning of the year.[23] However, Chief Miles was supported by many Austin residents, including a University of Texas professor and a former grand jury foreman, who said there were over 100 former grand jury members in the audience also supporting Miles. But

Friedman's proposal was voted down the following week, with council members voting unanimously "to do nothing about hiring a public safety director unless they are recommended to do so by the city manager."[24]

* * *

The man who would be an invaluable help to the NAACP during the fight for single-member districts shared the political limelight, albeit harsh, during early May 1974. Called the unofficial executive director of the Travis County Democratic Party, Peck Young made the news when he decided to cut back on political activities to attend law school.[25]

Volma became acquainted with Young when he volunteered to help in the NAACP's voter registration drive, when Young was still a teenager. Since then, Young had graduated from The University of Texas, and become very active in both student and local politics. He worked for Travis County Democratic Chairman Ken Wendler as his personal administrative aide.

The Austin daily called Peck Young "a lightning rod for controversy in the local Democratic Party during the last month . . ."[26]

* * *

Years after Old Anderson High School closed its doors, Northeast High School (later named Lyndon Baines Johnson High School) was in the advanced stages of construction, scheduled to open in the fall of 1974. The new high school, expected to provide a more even distribution of the city's diverse ethnic groups, also brought a new staff with plans to bring more personalized education to high school students.[27]

Newly assigned LBJ Principal Ron Beauford presented a school board study session with plans that included humanization of the educational process by staff development, decentralization of the decision-making process, the institution of program improvement committees, an administration that would be more in touch with teachers, and an officer manager to oversee building repair, food service, maintenance, attendance, and registration. A modern library, team teaching, and individual advisors were also included in Beauford's plan.[28]

In mid-June 1974 U.S. District Judge Jack Roberts approved boundary lines for LBJ High School that gave it 1,500 students. Of the 1,500 students, 15.5 percent were Black, 80.7 percent were Anglo, and 3.8 percent were Mexican American.[29] Judge Roberts' decision nullified the Mexican American Legal Defense Fund's (MALDEF) challenge that the boundaries as drawn did not place enough Mexican-American students at LBJ High. In compliance with the pending school desegregation suit and court directive, all boundary line changes were required to be approved by Judge Roberts' court.[30]

Volma and several other branch members convoyed by car to New Orleans in early July 1974 for the NAACP national meeting. Before leaving Austin, Volma granted Wendell Fuqua, staff writer for the Austin daily, an interview that was published July 2, 1974. Volma criticized the lingering discrimination that still pervaded the city, in terms of education, jobs, housing, and police brutality. "We're pretty fed up with discrimination. We're just getting tired of getting picked on," Volma said. "We want to get it [discrimination] off our backs." While conceding that "great strides have been made against discrimination in Austin," Volma said the end was not yet in sight.[31]

"I think one of the major problems is job discrimination," Volma said. "The high-paying posts—$15,000 to $20,000—are still denied Blacks."[32]

He said city departments, such as the water, electric and tax departments, were "lily white" in their employee makeup, with salaried positions in city departments almost exclusively white. "I would think by 1974, Austin would have crossed that point [fair employment], but we haven't arrived yet," Volma lamented.[33]

Concerning the lack of enforcement of housing codes, Volma said, "many of the absentee landlords in East Austin have property far below minimum standards."

Also, he said, "Some people might think that Austin does not discriminate in housing, but there are a lot of areas where [Blacks] are not buying. They [realtors] have a subtle way of keeping them [Blacks] out—like saying 'this one is already sold.'"[34]

Volma also criticized the fate of Black children and teachers in the educational process, saying that "Blacks are still bearing the burden of busing," with one of the new sixth-grade centers located in East Austin. He added that "The best Black teachers go to the white communities; the poorest white teachers go to the Black community."[35]

He also criticized the Austin Police Department, and called for creation of a citizens review board to handle complaints against police officers of alleged brutality. He added that Chief Bob Miles now seemed "more sensitive to minority problems than he was several years ago."

Volma also expressed a desire for the Black and Hispanic communities to work together to a greater extent than before. The Black and Mexican-American communities got together on certain issues, but normally had very little intercourse on matters vital to both groups. Volma said, "Once we get the money to build and to buy, then we become more competitive, then all of a sudden a man begins to think about his green stuff rather than the color of a man's skin."[36]

* * *

The Austin school district armed itself with a new salary schedule to attract minorities, while Black school board member Rev. Marvin Griffin criticized its efforts.

Reverend Griffin was dismayed at the low number of new Black teachers. "Has it been that difficult for the district to hire minorities?" Griffin asked.[37]

Officials at Huston-Tillotson College (HTC) were also critical of the district's low numbers in hiring minority teachers. LaVonne Marshall, HTC's director of recruiting, was critical of the fact that five of the students interviewed by AISD were offered jobs in other school districts. Marshall accused AISD recruiters of following a double standard for Black and white applicants. "I don't think they view a Black applicant as they do a white," Marshall said. She felt white teachers were hired to teach in Black schools where standards were not as demanding as in white schools, while Black teachers placed in white schools fell under the scrutiny of white parents and were judged by "stricter standards."[38]

HTC's Marion M. Curry, chairman of the educational division, expressed "misgivings about AISD's recruiting team which rated the twenty-two students interviewed with four-plus points on a five-point scale, but only made one job offer."[39]

However, AISD Asst. Supt. Hobart Gaines said the HTC students were qualified, and would be considered for employment notification later in the summer. Gaines said the AISD was in the process of establishing open communication with HTC, saying, "When they think they have a good prospect they will let us know and we will let them know when we have a vacancy." Gaines felt that competition with larger cities such as Dallas and Houston made it difficult to recruit qualified teachers to Austin. He also said AISD's recruiting teams "are not met with a lot of hospitality" at Black college campuses.[40]

* * *

Volma found that the face of discrimination was changing. He found that the obvious discrimination—the all-white water fountains and rest rooms, and the low-level jobs generally reserved exclusively for minorities—had changed. Now discrimination was more subtle, less apparent.

The NAACP's strategies to end discrimination also changed with the times. "The sit-ins, picketing, boy-cotting and marching days are gone," Volma told the Austin daily. "Our confrontations with employers are no longer publicized."[41] He stressed that state and federal agencies such as the Equal Employment Opportunity Commission, Department of Health, Education and Welfare, Housing and Urban Development, and the Office of Economic Opportunity should now provide assistance with complaints.[42]

However, the oldest civil rights organization in the nation still relied on lawsuits for legal changes.[43]

Volma was proud that the local chapter registered 25,000 voters in Travis County during 1974. But he told the daily that the low participation in the NAACP by young people saddened him. "They just don't know what we're all about," Volma said. "It used to be that during meetings, youth flooded the aisles and hallways."[44]

*   *   *

The year 1974 marked twenty years since the Supreme Court, led by Chief Justice Earl Warren, ordered public school integration with all deliberate speed.

The Civil Rights Act of 1964 put teeth into the *Brown* decision, forcing public school administrators, especially in the South, to seriously look at the less than one percent Black students attending integrated schools.[45]

The grade-per-year integration program begun by the Austin Board of Trustees in August 1955, in answer to the *Brown* decision, floundered until the advent of court-ordered busing in 1972.

*   *   *

Although Volma was no longer a member of the Human Relations Commission, he longed for the day when the protest marches and sit-ins of the 1960s would result in real power for the organization.

His wish came true—almost. In late August 1974 HRC members discussed a proposal for an ordinance that would give the HRC the power to force Austin businesses to comply with Equal Employment Opportunity Commission regulations.[46] If the proposal was approved by the city council, the HRC would gain the power to hear class action suits, assess fines for non-compliance, as well as audit the entire hiring, firing, and promotions practices of a business in all nine employment categories, from professional to maintenance levels. If passed, the ordinance would supplement the federal equal employment law. The new authority would also give the HRC the leverage to threaten termination of city contracts.

But in early January all hope of passage of an ordinance giving the HRC real enforcement authority was dashed when the city council voted it down 3-2.[47] Mayor Pro Tem Dan Love, Dr. Bud Dryden, and Lowell Lebermann voted against the ordinance, while Jeff Friedman and Bob Binder voted for passage. Mayor Roy Butler did not attend the meeting. David Strong, spokesman for the Austin branch NAACP, joined ten others in speaking in favor of passage of the ordinance.[48]

However, six months later, a reversal of fortune saw the Equal Employment Opportunity Ordinance sail through the council in a modified version. Councilwoman Betty Himmelblau suggested amendments that precluded HRC members from investigating complaints. They would instead serve as a review board in cases where staff members failed to resolve cases. The ordinance prohibited employment discrimination based on race, color, religion, sex, sexual orientation, national origin, age and physical handicap. The ordinance covered city government and private employers.[49]

* * *

In early January 1975 an East Austin group met to discuss their continuing problems with the police force. Some members felt police harassment of young Blacks would stop if the attitudes of some policemen would change.[50]

A week later, a public hearing of the Special Community Relations Task Force met at Rosewood Recreation Center in East Austin. The hearing drew three Austin citizens who aired complaints of police brutality.[51] East 12th Street barber Ray Dell Galloway said a police officer beat him when the officer thought Galloway was interfering in an arrest. Galloway, who told the group he was part of the buddy system with police officers, suggested the buddy system be expanded to provide "on the spot witnesses" for police activities. Two others alleged police harassed them by asking inflammatory questions about political activities, and refusing to tell one complainant why he had been stopped. "If you open your mouth again, I'm going to arrest you for disorderly conduct," the police officer allegedly said.[52]

In late February 1975 members of the Black community, university students, and others all but filled the LBJ Auditorium on The University of Texas campus to hear Coretta Scott King. The widow of the late civil rights leader Dr. Martin Luther King, Jr., spoke about the need for getting full employment legislation through Congress. She said it "will be far from easy" but "it will be possible to rally an equally impressive majority" as was raised on the civil rights issues of the 1960s.[53]

Volma sat with an ethnically mixed audience which politely applauded the genteel lady who had marched at her husband's side during the turbulent 1950s and 1960s. Volma couldn't help but compare King's low-key widow and the orderly crowd to the turbulent crowds of the sixties and King's powerful speeches that were now a part of civil rights legend.

The speech made Volma aware of how far things had come since he stood under the tree at the Washington Monument, while Martin Luther King, Jr., electrified the crowd with his "I Have A Dream" speech.

*   *   *

As Austin public school administrators struggled to write a satisfactory desegregation plan, The University of Texas faced its own mounting problems. The Department of Health, Education, and Welfare investigated UT Austin in the spring of 1974 and found many areas in need of correction. A year later, in early March 1975, the Austin daily's front page blared the headline, "HEW Criticizes UT Civil Rights Efforts." The article outlined areas pinpointed by HEW investigators in a twenty-five-page report. HEW cited areas in conflict with civil rights policies, including UT's discrimination policy, general admission policies, minority recruitment programs, supervision of student employment, student grievance procedures, athletic participation, and employment.[54]

HEW investigators suggested several things to bring the university up to par, among them the development of a systematic, university-wide recruitment program. The report cited no Mexican Americans and one part-time Black among the thirty-two staff members of the university's athletic department. The report also cited few Mexican-Americans on the football team, and none on the basketball and golf teams. Virtually no Blacks were in baseball, tennis, golf or swimming at UT.[55]

* * *

In March 1975 the branch received correspondence from Gloster B. Current, director of branches and field administration at the NAACP national office in New York. The letter advised of a march on Boston scheduled for May 17, 1975. Current listed the three-fold purposes of the march: (1) To celebrate the twenty-first anniversary of *Brown v. Board of Education;* (2) to support school desegregation in Boston; (3) and to support national opposition to the passage of anti-busing legislation as a first step in amending the Constitution.[56]

Volma knew that the Boston public schools had been experiencing racial difficulties since a federal court found them out of compliance with desegregation guidelines in 1974. Whites protested against forced busing of over twenty-five percent of the students by placing their children in private schools.[57] Boston was known for the protest march led by Martin Luther King in 1965 to achieve integration. Volma travelled to Boston by air. Over 50,000 people participated in the march. The marchers were in and out in one day, much like the march on Washington.

* * *

East Austin residents had long needed the services of medical doctors and mental health workers. Many low-income residents who did not have automobiles to make the drive downtown, nor the money to catch the city bus, were thankful for the Mental Health-Mental Retardation (MHMR) center located on Rosewood Avenue near Doris Miller Auditorium. Residents living in the predominantly Mexican-American neighborhoods near East First Street used the MHMR center on East First Street. Consequently, in July 1975, when MHMR administrators suggested a merger of the two centers, Blacks and Mexican Americans were decidedly upset. Both groups wanted to keep their own neighborhood centers.

MHMR Director John Weimer explained the reason for the suggested merger to members of the advisory boards of both centers, claiming it would be easier to keep a physician and psychiatrist at one center than at both.[58] MHMR officials asked both advisory board groups to select a central location favorable to both. But the groups maintained that finding a central location satisfactory to everyone would be very difficult. The limited budget increase for centers in East Austin for the coming year (1976) also brought accusations that they were being treated unfairly.

Two months later in September 1975, Sam Griggs, the president of the Rosewood Center's advisory committee, told the Austin daily that he was rounding up support in the Black community to prevent merger of the two centers.[59] In the end, the MHMR Board voted to keep both east side centers open, a decision which Rosewood Advisory Board members saw as both a victory and a defeat. The Rosewood Center would remain independent, but the prospect of a larger staff, something sorely needed, was put off for lack of money.

Volma and the local branch NAACP had watched MHMR operations in East Austin for some time. Many individuals were convinced that MHMR funding for East Austin centers was not going where it was supposed to.

In late October Austinites opened their evening paper to the front page headline: "MHMR Fiscal Probe Urged." Volma and the NAACP charged that money intended for East Austin mental health services was being funneled

off. The NAACP scheduled a meeting with the representatives of the U.S. Department of Health, Education, and
Welfare on November 10th.[60]

Volma said the NAACP had doubts that federal money
intended for "high impact"—or severe poverty areas—was
reaching its target. "It is that alleged 'disparity,'" Volma
said, "that is constituting the NAACP's complaint."

But prior to the scheduled November 10th meeting,
the MHMR Board of Trustees held a meeting (October
31, 1976) in which they voted to change the previous
vote. The board chairman, Dr. Bill Hill, called it a "decision not to make a decision." This change came about
after a board sub-committee visited the Rosewood
MHMR Center.[61]

The board voted to increase the Rosewood MHMR's
current funding level to a higher one. The board shifted
some funds away from MHMR centers in other neighborhoods in Austin to the east side centers.[62]

But Volma and representatives of the Rosewood
Recreation Center were still convinced that money allocated for poverty areas such as East Austin was not getting to the proper targeted areas.

The journey to Dallas to talk with officials of HEW
proved disappointing. The group presented their list of
grievances to HEW representatives. But the officials
responded that "MHMR is not bound formally to spend
specific funds in poverty areas. The only restriction on
the agency once it receives federal money is that the
entire city be served with facilities 'equally accessible' to
all residents."[63] But Volma responded, "What we find is
that we don't have the type services other (MHMR) centers have. Problems [in the Rosewood area] warrant better services than what we've been getting."[64]

But HEW staffer Glen Rawlins responded that it
appeared to him that MHMR had been taking positive
steps in meeting the needs of all Austin residents. Rawlins
also said that the Austin MHMR delegated the ultimate
"perogative and responsibility" for how that money is

spent to the local agency. MHMR officials told Volma and the group from the Rosewood MHMR advisory board to work with the local board for "actual development of the program."[65] Sorely disappointed, the group drove back home to Austin, and to the same cramped Rosewood MHMR facility that they had hoped to improve.

But January 1976 brought new hope for the Rosewood MHMR Center. In what seemed like a change of heart, the Austin-Travis County MHMR Board of Trustees voted the Rosewood Center a larger facility. The Rosewood Center would move next door into a building that would be leased when cited improvements were completed.[66]

During the controversy surrounding the proposed merger of the Rosewood and the East First Street MHMR centers, the Rosewood group suggested that a Black be appointed to the nine-member Austin-Travis County MHMR Board as a future project.[67] They felt Blacks needed a voice at the board level, allowing them some power in determining the destiny of their own affairs. They started the project with a letter-writing campaign to members of the city council, and planned to contact county commissioners and UT officials. Two names suggested for the post were veteran Austin branch NAACP worker Milton Gooden and local minister Freddie Dixon.[68]

* * *

The local branch ordinarily received complaints about conditions at the city jail. By August 1975 the number of complaints had mushroomed. Among eight written complaints by former jail inmates were allegations of abusive treatment, poor medical care, and inadequate beds. Volma decided it was time for the local branch to do something about the situation.

In late August Volma, as president of the local branch NAACP and the chairman of the disbanded Police Community Relations Task Force, wrote a letter to Austin Police Chief Bob Miles asking for a tour of the jail. "We have received an enormous amount of derogatory information about the jail," the letter stated.[69] When Volma and a group visited the jail, they found two or three inmates in tiny cells that were unclean. Most of the inmates were Black. The group wrote a report and left their findings for Chief Miles. But in the end, future action was not necessary. The situation took care of itself, with Miles' staff tidying up the jail cells more than in the past.

* * *

Members of the local branch frequently heard complaints from both Blacks and Hispanics about the difficulty they experienced in getting hired in various departments of the city of Austin.

On July 14, 1975, the local branch took action. They requested five federal agencies withhold funds from the city of Austin for "flagrant" racial discrimination in hiring, firing, promoting, training, and in numerous other areas.[70] The local branch NAACP forwarded the complaints to the departments of Housing and Urban Development, Health, Education, and Welfare, Transportation, Labor, and the Office of Economic Opportunity.[71]

* * *

Although sympathy for Dr. Martin Luther King, Jr., and his fight for non-violent racial equality was strong in Austin, a controversy erupted when Blacks wanted to rename a street in King's honor. Over a two-year period, the controversy became heated, forced most Austinites to choose sides, contributed to the death of a seasoned political activist and East Austin educator, brought about a court battle, and ended with the city council passing an ordinance.

Supporters of the proposal to rename the street contacted Volma for the NAACP's position on the matter. Dubbed the Austin Black Assembly, the group listened to the NAACP's plan to attempt to rename Rosewood Avenue, a short street in the heart of East Austin, for Dr. King. But members of the Austin Black Assembly wanted to select a street that spanned the entire city. They selected 19th Street, a major thoroughfare which crisscrossed both the Black and white communities.

The Austin City Council agreed to rename 19th Street for Martin Luther King for one day, as an honor. However, members of the Austin Black Assembly felt that the name change should be made permanent. The group at first asked that the name be made permanent for the section of 19th Street running through East Austin. This the city council did. But later, the group asked that the entire street be renamed for King. The prospect of renaming a major thoroughfare for a slain civil rights leader caused controversy that filled city council chambers and made the front page of the Austin daily.

Thursday, April 10, 1975, was an historic day for civil rights in Austin. The Austin City Council, after hearing ninety minutes of arguments for and against the name change, voted 4-2 to rename 19th Street Martin Luther King Boulevard. Mayor Roy Butler and Mayor Pro Tem Bud Dryden voted against the measure.[72] Other individuals who spoke against the measure included property owners along 19th Street, and business persons with offices on the thoroughfare. The business people all said it would be expensive to reprint stationery and risk lost mail.

The cost to the city for changing street signs was also a source of controversy. City officials estimated new exit signs on IH-35 would cost in the neighborhood of $50,000.[73]

Councilman Jimmy Snell made the motion to change the name of the street to Martin Luther King Blvd. Despite this, a heated controversy lingered, with opponents trying to rescind passage of the measure.

Just three weeks after the name change passed the city council, Dr. J. J. Seabrook, president emeritus of Huston-Tillotson College and a former minister, rose during a council session to speak on behalf of retaining the name Martin Luther King Blvd. A few moments later, Seabrook slumped to the floor. Attempts to revive him failed. He died at 5:45 P.M.[74] Seabrook's death left a pall over council chambers. His death also galvanized civil rights proponents to make sure the measure to pass the name change was not rescinded. They had to do it in Dr. Seabrook's memory and for the cause of civil rights.

However, a segment of the Austin community remained adamantly opposed to changing the name. A conservative group dubbing itself the 19th Street Association filed suit against the city of Austin on September 4, 1975, for a temporary injunction to stop the placement of Martin Luther King Blvd. signs on IH-35. The group also asked for $250,000 in damages for the taking of property rights (changing the street name) "without just compensation."[75] This occurred after the group collected over 17,000 signatures to force a referendum, or public vote, on the name change. But the action met resistance from the city's legal office, which held that the name change was not a suitable subject for a referendum since the council's action was not "legislation."[76] The 19th Street Association's petitions were, therefore, ruled invalid by the city council's legal staff.

The NAACP and the Austin Black Assembly, represented by attorney Sam Biscoe, filed a petition requesting friend of the court status.[77] The friend of the court designation would allow both groups to present their side during the hearing.

Volma felt the lawsuit filed by the 19th Street Association reeked of racism. Volma, president of the local branch NAACP, and Joel Bennett, chairman of the Austin Black Assembly, said the lawsuit was representative of "the narrow-mindedness of a few persons with business offices on (the) . . . boulevard who simply cannot stomach the idea of working on a street named after a Black person." Volma also said the city council had renamed at least fifty-eight streets since 1965, and not one was put to a citywide vote, an exercise the 19th Street Association demanded.

However, Marion Findlay, leader of the 19th Street Association, charged Councilman Jeff Friedman with using the name change to "pay off a political debt to East Austin voters and democratic organizations."[78]

In a court hearing, Judge Herman Jones ruled in favor of the 19th Street Association, invalidating the name change to MLK Boulevard. Judge Jones ruled the "renaming of the street was a legislative act, that the city charter allows legislation by ordinance only, that the name was changed by motion rather than ordinance and was therefore not valid."[79]

"The judge gave us our street back and we're very happy," Marion Findlay said after the ruling. "We do hope the city will be as prompt in restoring 19th Street signs as they were in putting up the King Boulevard signs (after council renamed the street last spring)."[80] But Judge Jones refused to order that the name be changed back to 19th Street.

Thursday, June 24, 1976, saw the city council pass an ordinance to approve the renaming of Martin Luther King Blvd., after which Findlay spoke. Findlay said the passage of the ordinance "violates a basic property right that is ours. Never in Austin has a street name been changed without consent of the property owners."[81] Findlay's group refused to let the matter die. In October 1976, the 19th Street Association, led by Findlay, began another petition drive to bring the matter to a referendum. But his efforts came to naught. MLK Boulevard survives as one of Austin's major thoroughfares.

Another victory came for East Austin when, after years of pushing, residents found that Givens Park would finally be allocated funds for expanding the park. Volma and members of the Givens Park Advisory Board were elated when over $1 million was set aside for a recreation center at Givens Park. The funds were made available through the Capital City Improvements Program.[82]

* * *

She had been Volma's mentor for as long as he had been involved with the NAACP. Looking down at her serene face wizened with the experience of age, but closed in death on October 25, 1975, Volma felt as if a part of himself lay in the satin-fringed casket.

Mrs. U. V. Christian paid her dues to Austin's Black community in a way that few others ever would. Now in death, accolades poured in by the hundreds for this remarkable woman—owner of the first beauty school for Blacks in central Texas, wife of a prominent physician, former president of the Austin branch NAACP, watcher of Austin politics, and DeWitty Award winner in 1968.

Hundreds of people crowded into the funeral services held for Mrs. Christian at Ebenezer Baptist Church, the largest Black sanctuary in East Austin.

When Volma rose to speak of Mrs. Christian's accomplishments in behalf of the Austin branch NAACP, he knew he did not have enough words to describe her contributions:

> The death of Mrs. Christian robbed the Austin community of one of its stalwart and productive members. She was in a real sense the shaper and finisher of the branch activities and programs. Her involvement in the NAACP was complete and everything that is characteristic of the NAACP in Austin was molded by Mrs. Christian.[83]

Two or three years later, the Austin branch NAACP voted to erect a statue in Mrs. Christian's honor in Rosewood Park. The city's parks and recreation department approved a space in the park for the statue. But the group was never able to raise the $13,000 necessary to commission the statue. The $800 raised by the local branch was eventually placed in the U. V. Christian Scholarship Fund. Since 1996, a $1,000 scholarship has been awarded yearly to a deserving student in Christian's name.

7

SCHOOL DESEGREGATION PLAN— BACK TO SCHOOL DISTRICT

Despite the best efforts of the Austin School Board, HEW officials, a specially appointed Tri-Ethnic Committee, parents, and other interested individuals, the struggle to write a desegregation plan that would be acceptable to all segments of the community proved to be a bitter one.

Volma watched as the sparring continued on the tide of public opinion. During the hearings that dragged on until the final settlement of the suit in 1983, he remained an interested bystander. However, he was always there when Sam Biscoe, local branch NAACP attorney, needed to consult with him in areas where he was knowledgeable.

The Fifth Circuit Court of Appeals in New Orleans issued a decision reversing Judge Jack Roberts' court-ordered one-way busing of African-American students. The court found that no race should have to bear the burden of busing. They also found discrimination against Mexican Americans, and took issue with the elementary plan wherein students of different ethnic backgrounds would be mixed during some part of the school year.

After putting their heads down for the fourth time, the Austin School Board agreed on a desegregation plan which was filed in federal district court on April 15, 1973.

Although the plan was approved by the members of the school board, comments by Trustee Gus Garcia indicated that the final product had been agreed upon simply to get the document filed. Garcia said that while the plan, in his opinion, did not address the issues in the ruling from the Fifth Circuit Court of Appeals, it was a plan that approached the minority problem "in a way that can be healthy."[1]

The plan showed that although boundary line changes resulted in an improved racial balance in junior and senior high schools, it was not feasible for elementary students. The plan also emphasized stepping up recruitment efforts for Mexican-American teachers at all levels, increasing special programs targeted towards helping minority students, and a detailed study of busing.

* * *

During the first day of the trial, lawyers for the U.S. government called five witnesses, all of whom attended East Austin schools in the 1930s, 1940s and early 1950s.[2] Under extensive cross examination by lawyers from both sides, witnesses said Spanish could not be spoken on campus and teachers spoke only in English. No special programs were available to meet the needs of the Mexican-American student. Each witness said they made good grades, but at times a grade had to be repeated.[3]

Mary Grace Herrera, who taught at Palm Elementary School from 1938 onward, said she had only Mexican-American students who could not speak English when she first began teaching. She spoke only English to them, sometimes using a student to interpret. She said teachers were told not to use any other language but English. She did not recall who gave those instructions. Of the bilingual program in place at Palm Elementary School in 1973, Ms. Herrera said it worked with students who spoke both English and Spanish.[4]

Another witness, Charles Jones, testified about his experience at the Biclar School. The school accepted students who were two years behind their own age group and attempted to provide extras for them. Jones stated language difficulty was one reason the students were behind. The students were taught only in English because they were in an "English speaking country," Jones said. The students included Mexican-American, Anglo, Chinese, and other nationalities.

Ed Idar, attorney for MALDEF, stated that Mexican Americans had not been segregated by state statute, but segregation had "come about by custom, practice and tradition." He said the state's prohibition of Spanish in the schools was "unrealistic."

Testimony by Dr. John A. Finger as an expert witness during the court session also drew avid interest. Dr. Finger was a Rhode Island professor of education who gained nationwide attention when he wrote the plan for the Charlotte-Mecklenburg, North Carolina School District in 1971.[5] But his preparation of a school desegregation plan submitted on behalf of the NAACP and MALDEF drew fire.

During his testimony, Dr. Finger said his plan was prepared while he was in New York City. It had been completed in three or four days. He admitted the plan was prepared under great pressure and filed without calculating the cost. Finger never set foot in Austin and admitted having "insufficient information." He said "some errors" existed in the plan.[6] Segregated housing patterns in Austin caused the district to have major problems implementing a desegregation plan, and Dr. Finger testified he "had to do some awkward things" in writing the plan for Austin. "There is no way to desegregate schools where there are segregated housing patterns except by busing," Finger testified. But he did see the need to change some of the provisions in his plan. The 4-4-4 plan submitted, where kindergarten through fourth grade would be in one level, fifth through eighth grades in a second level, and ninth through twelfth grades in a third level, would be changed to a 5-3-4 sectioning of grade levels. Minority students would be bused eight years and whites four years.[7]

Attendance zones encompassing minority schools would be restructured. But the main impetus of the plan would remain the busing of younger students. Finger said the school board's plan to mix younger students through field trips and other school activities, a plan critics called "part-time" desegregation, would be "very difficult." He felt that students would not "rub shoulders" and "get acquainted" like they would under his plan.[8]

However, under cross-examination, Dr. Finger said that there more satisfactory devices to achieve desegregation than crosstown busing. He added, "with the segregated housing patterns in Austin there is no way to rezone, and no other way than crosstown busing." Dr. Finger also stated that problems created for small children who are bused were "not insoluble."[9]

* * *

Other testimony in the desegregation case centered on the current level of education for Mexican Americans.

The city's predominantly Mexican-American high school was named for Albert Sidney Johnston, a Texan who became a Confederate general during the Civil War.

Built in East Austin, the student body was drawn from predominantly Mexican-American neighborhoods in East Austin with some African-American students thrown in.

Johnston High School counselor Leonard D. Jordan had been assigned to the school for thirteen years. He testified that students entering Johnston High School were two or three grade levels below the norm at other schools. "It has been felt that Mexicans and Blacks just aren't quite as bright as we are and it is normal for the achievement levels to be low, and there is not any need to do anything about it," Jordan said.[10]

But when he was cross-examined by Donald Thomas, attorney for the school district, Jordan conceded that the school district, and "educators generally," believed that disadvantaged children of any race underachieve. Difficulty in language skills, he said, caused difficulty in all other subjects.[11]

Jordan stated the primary problems faced by Johnston High School were absenteeism and drop outs, which were termed as worse at Johnston than at any other school district. He also cited discipline, difficulties with the language and a curriculum planned by the administration, not by "teachers and kids," as being the problems. However, Jordan did concede during testimony that the "school district has always bent over backward in a real effort to provide the same academic courses at Johnston that are available at other schools."[12]

Conditions at minority schools in East Austin were compared to schools in north and northwest Austin by Pete Reyes, who took the stand as president of Concerned Parents for Equal Education. Reyes said Mexican- American leaders had previously appeared before the school board, making at least twenty demands at one meeting, some of which were acted upon, others not. Reyes said that Johnston High School athletic facilities "are pitiful" compared to Reagan's which "are tremendous." Metz Elementary was "an eyesore" and in need of painting, and the grounds were in "a deplorable condition." The grounds at Govalle were "still in very bad shape," even though the inside had been improved. The desks and chairs at Govalle looked like "something from the WPA."[13]

In an effort to show that segregation of Americans "came about by custom, practice and tradition," attorneys for MALDEF introduced a report containing documents showing 176 restrictive housing covenants existing in Austin between 1923 and 1960.[14] Restrictive covenants were common in Texas and numerous states in the early part of the century. The report included a color-coded map pinpointing tracts of land having housing covenants. The tracts were located in west Austin in an area bounded by North Lamar Boulevard west, Enfield Road on the south, and Anderson Lane to the north. Another area was located in northwest Austin, bounded by North Interregional, Airport Boulevard, and Manor Road. Other areas were scattered throughout the city, except in downtown Austin and East Austin.[15]

The report showed four categories of restrictions: eighty-seven deeds specified housing must be occupied by either "strict Caucasian blood," or "white race only";

twenty-two prohibited residents of African descent, and six others excluded "Mexicans." The fourth category prohibited housing construction ranging from no more than $1,500 in 1932 covenants, to $30,000 in 1955. The study listed "nearly all covenants found in deeds recorded after 1952 as economic restrictions."[16]

An example of two covenants written into subdivision deeds allowed that although Negroes and Mexicans were banned from the neighborhood, "this restriction shall not prevent the employment of such excluded persons as domestic servants and furnishing for same the customary servants' quarters and accommodations."[17]

Charles Miles was a former school teacher at Old Anderson High School. At the time of the trial, Miles had been the executive director of the Human Relations Commission for over two years. He testified during the trial concerning Austin's housing patterns.

Miles testified that the African-American community was against the closing of Kealing (closed in 1971 by federal court order), and disliked "putting the burden of desegregation on Blacks 100 percent." Miles also criticized the city. He accused them of rejecting or not acting on Human Relations Commission recommendations concerning housing.[18]

Attorneys for the NAACP and MALDEF also sought to show that the site selection by the school board was an attempt to isolate and segregate minority schools.[19]

Arthur Cunningham, Jr., retired former director of pupil personnel, defended his recommendations concerning school locations in what turned into a day-long testimony. Cunningham stated it "would have been easier" to integrate schools in East Austin in 1950, when whites, blacks, and Mexican-American pupil groups were nearly equal."[20] Whites moved out of East Austin, leaving only seven percent white students in East Austin in 1970.

In answer to attorney Idar's question of whether the trend of whites moving away from East Austin could have been reversed if the location of schools had been different, Cunningham answered, "That's some more of your hindsight business."

In 1947 the Gubbels Report said a high school should be built in East Austin first. However, on Cunningham's recommendation, the school board constructed McCallum High School in North Austin first, and Travis High School in South Austin. A new high school in East Austin was built in 1953 at Cunningham's urging.

But Cunningham felt there was a greater need for schools in North and South Austin. "He [Gubbels] just didn't know what he was talking about," Cunningham said. He said the consultant based his East Austin figures on children living in the area. But Cunningham's calculations were based on the number of area children actually in school. He urged that an east side school be built when more students from that area were graduating and "the proximity of a school would be helpful in improving attendance."[21]

In the last eight days of testimony, Dr. Thomas Carter, dean of the school of education at California State University in Sacramento, was called as an expert witness. Dr. Carter said, "This is not an integration . . . in fact, it justifies separate but equal schools as a viable concept." He said programs designed to promote equality between races and ethnic groups could not work if the groups were kept separate from one another.[22]

* * *

Judge Roberts spent the next two months pondering the alternatives before the court. On August 1 he issued an eleven-page ruling approving the desegregation plan submitted by the Austin school district involving creation of eight sixth-grade centers.

8

SCHOOL SUIT CONTINUES

The minority community often felt police officers harassed them and concentrated policing efforts on the streets of East Austin. Consequently, when Chief Miles retired and the city council began an active search for a replacement, many East Austin citizens felt they should have a say in the selection.

The Human Relations Commission called a special meeting on Monday, January 12, 1976, to give East Austin residents the opportunity to talk to city council members.[1] Mayor Jeff Friedman, City Manager Dan Davidson, Mayor Pro Tem Jimmy Snell, and Councilwoman Margaret Holman spoke to a group of about seventy-five Black and Hispanic residents at the Oak Springs Library in East Austin. Volma also attended the meeting.

Some East Austinites wanted a citizens' review committee which would interview applicants for police chief before the city council made a final selection. But City Manager Dan Davidson downplayed the idea. He said names of applicants would be kept confidential so that their present jobs would not be placed in jeopardy. Davidson also said only one name would be forwarded to the city council. Mayor Pro Tem Snell urged the group to provide their input by writing letters to council members.[2]

* * *

Volma marked his fourteenth year as president of the Austin branch in 1976 when NAACP members decided to hold an appreciation ceremony in his honor. A committee chaired by Mrs. Willie M. Kirk and co-chaired by Rev. Freddie Dixon planned the event from start to finish. Many friends, acquaintances, and supporters of the NAACP wanted Volma to know that his efforts to make Austin a better place were appreciated.

Dubbed "Volma Overton Appreciation Day," the ceremony was held Friday, February 13, 1976, at the elegant Stephen F. Austin Hotel in downtown Austin. The Houston-Bowie Room was packed to the walls with government officials, political dignitaries, Austin branch members, friends and relatives.

Many of Volma's life-long friends and acquaintances were part of the festivities. People such as Rev. N. W. Bacon of Greater Mt. Zion Baptist Church, Rev. Lawrence V. Wicks of Olivet Baptist Church, and Mrs. Beaulah Agnes Jones, musician at Huston-Tillotson College, came to celebrate. Politicians also attended. Mayor Jeff Friedman, Mayor Pro Tem Jimmy Snell, AISD Trustee Gus Garcia, and State Representative Wilhelmina Delco all praised Volma for his efforts in the field of civil rights. National NAACP officials Richard Dockery, regional director, and Rev. Emerson Marcee, NAACP national board, also praised Volma's civil rights gains.

After numerous speeches lauding Volma's accomplishments, the committee presented him with a gift that would ignite a passion in his life and a change in his personality. He was presented with a ticket for a ten-day tour of Liberia, a travel packet offered as part of the 70th Anniversary Convention, Alpha Phi Alpha Fraternity, Inc., held in both New York City and Monrovia, Liberia.

Volma was excited at the thought of travelling to the African continent. He wanted to really enjoy himself and not be a wallflower. He often saw couples gliding effortlessly across the dance floor. He decided to take dance lessons, something he had never done before. After spending several days in New York City, Volma and enough of his fraternity brothers to fill two airplanes left for the African continent, land of their forefathers. They crossed the Atlantic Ocean and landed at Roberts International Airport, one of the two airports in Monrovia, the capital city of Liberia, on August 4, 1976.

Volma stayed at the Carlton Hotel in downtown Monrovia, one of several hotels used by the conventioneers. The city's mayor, Edward A. David, said "Your meeting in Monrovia is an historic occasion not only for Liberia but for the entire continent of Africa because this is the first time that this organization has met on the Continent."[3]

The days were filled with breakfasts, receptions, lunches, business meetings, and activities for children who came on the trip. Volma and his companions toured the churches, rubber plantations, and schools in the city and countryside. They saw an economically deprived population that loved the game of soccer, but suffered severely from the country's stagnant economy. They learned that Liberia was the oldest independent Black nation in Africa.[4] When the young people learned that the visitors were Americans, they asked the conventioneers to sponsor them to come to America. Volma still received letters from some of them long after he had returned home.

Nights were filled with various functions planned especially for their tour group. The head of state, William R. Tolbert, Jr., held a dinner, and officially welcomed the group to Liberia. It would be four years later (1980) that a military revolt would unseat Tolbert's government and end with his death.

And there was dancing. Volma donned his black tuxedo that only came out of the closet on special occasions. When he spied a woman standing alone or in the company of other women, he did something that he would have never done before. He crossed the room and asked her to dance.

While they swayed to the beat of a fox trot, samba, or waltz, Volma discovered something else. Dancers were social animals. They talked to each other.

He not only talked to his dance partners. He also met

their friends, husbands, boyfriends, and relatives. As time wore on and the trip neared an end, Volma noticed the change that knowing how to dance had made in his life. When before he would have seldom struck up a conversation with someone he did not know, now he found himself crossing the room to shake hands with total strangers. He boarded the plane to leave Liberia with more new friendships than he had ever made in his life. He was also convinced that dancing was "the universal language."

When he returned to Austin, he arranged for more dance lessons at the Arthur Murray Studio where he first started. Volma's relationship with the studio and the dance instructors was to continue for the rest of his life.

Many of his friends noticed the change in him. "When Volma started going to Arthur Murray and learning how to dance and what have you, this brought him out of his shell," Fay Willis said of the change in Volma. "Volma is a very quiet person. When he started that dancing, honey, he started going up to anybody and asking them to dance."[5]

One of Volma's many dance instructors over the years, Dean Stitt, felt he already had the "soul of a dancer" when he first came to the studio: "All I did was take what he had already developed in his dancing and continue to mold and shape it. He is one of the smoothest dancers I know. Sometimes this takes a long time to develop. He has the grace and polish of a good dancer."[6]

His dance partners came to know him, not as the firebrand who gave impassioned speeches before the city council and other audiences, but as a soft-spoken, considerate, and thoughtful man.

Volma's wallflower days were behind him now, as attested by the wall of trophies lining the walls in his home. He took lessons at the studio as often as he could, often leaving meetings early. He also danced regularly with the Austin Ballroom Dancers, an organization that sponsored "tea" dances. He also got to know many of the band leaders around town, and they would play his favorite dance numbers.

Volma Overton dances with Rose Redfield during an Arthur Murray Showcase. Photo courtesy of the Overton Family Collection.

* * *

The Human Relations Commission was still considered an advisory arm of the Austin City Council in February 1976. That year, the council approved an Equal Employment Opportunity Office for the HRC by passage of an ordinance.[7]

The EEOC ordinance prohibited discrimination based on race, age, sexual orientation, religion, or physical handicap by businesses with fifteen or more employees.[8]

Frank Dyson was selected as Austin's new police chief. He met with a combined group of about thirty Austin branch NAACP and Youth Council members in April 1976. Dyson stressed the "team" approach to stemming youthful crimes. He reemphasized citizen and police cooperation and said the APD's storefronts offered a means for police and officers and youths to meet under "non-stress conditions."[9]

Some NAACP members questioned Dyson on the oversaturation of police officers assigned to East Austin, where they concentrated on minor crimes. Dyson responded that the APD's research and planning office was studying the reallocation of manpower in that specific area and a report was due on the matter by next week.[10]

* * *

By 1976 Volma had been employed by the U.S. Postal Service for twenty-three years. During that time, he served as president of the National Alliance of Postal

Employees, as well as president of the Austin branch NAACP. He also advocated for the rights of postal employees, many of them minorities, when he felt they had a valid complaint.

Many people, both inside and outside the postal service, were thankful for Volma's strong voice and reasoning power. But Volma knew his civil rights activities were the major reason that employees who began working for the post office years after he began were ultimately promoted to positions above him.

In late June 1976 Volma filed a class action suit against the postal service for himself and "all others similarly situated." Volma's suit charged the postal service with refusing "to promote and advance black employees on the basis of race," and for following "a policy . . . of limiting the employment and promotion opportunities of Blacks," in violation of federal law.[11]

As compensation Volma sought a declaratory judgment "that the actions of the postal service violate the rights of blacks and other minorities," as well as a permanent injunction prohibiting the postal service and its employees from "engaging in the policies and practices complained of." Volma's suit also asked that Volma and Blacks be granted "promotions and advancements as are necessary, and back pay and front pay, which they would have earned from the date of the wrongful denial of promotion and advancement, together with interest."[12]

Volma engaged attorney Sam Biscoe to represent him in the lawsuit. The process of settling the suit dragged on for a couple of years before Judge Jack Roberts threw it out. He maintained that there was not enough evidence to go to trial.

* * *

In early October 1976 the U.S. Department of Justice filed a brief to the Austin School Board's appeal of the May 13, 1976, decision by the U.S. Fifth Circuit Court of Appeals.[13]

The Austin School Board, led by President Carol

Volma Overton is sworn in as postmaster of Cedar Creek, Texas, by Austin Postmaster Glynn Vorick in 1978. Photo courtesy of the Overton Family Collection.

McClellan, filed its appeal with the U.S. Supreme Court, taking exception to the circuit court's findings in two areas. First, the court's finding that Mexican Americans and Blacks were deliberately segregated in the school system went against the grain of everything the board felt had happened historically in education in Austin. Second, the court's order for large scale busing to remedy discrimination would only increase the district's expenses, and create serious discord throughout the community.[14]

The school board countered that local housing patterns were responsible for existing segregation, something the school board could not be expected to shoulder responsibility for.[15]

John Wilson, assistant public information officer for the Justice Department, said the Supreme Court "may want" to hear the case to clear up "conflict" among the judges' opinions in the U.S. Fifth Circuit Court of Appeals order. Part of the confusion involved "legal standards for desegregation" and a legal definition of what constitutes official action to discriminate against minorities in school assignment.

Lino Graglia, The University of Texas constitutional law expert who also helped write the school board's petition for Supreme Court review, liked the idea that the Justice Department was also requesting a review. "We are asking the Supreme Court to hear the case and the government is agreeing with that," Graglia said. It is "unusual" in a school integration case that the "government winds up supporting a [review] petition of the defendant," Graglia added.[16]

Graglia proved to be a strong advocate for anti-busing. On November 7, 1976, he appeared on a nationally televised debate with U.S. Civil Rights commissioners in Washington, D.C.[17] Graglia voiced the opinion that since 1968, Supreme Court decisions had gone beyond the tenets of the findings in *Brown v. Board of Education.* "Forced busing for racial balance is not a constitutional imperative," Graglia said. He further called it "a perversion of the Constitution."[18] He was also a member of two anti-busing groups, the National Association for Neighborhood Schools (NANS), a national group, and Action for Neighborhood Schools, a local organization.

Back in Austin, one of the intervenors in the school desegregation case, the NAACP, was disappointed at the school board's lack of progress in producing a desegregation plan for the 1977 school year. In early November NAACP attorney Sam Biscoe threatened to take the school board back to federal court if the 1977 plan was not ready by the following week. Biscoe said a decision with Mexican American intervenors in the desegregation case would be made soon about whether to ask U.S. District Judge Jack Roberts to compel the school board to reveal its 1977 school integration timetable.[19]

Biscoe also wrote a letter to AISD attorney Bill Bingham, dated October 28, 1976. In the letter the NAACP demanded that a new school be built in East Austin to replace Old L. C. Anderson High School, the city's only African-American high school, which, along with Kealing Jr. High School, was closed by order of Judge Jack Roberts in 1971. Biscoe said the NAACP was requesting a new school be built to ease the busing burden for Black students, as "every black school student in central and East Austin has been bused since Anderson was closed."[20] The NAACP wanted the proposed new high school for East Austin built in the area north of Seventh

Street, south of Manor Road, east of Interstate Highway 35, and west of Webberville Road.[21]

The school year 1976-1977 also revealed a marked drop in white enrollment in the Austin school district, after a twenty-year pattern of stability.[22] White enrollment in the district dropped by 1,200 students from the previous year's statistics, while Black and Mexican-American student enrollment rose by one percent, respectively.[23] Pupil Services Director Hugh Echols attributed the decline in white students to a lack of "in-migration." The drop in white students meant that white student enrollment went from sixty-five percent to sixty percent.[24]

But student figures for minorities showed that Blacks and Mexican Americans were moving into the district in even greater numbers. Statistics showed a gain in Mexican-American students of 667, while black enrollment increased by 268.[25]

The decline in white enrollment did not bode well for the school district, especially since the 1977 desegregation plan calling for mandatory busing was still in the planning stage.

But in early December 1976, the Supreme Court released its ruling. The ruling read: "The petition for certiorari is granted, the judgment of the Court of Appeals for the Fifth Circuit is vacated, and the case is remanded for reconsideration in light of *Washington v. Davis, 428 U.S. 229* (1976)."[26] In a vote of seven to two (7-2), the Supreme Court overturned the U.S. Fifth Circuit Court of Appeals finding that ordered large scale busing to achieve integration. In a decision that took only one paragraph, the Supreme Court ruled that racial imbalance alone is not sufficient evidence of discrimination.[27]

A separate opinion written by Justice Lewis F. Powell, Jr., and supported by Chief Justice Warren E. Burger and Justice William H. Rhenquist read:

The lower court in Austin seemed to have assumed too much about the duty of the local school board to arrange its schools so as to break up neighborhood segregation patterns . . .

The principal cause of racial and ethnic imbalance in urban public schools across the country—North and South—is the imbalance in residential patterns.

Such residential patterns are typically beyond the control of school authorities.[28]

Justices Thurgood Marshall and William A. Brennan, Jr., dissented from the ruling, noting that the Fifth Circuit Court had "correctly interpreted and applied the relevant decisions of this court."[29] The justices told the lower court to look again at the Austin desegregation case in light of the findings of a June 7, 1976, case in which the Supreme Court said that all forms of racial discrimination were not automatically unconstitutional.[30] In the June 7th ruling the Supreme Court said, "The Constitution is violated only when discrimination is a result of the intentional policies of government officials. The mere fact that one race may suffer more than another because of some policy is not, by itself, enough to prove a Constitutional violation . . ."[31]

The news was a setback for the NAACP, but attorney Sam Biscoe said it "has more impact on the brown [than the black] citizens of Austin."[32]

Attorney Biscoe's reaction to the decision was simple. The fact that Blacks were segregated by state law until the 1954 *Brown v. Board of Education* decision "is de facto segregation and undisputed evidence of discrimination."[33]

But others could not have been happier with the Supreme Court decision. Austin school officials were elated. Carol McClellan, school board president, told students in a University of Texas [at Austin] government class that the courts are more concerned with legal issues of school discrimination, like enrollment, than with the quality of education. But that does not mean the courts do not care about education.[34]

McClellan said although the court order did not achieve landmark status, it "picked up national attention."[35]

Desegregation plans for the 1977-1978 school year would be curtailed because of the Supreme Court decision, McClellan said.[36]

But Lino Graglia, the UT professor who helped draft the Austin School Board's appeal of the Supreme Court decision, warned that the district may not have heard the last of the busing issue from the courts. "The Supreme Court seems to have lost some enthusiasm for court ordered busing," Graglia said. "The school district can expect the panel to continue to order busing for racial balance until the Supreme Court very directly orders that they cannot."[37]

But others took the Supreme Court justices to task for a ruling that appeared murky and confusing at best. In an article in the *Christian Science Monitor*, Mark G. Yudof, professor of law at The University of Texas at Austin, said the ruling "offends my sensibilities as a sometime apologist for the judiciary . . . the combined scholarship of six justices produced only two sentences in addressing one of the most serious social, political, and legal problems of our time."[38]

9

MORE CHANGES—1977

As the new year came in, Volma and members of the Austin branch NAACP realized that uneven treatment of Black students and educational issues were to take up much of their time. Poor treatment of Black students by school teachers and principals, some of whom were openly hostile to minority students, continued to crop up in ever-increasing numbers.

Sometimes Volma locked the front door of the small NAACP branch office on East 12th Street with the words of African-American parents and their children still ringing in his ears. When complaints came in, Volma and a special team of investigators went into action. Milton Gooden, Ezell Green, James Sheard, David Strong, and Fay Willis often spent hours pouring over documents and discussing the pros and cons of taking action on specific matters.

One such investigation in April 1977 resulted in the NAACP asking for the removal of an assistant principal. In a report to Supt. Jack Davidson, the NAACP charged George A. Goethe, assistant principal at Burnet Jr. High School, as "rude, insensitive and sarcastic to students and parents."[1] The report listed eighteen recommendations for improving motivation and achievements of Black students. The recommendations included hiring a Black counselor, regular parent meetings at an eastside recreation center, bus transportation for parents to night school meetings, and a "we care" attitude for minorities.[2]

176

Burnet Principal Henry K. Henley termed the NAACP's charges against Goethe as untrue, calling him a strict disciplinarian who primarily handles problem students. Henley also expressed reservations about how much the NAACP could learn about the school during four visits.[3]

* * *

The NAACP's national leadership was also changing. Volma had always taken pride in his friendship with Roy Wilkins, executive secretary of the NAACP. Wilkins provided a strong role model for Volma. But the organization's national board began to change in the mid-1970s, and Wilkins found that "some board members were quite eager to see me step down."[4]

Wilkins retired from the NAACP's top leadership position in July 1977. In so doing, he ended an almost fifty-year relationship with the organization he helped to shape into the most powerful civil rights organization in the country. Wilkins was succeeded by Benjamin Hooks, a Memphis attorney and minister.

* * *

The U.S. Fifth Circuit Court of Appeals dropped a bomb on the Austin School Board on November 21, 1977.

In a surprise ruling that caught the appealing parties off guard, the Fifth Circuit Court found: "the evidence demonstrates that the segregation of Austin's Mexican-American students was pervasive and intentional."[5] This marked the third time the lower court found the district at fault in the segregation of Mexican-American students.

Although School Board President Gus Garcia originally voted against filing an appeal, he agreed with the Fifth Circuit Court's findings. Garcia said the "pervasive intent" to segregate Mexican Americans "has prevailed" through past Austin school boards, and has continued to an extent with today's board.[6]

For the same reason, Garcia later voted against a proposed Southwest high school site, saying the plan "clearly shows what the board was not thinking about." He said even though the present board may not have consciously intended to segregate Mexican Americans, there wasn't enough conscious attention paid to integrating minority students. Futhermore, building schools in predominantly Mexican-American communities "clearly establishes that they were trying to separate those students."[7]

Also surprised at the court's decision was Supt. Jack Davidson. Regardless of the court's findings, Davidson said he expected the district to maintain its legal position that it had not, at any time in the past or present, discriminated against Mexican Americans. Gabe Gutierrez, attorney for MALDEF, said the ruling was "what we anticipated," but he expressed surprise that "it came so early."[8]

But school board members, this time without former president Carol McClellan who had gone on to the Austin City Council, felt their exceptions to the past and present lower court decisions were valid ones. In a closed board meeting on November 28, 1977, the trustees voted 5-2 to appeal the lower court ruling to the Supreme Court for the second time.[9] The five board members voting for an appeal were DeCourcy Kelly, Will Davis, M. K. Hage, Jerry Nugent, and Winnie Gage. African-American board member Rev. Marvin Griffin and Mexican-American board member Gus Garcia voted against an appeal.[10]

While the Austin School Board took steps to file an appeal with the Supreme Court for the second time, it also took steps to begin implementation of forced busing. Members of the Austin School Board realized that community input was vital to having even a remotely successful integration plan.

But the board soon found that the community did pretty well in organizing its own interests and agreeing on an agenda of common interests. The League of United Latin American Citizens (LULAC) and the G.I. Forum, two groups deeply involved in better education and opportunities for Mexican Americans, appointed a twelve-member education task force. The task force consisted of teachers, students, and community leaders who would try to determine how Mexican Americans felt about the public schools, as well as vocalize their opinions.[11]

But Gus Garcia, Austin's first Mexican-American school board member, said, "There has always been a strong community sentiment towards education and those sentiments have been expressed strongly. Organizing the effort is what's needed." The organization was targeted towards assisting Gabe Gutierrez, attorney for MALDEF, as a voice for the community in the lawsuit.[12]

* * *

The Austin branch NAACP was dissatisfied with the pace and amount of hiring of minorities by the city of Austin, one of the largest employers in Austin. In early 1978 Volma called a press conference. He called for an investigation of Austin's "dismal record of minority hiring" in federally financed job programs. Volma said Davidson's report on the city's job placement and training programs showed that despite high levels of minority unemployment, the city had not filled all the jobs available under the Comprehensive Employment Training Act (CETA) grants.[13]

"While the problem of unemployment and underemployment lingers in the Black and Mexican-American communities, most jobs under the manpower programs are going to whites," Volma said. "And jobs that could and should be made available are going unfilled because of mismanagement of the program and laxity on the part of the city manager and city council."[14]

* * *

Developments in two desegregation suits pending before the U.S. Supreme Court (involving court-ordered busing similar to Austin's case) gave the school board a needed excuse to file for a delay in the scheduled "remedy trial."

The district attorney filed a motion in U.S. district court, requesting a postponement from June 11 to July 9, 1979, of the "remedy trial," in order to take advantage of "additional guidance from the Supreme Court."[15]

The desegregation cases were the Dayton and Columbus, Ohio, desegregation suits, and involved questions over intent to discriminate, and how widespread the discrimination must be to justify a systemwide remedy.

Lawyers for both school boards argued that the federal courts should not interfere in situations where segregation is unintentional, but actual (de facto), stemming from housing patterns rather than law, or gerrymandered attendance zones.[16]

But the intervenors in the school desegregation suit, the NAACP and MALDEF, expected the ultimate decisions to have a minimal impact in Austin. NAACP attorney Sam Biscoe said, "Probably all parties would like to see what the U.S. Supreme Court says. But what they say will not impact Blacks in Austin. The Dayton and Columbus cases affect de facto segregation and would impact more on browns than blacks."

True to its ongoing effort to desegregate all grades in the public school system, the NAACP came up with a plan for desegregating the remaining grades, one through six. Since no African-American high school or junior high school existed in East Austin, the plan also called for an integrated junior high school in East Austin, and a sixth grade center in East Austin.[17]

An out-of-court settlement would have eased the burden on all concerned, especially considering the negative connotation of a trial. The intervenors, the AISD, and the community would have all benefitted from being a part of out-of-court settlement. But in late May 1979, Mexican Americans charged the school district with negotiating in bad faith. Representatives of MALDEF presented an educational proposal for Mexican-American students on April 9, 1979. Ernest Perales, district director of LULAC, charged that the school district was selective in picking items from the plan. The plan included a call for desegregation in grades five through twelve, and changes in the curriculum to achieve voluntary integration at Johnston High School.[18]

After a year and a half of working on the education plan, Perales said, "We just feel like we've been cheated out of a lot of good time and hard work, trying to minimize the amount of busing that might come out of a court settlement." The Mexican Americans refused to negotiate further, a situation which practically killed all hope for an out-of-court settlement. A trial appeared imminent.

* * *

A hearing in Judge Jack Roberts' district court was only a week away when the U.S. Supreme Court handed down a decision on the school board's request for an appeal of the November 21, 1977, ruling by the Fifth U.S. Circuit Court of Appeals. The ruling found the Austin School District guilty of intentionally segregating Mexican-American students.

The Supreme Court refused to hear the case. By its decision not to make a decision, the Supreme Court let stand the ruling by the Fifth Circuit Court of Appeals that the school board intentionally discriminated against Mexican Americans.

The hearing scheduled for July 9, 1979, was to determine the school district's constitutional violations and develop a plan to remedy those violations. The crux of the issue continued to revolve around forced busing. The Justice Department and the NAACP wanted some busing in grades one through five. But Judge Roberts had ruled previously that, "the time required for transportation, risk to health, and probably impingement of education of students younger than the sixth grade would be prohibitive under such plan."[19]

In its court order overturning Judge Roberts' ruling, the Fifth Circuit Court of Appeals said, "the district's plan has 'put the entire burden of transportation on blacks.'"[20] The court also found that the Austin School District used the neighborhood assignment plan to selectively discriminate.

* * *

The approach of the July 9, 1979, "remedy" hearing before Judge Jack Roberts found the community wrestling with ways to find a solution for several very distinct problems.

African Americans were segregated by law until the Supreme Court ruled the practice unconstitutional in the landmark 1954 case *Brown v. Board of Education*. African Americans, therefore, felt they had borne the full brunt of the school district's desegregation efforts. Both Old Anderson High School and Kealing Jr. High School, the city's two African-American secondary schools, had been ordered closed in 1971 by Judge Roberts' court order. African-American students were then bused one way across town to integrate formerly white schools. The NAACP represented African Americans, and contended forced busing should be shared.[21]

Mexican Americans contended they, too, had been discriminated against in the educational process, but not by law, as in the case of African-American students. Represented by MALDEF, Mexican Americans contended they were discriminated against by the actions of the school board.[22]

The Austin School Board felt that further integrating grades one through five, and instituting forced busing, would place too great a strain on the educational development of younger children. The board also denied intentionally discriminating against Mexican Americans, and claimed the segregation that did exist occurred as a result of neighborhood housing patterns.[23]

In its third opinion in the case, the Fifth U.S. Circuit Court of Appeals ruled the school board had historically used dual-overlapping attendance zones, student assignment policies, teacher assignment policies, school site selection, and gerrymandering to produce "more racial and ethnic separation in the schools than in the residential patterns of the district as a whole." In addition, the court found "the wholesale exclusion of entire grades (one through five) from a desegregation plan" as unacceptable.[24]

The beginning of the trial in Judge Roberts' court saw all parties in the suit poised to give testimony—including the AISD, the Justice Department, NAACP, and MALDEF. The first day of the remedy trial in Judge Roberts' court saw NAACP legal counsel Napoleon Williams ask Roberts to order the district to prepare a desegregation plan for Blacks as soon as possible. As justification, Williams' cited the Fifth Circuit Court's ruling that the dual system had never been completely done away with.[25]

But school board attorney Bill Bingham felt the intervenors, the NAACP and MALDEF, did not have the best interests of all public school children at heart. "The educational interests of the children are at best of secondary concern," Bingham said during the first day of the trial.[26]

In his opening statement before the court, Bingham cited the Supreme Court's findings in the Dayton, Ohio segregation case. The case held that a remedy in cases where mandatory segregation by law has long ceased (or never existed) must be based on the "incremental segregative effects" of school board policies.

As in the previous trial heard before Judge Roberts in 1973, the school district attorneys sought to show that the selection of sites for construction of new schools and the resulting assignment of students was determined by housing patterns. School board attorneys maintained throughout the trial that the district had no control over residential patterns.[27]

Under questioning by school district attorney Bill Bingham, the director of pupil services for the school district, Hugh Echols, testified at length about the history of AISD's school construction.

However, the Justice Department's attorney, Joe Rich, objected that Echols' testimony before the court was simply a rehash of evidence already on record. Rich said the testimony was "repetitious and irrelevant to the purpose of the trial." Rich pointed out that the U.S. Fifth Circuit Court of Appeals in New Orleans had already ruled that constitutional violations did occur.[28]

But Roberts overruled Rich's objection. Roberts said he would allow all parties to the suit wide latitude in introducing evidence into the trial record in case any of the parties decided to appeal his ruling.[29]

As Echols enumerated details on selection of each new school site, Bingham had him provide the court information on the earliest record of Mexican Americans in attendance at each school. Bingham then questioned Echols on whether the school district had any other alternative for selecting construction sites at the time. Echols also said the most important factor was real estate developers, who often led people seeking to purchase new homes to believe the suburbs offered the best schools— and not the inner city.[30]

Bingham sought to show that school officials planned new school sites in response to growth patterns, rather than attempt to control them. Under cross-examination, Rich, the Justice Department attorney, said that every Black school in the district since the 1930s had been built in East Austin, with the exception of the old St. John's Elementary School. "If Blacks can only attend black schools, wouldn't they be drawn to such schools?" Rich questioned Echols.[31]

But Echols said a school district study didn't show any impact on Black areas outside of East Austin, such as Clarksville. He said a review of a "small percentage" of Black students showed only fourteen cases of families moving to East Austin so their children would be closer to school.[32] Echols' testimony went against the federal appeals court finding that the Austin school district shuffled attendance zones and made school site selections in a method which produced "more racial and ethnic separation in the schools than in the residential patterns of the district as a whole."[33] He said that racial and ethnic concentrations would exist regardless of school board site selection policies. But Echols did concede that the "configurations" of the residential patterns might be different.

School district attorneys continued to expand on their theme that the selection of sites for schools did not contribute to segregated housing patterns when they cross-examined Dr. Joe Feagan. Feagan, professor of sociology at The University of Texas, was questioned as an expert witness. He authored *Discrimination, American Style,* in which he found a network of institutional discrimination in housing, schools, and employment, each reinforcing the other. Dr. Feagan was also the author of a study for the Hogg Foundation on mental health, in which he looked at discrimination in the delivery of public services to East Austin. He also cited the Koch-Fowler Report of 1928, a city master plan, as clearly indicating that the city's policy was to concentrate services for Blacks in East Austin.[34]

School District Attorney Shannon Ratliff questioned Dr. Feagan at length on the efforts involved in school site selections. Ratliff sought to show that white movement to the suburbs since World War II was attributable to a desire to improve their economic lot, not an avoidance of central city concentrations of minority groups. Ratliff further cited the restrictive covenants contained in policies of the Federal Housing Authority (FHA) and the Veterans Administration (VA) before 1948. Ratliff proposed that it was these policies which encouraged the homogeneity of neighborhoods. While conceding that FHA and VA policies could be seen as the primary cause of segregated neighborhoods, Dr. Feagin argued that school board violations found by the U.S. Fifth Circuit Court of Appeals in New Orleans "reinforced other things that were going on such as real estate discrimination."[35]

Ratliff questioned Feagan on whether the use of overlapping attendance zones between Zavala and Metz elementary schools had a systemwide impact. Feagan responded that he couldn't say for sure whether the impact was systemwide, but said discrimination has "tentacle-like" effects throughout a community.

Ratliff also questioned Dr. Feagan about whether West Austin schools which had Mexican-American students would have offset the effects of Mexican schools like Zavala in attracting Mexican Americans to East Austin.

Dr. Feagan answered that such schools probably gave "conflicting signals" to Mexican-American parents at the time.[36]

However, when NAACP lawyer Sam Biscoe cross-examined him, Echols seemed to reverse himself on several key points. "Do you agree with me that the housing patterns and the school patterns developed at pretty much the same time?" Biscoe asked. Echols answered "yes" after a long pause. Upon continued questioning from Biscoe, Echols read from his own deposition where he stated, "I don't know which comes first, the housing pattern or the school pattern."[37]

Biscoe also raised questions to Echols concerning the percentage of African-American students in the district's elementary schools during the 1970-71 school year (the last year East Austin had Anderson High and Kealing Junior High schools) and 1978-79 school year (prior school year before court hearing).

The NAACP's case centered on the premise that the dual school system mandated by law prior to 1954 had not been completely eliminated. Student statistics showed St. John's Elementary School in north Austin as having the district's highest percentage of African Americans—ninety-four percent in the 1970-1971 school year. Blackshear Elementary School in East Austin was shown as having a high percentage of African-American students attending an elementary school in East Austin at ninety percent.[38]

For MALDEF, intervenor on behalf of Mexican Americans, the main issue centered on the "incremental, segregative effects" of school board policies over the years.[39]

The federal appeals court said in its first ruling that Zavala Elementary was located three blocks from the then closed Mexican-American Comal Street School. The court found Zavala shared a dual-overlapping zone with Metz Elementary School. In its 1977 ruling the court described Metz Elementary School as "one of two predominantly white schools with significant numbers of Mexican-American students." Mexican Americans were expected to and did attend Zavala Elementary; whites attended Metz.[40]

Justice Department attorney Joe Rich noted during the trial that even after the 1954 *Brown* decision, the Austin school district had an optional attendance zone, which permitted whites in the zone of Old Anderson High School to attend Austin High School. Rich also quoted from the Gubbels Report, a plan for future site acquisitions written in 1948 by Joe Gubbels. The report said the concentration of Austin's non-white population was in their "economic and social interest."[41]

Two University of Texas professors hired by the Austin school district also testified. Dr. Terry Kahn, associate professor of community and regional planning, and Dr. Charles Wurstbach, assistant professor of finance, testified they were hired by the AISD to determine how housing patterns affected racial segregation in the community. The Kahn study found that median housing costs and median family income were among the economic factors found to be critical in producing ethnic and racial residential concentrations.[42]

Kahn said that because of economic factors, "there is a very restricted number of places low-income families in this community can live."[43]

However, upon cross-examination by Justice Department attorney Rich, Kahn was unable to explain why families with the lowest median incomes in the city in 1949 were living in an area with one of the highest median housing values. He also said he couldn't explain in purely economic terms why low-income whites didn't usually live in the same neighborhoods with low-income minority families.[44]

Dr. Charles Wurstbach testified that school quality was listed fifth as a determining factor in where families chose to purchase a home. Wurstbach testified seventy percent of families nationwide consider the cost of a home as the primary concern when deciding where to move. But for individuals in a higher income range, school quality was shown to be a more important factor, Wurstbach testified.[45]

School Supt. Jack Davidson took the stand on July 19, 1979, the seventh day of the court case. He testified that he had "come to the conclusion there may be a possible incremental segregative effect" in fourteen Austin schools as a result of previous school board actions.[46]

The fourteen schools were Johnston High School, Martin and Allan junior high schools, Blackshear, Campbell, Norman, Rosewood, Oak Springs, Ortega, Sims, Brooks, Govalle, Metz, and Zavala elementary schools.[47]

Supt. Davidson said that, in his opinion, there had not been an "incremental segregative effect," although he believed school board policies had such effects in the past for both blacks and Mexican Americans. However, "the effect has become dissipated" since the district's desegregation efforts began in the 1950s.[48] The U.S. Fifth Circuit Court of Appeals in New Orleans found that the "incremental segregative effect" was the difference between present ethnic and racial distributions and what they would have been without the district's constitutional violations.[49]

In cross-examination, U.S. Justice Department Counsel Joe Rich questioned parts of Davidson's testimony. Rich felt Davidson's views were inconsistent. Davidson seemed to say there were no remaining effects of segregation, while at the same time saying the effects had dissipated.[50]

Rich's cross-examination delved into Davidson's earlier testimony that white flight percentage losses of Anglo students was as high as eighteen percent. When cross-examined, Davidson conceded that in some instances Anglo percentages had actually increased by two or three percentage points after the adoption of desegregation plans.

Davidson told the court he regarded himself as an expert in race relations and the practical aspects of school desegregation, based on his experiences as school super-intendent in Tennessee, Florida, and Austin.[51]

On July 23, 1976, Judge Jack Roberts denied an NAACP motion to end segregation in East Austin schools. The NAACP plan called for pairing eight Black East Austin schools with white schools in north and west Austin.[52]

* * *

The Justice Department opened its case with testimony by Dr. Joe Feagan. "Segregated schools are like a magnet, attracting segregated housing," Feagan said. He also said Black schools were scattered throughout Austin between 1881 and 1900, but became increasingly concentrated in East Austin in this century. He cited construction of Sims and Oak Springs Elementary Schools in East Austin as examples of school site decisions that reflected "a desire to reinforce the boundaries between white and minority concentrations in Austin."[53]

The key witness in the Justice Department's presentation was Dr. Andrew Robinson, who prepared the NAACP and MALDEF-sponsored desegregation plan in 1976. He had also drawn up two other plans for school districts in Florida. Robinson's plan, if implemented, would close sixth grade centers and pair ten predominantly Black elementary schools with nine predominantly Anglo elementary schools. His plan also called for rebuilding Kealing Jr. High School in East Austin and either renovating Old Anderson High School and closing Johnston High School, or closing Johnston and constructing a new high school in East Austin.[54] At the end of the thirteen-day trial, Judge Roberts turned down a motion by NAACP attorneys that Dr. Robinson's plan be implemented. "We're gonna take a little time with this and I want everybody to understand that," Roberts told the parties of the desegregation suit after closing arguments in late July 1979.[55]

* * *

The Arthur B. DeWitty Awards Banquet was held in early December 1977. Myrlie Evers, wife of Medgar Evers, the civil rights leader who was assassinated in

Mississippi in 1963, was the speaker. Evers would later become chairman of the board of the NAACP. Evers said the first battle for civil rights was against slavery. In the 1950s and 1960s it reared its ugly head again, and at that time, Blacks had the police dogs and the beatings as a unifying force. She said she became disturbed when she visited high schools and colleges and found Black students unaware of the struggle that brought about social changes they now took for granted.[56]

The DeWitty Award was presented to Dr. Charles Urdy, chemistry professor at Huston-Tillotson College and the Black city councilman who had worked for the Fair Housing Ordinance and on community relations committees.

Volma found that some of his obligations were lifted during 1977. He retired from the U.S. Army Reserve at the rank of lieutenant colonel, an achievement he never imagined when he was a young, green recruit headed for Camp LeJeune in a segregated railway car.

10

JUDGE ROBERTS ISSUES
FINAL ORDER—1979

Roberts took until early November to issue a final ruling in the desegregation case that had dragged on for almost ten years. On November 5, 1979, Judge Roberts issued a fifty-one-page order calling for formation of a school desegregation plan targeted at achieving an Anglo enrollment in each school in "rough proportion" to the percentage of Anglo students in the Austin Independent School District. Roberts stated, "This does not mean that every school in the system necessarily must reflect the racial and ethnic composition of the scholastic population in the entire district, but the court will closely scrutinize any plan which contemplates the continued existence of schools which are predominantly minority or disproportionately Anglo . . . The court emphasizes that this Anglo-majority standard is a goal, but not an absolute requirement." Roberts also called for a plan that minimized "extensive or long distance busing of children in the lower grades . . ." The judge also said that the continued existence of "essentially one-race schools resulting from geographic or demographic accidents and surviving as minor anomalies in a broadly integrated program may be found acceptable by the court. The AISD will bear the burden of demonstrating that any such one-race school assignment is genuinely nondiscriminatory." Judge Roberts ordered all parties to the suit—AISD, NAACP, MALDEF and the Justice Department—to participate in drawing up a plan.[1]

Dr. Jack Davidson felt Roberts' new order would easily require the busing "of at least 10,000 to 20,000 students."[2]

The Austin branch NAACP was happy with the court order. "We welcome the court order by Judge Jack Roberts," Volma told the press. "This ruling is long overdue—we felt our position would prevail in the end." However, Volma felt Judge Roberts gave the school district too much time to implement a plan. "The school (district) has the expertise and staff to implement a desegregation plan in the spring semester," Volma said.[3]

Volma was also deeply concerned with the possible continuation of one-race schools as outlined in Judge Roberts' court order: "The judge said one-race schools might be acceptable in some instances—this could encourage white flight. We could find ourselves back in court again if one-race schools are allowed."[4] Austin citizens expressed mixed responses to this, the last in a series of orders concerning the segregation issue from Judge Roberts' court.

In an editorial in *The Daily Texan*, the student publication of The University of Texas at Austin, Beth Frerking wrote, "Judge Jack Roberts made a wise decision . . . until school systems can insure equal distribution of funds and resources between all district schools, forced segregation will become a fact of life in many Texas cities. It can work . . ."[5]

Lucille Crawford, a long-time physical education teacher at Old Anderson High School, expressed the sentiments of many educators. Crawford, president of the Austin Association of Teachers, said, "Our job is to teach the children wherever they are."[6]

School Supt. Jack Davidson called for actual desegregation of the races, not simply instituting new programs. "The court gives desirable emphasis to the educational programs (such as bilingual programs), but none of these programs will take the place of physical programs," he said.[7]

Gabe Gutierrez, attorney for MALDEF, said Roberts'

finding was "a good opinion." However, Gutierrez expressed disappointment in Roberts' failure to find a systemwide impact in the constitutional violations against Mexican Americans.[8]

Former School Board President Carol McClellan responded to Judge Roberts' criticism that the board "has not demonstrated a willingness voluntarily to take the necessary steps to effectuate complete desegregation of the AISD schools." McClellan said AISD had been under various desegregation plans since 1971, and that "Each step has been very successful, though possibly slower than people want."[9] One of those people who felt progress towards integration was too slow was Volma Overton.

NAACP officials took a closer look at Judge Roberts' order calling for submission of a plan to his court by January 15, 1980. They also considered Supt. Jack Davidson's estimate of an effective date of September 1980 for full implementation of the plan. Davidson's estimate took into consideration the logistics problems of busing 10,000 to 20,000 students. Volma and NAACP attorney Sam Biscoe decided the final desegregation plan could be implemented sooner than the fall of 1980. They decided to file an appeal with the U.S. Fifth Circuit Court of Appeals for implementation of the plan in the spring of the following year. "We're letting the (AISD school) board know we're putting as much pressure on them as we can," Biscoe said.[10]

The memory of Judge Roberts' stinging denial in July 1979 of immediate implementation of the NAACP's desegregation plan was still fresh in their minds. The plan was unacceptable to the court because it dealt with whites and Blacks only. It did not include Hispanics. But Volma and Biscoe decided to submit the request for immediate desegregation of the schools to the court of appeals in hopes of quicker action.

Less than a week later, Volma, Biscoe, and other NAACP stalwarts were celebrating victory. After a hearing before a three-judge panel of the U.S. Fifth Circuit Court of Appeals in Fort Worth, a mandate was issued requiring parties to the Austin desegregation case to submit their plans by December 17, 1979, to Judge Roberts. The court also ordered that the plan be implemented by January 21, 1980.[11]

Criticisms of the NAACP and the court mandate were not long in coming. Supt. Dr. Jack Davidson predicted chaos in the schools, reiterating his estimate that 10,000 to 20,000 AISD students would have to be bused.[12]

M. K. Hage, board member and former board president, requested NAACP and MALDEF attorneys attend a meeting so that "board members can personally discuss with them the difficulties and the risks of immediate implementation." Hage feared the entire school district would have to be shut down so that the desegregation plan could be fully implemented. The school district also filed a "motion for reconsideration of the mandate" with the appellate court. "What we want is a reasonable time to plan for a school program that will work," Hage said. "To shut down for immediate implementation would cost about $360,000 a day, would extend the school year about two weeks, and would be a complete waste."[13]

However, Volma remained unmoved. "They [the district] have been dragging their feet for nine years," Volma said. "They don't need any more time than they have— they can say anything they want to, but they're just talking."[14] Volma was steadfast in his opposition to further delays of integration of Austin's public schools. The *Brown* ruling handed down in 1954, declaring that the nation's public schools be integrated "with all deliberate speed," often crossed his mind during those final days before all parties of the lawsuit entered into a consent agreement less than a year later.

And he often thought of DeDra. The plump baby girl of the Overton family who slumbered in a friend of the family's arms in council chambers in 1964 while her father and other members of the Austin branch NAACP took turns reading from *Black Like Me* to disbelieving Austin City

Council members. The mischievous nine-year-old was a smiling sixth grader when Volma penned her name as plaintiff in the NAACP's desegregation suit against the Austin school district.

DeDra was now eighteen years old, and the suit, initially filed in 1970, still remained unsettled in the courts. Throughout the years, DeDra's school friends often asked questions about her name being read over the news broadcasts and printed in newspaper stories. DeDra was now a young woman, and complete integration of Austin's public schools was not yet a reality.

Looking back, Volma could still see the pained expressions on the faces of Austin's movers and shakers, and public officials who soon realized that behind Volma's quiet, unassuming exterior lay a will of iron. He would not back down on the integration issue but he made a point of never backing his opponents into a corner without giving them room to get out to save face. Volma knew from bitter reality that saving face, eating a little crow, was often all a person had left.

He would not back down on integration, but he would compromise. And that is just what the next few months brought—compromising, strategizing, planning, talking. But in the end, he never gave up on the central issue—complete integration of all grades.

The following week, after a meeting between school board trustees, NAACP and Justice Department officials, Volma confirmed that the plaintiffs would consider delaying the deadline for desegregating high schools to March 3, 1980.[15] But the plaintiffs said they had to be given the latitude to look at the district's proposed plan before a final decision was made. They also told the trustees of specific elements they wanted considered during formation of the district's plan.

But they remained adamant in their belief that all grades be integrated. They told Supt. Davidson, "they did not see any negotiating room with regard to excluding any grades from integration . . ."[16]

However, the plaintiffs' insistence on a plan that met with their approval proved to be the breaking point for some board members, community observers, and concerned parents. As Judge Roberts' deadline for submission of a plan agreed upon by the school board, NAACP, MALDEF, and the Justice Department grew nearer, tempers flared.

On December 4, 1979, the plaintiffs found AISD's carefully drawn-up desegregation plan "inadequate." The proposed plan "left too many minority schools in the East side segregated. They [predominantly minority East Austin schools] need to be desegregated grades one through twelve," Gabe Gutierrez said. Gutierrez also said the AISD must be prepared to bus more Anglo high school students to meet federal court mandates, which had set early 1980 deadlines for ending racial and ethnic segregation of the city's eighty educational facilities.[17]

A storm of criticism followed. School board member M. K. Hage told the City Council of PTA's, a predominantly Anglo group of about 140 members, that complying with the plaintiffs' demands "would destroy Austin." Other board members speaking before the same group urged "calmness" and "reason."

Board member DeCourcy Kelly, speaking before another group, said, "If you allow panic to take over we can have destruction of the (public school) system . . . If we don't panic and desert the ship, we can do it again."[18] One group even suggested the school board ignore the court order as illegal. Action for Neighborhood Schools, organized in 1976 to oppose desegregation plans, urged board members to file another appeal with the Supreme Court. The group's president, Fred O'Connor, said large-scale busing could destroy the Austin school system and change the character of the community.[19]

On December 10, 1979, over 2,000 people packed a meeting in which proposed desegregation plans were discussed. Several hundred persons staged a walk-out as school board members discussed the proposals.[20]

But perhaps the most vocal critics of the school desegregation plan were the students themselves. Chanting "hell no, we won't go," over 300 Anderson High School students marched on the Carruth Administration Building in north Austin on a morning in early December 1979. The students carried signs with anti-busing slogans: "Busing is Anti-American"; "Bus Judges, Not Students"; "Make a fuss, don't get bused"; "Honk if you hate forced busing." They said they would not be forcibly bused.

"We'll find a way to get out of it," one student said.

"I promise you, none of us will go," another student said. "They call us a bunch of rich snobs, but the fact is, we'll stay at Anderson and stand up for our rights."

An AISD employee told the student protesters, "You should go march at the NAACP office. They're the ones who did it."[21] The NAACP continued to get the brunt of criticism levelled at the intervenors. Volma took note. He sympathized with the pain on the faces of white parents whose children faced forced busing for the first time in their lives. He knew that white students, who were for the most part free of the threat of busing, really felt the sting of change for perhaps the first time in their young lives.

He also heard the concerns of Black parents whose children faced busing from their neighborhood schools to unfamiliar schools in white sections of Austin. He heard complaints that despite the court order, Black children would be bused more than white children.

But it was when he heard from parents like himself—Blacks who knew the humiliation of inferior schools, dog-eared books that the white schools no longer wanted, and heating and ventilation that were made up of space heaters and windows propped open with sticks—that Volma knew the fight for integration through busing had to be waged until the last. And in the end, Volma found that compromise played an important role in the final decision.

Sunday, December 16, 1979, saw over 600 anti-busing protesters massed on the steps of the state capitol, listening to speeches and waving flags.

But later that same day, the Austin School Board made history. The board announced it would enter into a consent agreement in Judge Roberts' court to settle the school desegregation suit once and for all.

Under the consent agreement, implementation of the plan would be delayed until August.

Glaring headlines appeared in Austin's newspapers the following day (December 17, 1979): "15,000 to be Bused—Desegregation Agreement Reached, Judge Roberts to Get Proposal";[22] "Protesters Unhappy With AISD Vote";[23] "Board Vows to 'Obey the Law.'"[24]

* * *

The final consent agreement was hammered out at a planning session between Austin School Board attorneys, including Bingham and representatives of the intervenors.

After many hours of discussion, some emotional board members cast their votes on the final plan. The plan submitted to Judge Roberts' court contained a delay in implementation until August 1980. It also guaranteed a new Kealing Jr. High School for East Austin. The plan also left in place an option between Plan A and Plan B, to be decided by January 15, 1980. Plan A required busing of approximately 15,000 students to include about 7,000 in the first through sixth grades. Plan B included the same provisions as Plan A, with the exception of pairing Anderson and Johnston High Schools. Both schools would become two-year high schools with students from both schools attending Anderson during the ninth and tenth grades, and Johnston during the eleventh and twelfth grades. The school board planned to hold public hearings to get community input on the final adoption of Plan A or Plan B in January 1980.

* * *

The prospect of the adoption of Plan B threatened to upset the athletic programs at Johnston and Anderson High Schools. Coaches at both schools worried they would lose their jobs.[25] With the possibility of the consolidation of two varsity programs, only one coaching staff would be needed. There was also concern that tenth grade athletes with the ability to play on a varsity squad would have to be shuttled between campuses. Also, junior and senior level athletes from two different high schools assigned to one school would create such a wealth of talent as to "corner the market," creating a disadvantage for their opponents.[26]

As school officials and Judge Roberts' court smoothed out plans for a peaceful transition into busing, other educators were defending their role in desegregation issues. Bishop Vincent Harris and the pastors of fifteen Catholic churches of the Roman Catholic Diocese of Austin attended a closed meeting on December 18, 1979, to discuss the impact of busing on private parochial schools. "Enrollment is frozen and we won't be taking any more students," Monsignor Lonnie Reyes, diocesan chancellor and pastor of Christo Rey Church, said following the meeting.[27]

Bishop Harris said, "I feel as responsible members of the Austin community all of us should work for a smooth transition. We can't put ourselves in a position of cooperating with white flight."[28]

The Catholic schools would continue to accept the children of parishioners, but not children of nonmembers, the Catholic officials said.

Volma was pleased with the turn of events that led to the consent agreement. He felt that after years of monitoring and appealing the court order, it was time to start all children with the kind of quality education that he knew the district could provide throughout the school system.

11

RETIREMENT—THE EIGHTIES

As cheerful crowds celebrated the coming of the decade of the 1980s, Volma danced the fox trot and the Australian waltz at a New Year's Eve party. He faced the new decade with optimism, now that a firm desegregation plan for Austin would soon become law.

He also realized that Austin and the entire nation were changing. Solutions to the problems of today would not always fit the city's problems of tomorrow. He was very proud of the branch's involvement in the total integration of Austin's schools. But it had not been easy. As the pages of the calendar turned to January 1980, a segment of the anti-busing group still held hope that integration could be achieved without busing.

On the day scheduled for final approval of the consent decree, people having objections were invited to present them. James Dunlap filed an alternate, student choice desegregation plan in a friend of the court brief. His plan called for ethnic quotas for each school based on current district-wide ethnic enrollment percentages. Students would be allowed to choose a school until target enrollments were reached. Students who selected schools which had already reached the targeted enrollment would be allowed to select an alternate school.[1]

Attorney William C. Bednar, Jr., filed a petition containing 5,477 names on behalf of parents who objected to both Plan A and Plan B. Bednar termed the signers, most of whom were residents of Northwest Hills, as "not adamantly opposed to the busing of students over reasonable distances and times." He predicted that implementing Plan A or Plan B would "convert the AISD into a predominantly Black and Mexican-American school district in a relatively short time."[2]

But Judge Roberts said that interested parties filing objections to the plans could not legally become intervenors at this stage. Roberts said the parties' objections were legitimate concerns, but did not justify rejection of the decree.[3]

The following day (January 3, 1980) Judge Roberts issued a memorandum of opinion giving final approval to the consent decree. Judge Roberts also addressed what he termed "commonly cited objections" to the plan. With the exception of making a choice between Plan A and Plan B, Judge Roberts' memorandum of opinion and order gave final approval to the consent degree and settled Austin's desegregation suit.

The following week, however, residents of South and North Austin remained sharply divided over which plan the school board should accept and implement. A cross-section of Austin residents from neighborhoods in North and South Austin expressed their opinions to school board members at a hearing at KLRU on The University of Texas campus. But board members noted that parents argued for the plan that would have the least effect on their own children. Residents of North Austin were favorable towards Plan A, which would allow Anderson and Johnston to remain four-year high schools. Plan B would exempt Crockett High School from busing to integrate Johnston and was, therefore, supported by South Austin parents. "Anybody who testified last night wanted that plan because he was least affected by it," board member Will Davis said. "That's human nature— and we knew that going in."[4]

The following week, in front of a packed room, school board members held the audience in suspense for over half an hour before they voted. The vote was 4-3 in favor of Plan A. Board members Griffin, Navarro, Davis, and Hage voted for Plan A. Board members Nugent, Kelly, and Clayton voted in favor of Plan B.

A range of emotions ran through the room. Some Plan B supporters shed tears. Several Oak Hill residents shouted that the board had "shafted South Austin again." One South Austinite called for Reverend Griffin's resignation because he had "not kept an open mind."[5]

Another resident delivered petitions containing 16,773 signatures demanding board members' removal from office through recall or resignation before the vote was taken.

A spokesman for Winn Elementary School parents asked for an exemption from both of the proposals, stating their neighborhood was already naturally integrated. Students enrolled at Winn Elementary in grades 4-6 were scheduled to be bused away from their neighborhood under both Plan A and Plan B.

Other distraught parents joined about 150 members of Action for Neighborhood Schools, an affiliate of the National Association of Neighborhood Schools, for a meeting with U.S. Representative Jake Pickle. But Congressman Pickle left the anti-busers with little hope for changing the law.

He said HR 1180, a bill that would deprive federal courts of the jurisdiction to order busing for desegregation purposes, held "false hope." "I don't think you can take away the jurisdiction of the federal courts on a constitutional question," Pickle said.[6]

Pickle was also firm in his opposition to a constitutional amendment to ban court-ordered busing. "I am not going to support a constitutional amendment," he told the group. He also stated he voted against appropriations for busing over the years and felt that "massive" court ordered busing is bad, but agreed with the U.S. Supreme Court that busing is "one tool" for bringing about school desegregation.[7] The group left Pickle's office dejected, many of them feeling he had been evasive about the real issue.

* * *

The following April brought school board elections to a community still deeply divided by the busing issue. A new crop of political hopefuls running on an anti-busing platform made headway in the election, causing three runoffs. DeCourcy Kelly was defeated in Place 2 by physician Peter Werner. Werner was supported by the anti-busing group Action for Neighborhood Schools.[8]

Rev. Marvin Griffin did not run for Place 1, choosing instead to run for the Austin City Council. Candidates Steve Ferguson, supported by Action for Neighborhood Schools, and Dr. June Brewer, both African Americans, went to a runoff. Ferguson was elected.

Dennis Bauerle, also an anti-busing candidate, and Ed Small were in a runoff for Place 3. Small won.

12

END OF OVERTON ERA
WITH NAACP—1983

In early 1983 Volma told the members of the Austin branch NAACP that he would not seek re-election to the presidency. He later told a news reporter that he hoped new blood might infuse some enthusiasm into the NAACP.[1]

Many important issues still remained. A new Austin branch president had to be selected and trained, the issue of the Austin school district receiving unitary status was still a divisive subject, and there remained the thorny question of the location of newly built public schools. There was also the ongoing controversy surrounding single-member districts.

Volma would be a behind-the-scenes supporter of the NAACP for years. After the election he kept busy bringing the new branch president, John Hall, into the job that had been his second life for over twenty years. His advice to his successor was simple: "Be patient and stick to it. You'll have a lot of disappointments, but you can't give up, because the forces are out there and they'll be coming at you from all directions."[2]

The school desegregation issue quieted down. The Austin schools remained under the the eye of the federal court until it achieved unitary status.

Austin voters approved thirteen new schools for the district in a bond election held in February 1983. Members of the NAACP and MALDEF, who were plaintiffs in the school desegregation case that had dragged on from 1970 to 1980, wanted to insure that the new schools would not be one-race schools.[3]

Representatives of MALDEF and the NAACP met with an NAACP attorney from New York on Monday, March 7, 1983. The group collaborated on objections to the AISD's request to the federal court that the schools were no longer segregated.[4]

John Hall objected to the district's affirmative action posture. Hall said he did not feel the district was hiring enough minorities.[5]

The Austin branch NAACP was also losing the services of attorney Sam Biscoe. Biscoe had steered the Austin branch through the desegregation lawsuit against the school district and provided invaluable assistance in busing issues and the final consent decree. Biscoe accepted a job with the Texas Department of Agriculture in 1983.

In March NAACP attorney Napoleon Williams indicated that "it might be possible" for the parties involved to agree that the district had reached "unitary" status. But Williams asked that the federal court continue "jurisdiction for a reasonable length of time."[6] Unitary status meant the school district had eliminated the dual-school system that automatically sent Black and white students to separate schools.

NAACP branch President John Hall listed fifteen schools where Anglo enrollment had gone below 1980 predictions, causing some to become one-race schools.

Also, the Austin school district, as well as two other school districts in Texas, brought their lawsuits to a close after many years.

The Waco school district and NAACP and MALDEF representatives reached a tentative agreement that the school district would close some schools and consolidate others. In Fort Worth, NAACP attorney Clifford Davis stated his approval of a proposal that would reduce busing by seventy-five percent.[7]

However, some Austinites were not convinced that

the schools were completely integrated. The provisions of the consent decree reached in 1980 called for federal overseeing of the schools to end in January 1983.

Parents of LBJ High School students, represented by Carmen Gonzales, carried a petition containing 200 signatures to Judge James Nowlin. Another group, the Mexican American Coalition for Desegregation, an umbrella group for thirteen community-based groups, said it would also deliver Nowlin's court a petition.[8]

LBJ High School was a good example of what both groups wanted to achieve. LBJ had a student body consisting of twenty percent Black, five percent Hispanic, and seventy-five percent Anglo in 1974. By 1983 the percentages had changed to fifty-five percent Black, nine percent Hispanic, and thirty-six percent Anglo. Enrollment figures also changed. In 1974 1,590 students attended LBJ. By 1983 the total enrollment figure was 1,298 students, triggering concerns about white flight and the effect it had on public schools.[9]

NAACP President John Hall moved to settle the suit, despite nagging problems.

School board members voted 6-1 to accept settlement of the district's desegregation case. Other parties to the suit were given the right to reopen the case until January 3, 1986, if they felt the district practiced discrimination.[10]

The school district and plaintiffs in the case agreed to hire, promote, dismiss, assign, and pay professionals, administrators, and other staff members without regard to race, color, or national origin, with a commitment to affirmative action. This included placing minorities in positions of high visibility, the construction of Kealing Jr. High School in East Austin, for which architectural plans were already prepared, studying the effect of the construction of new schools on racial makeup of schools, and consideration of alternatives that would maximize integration. The agreement also included retaining the majority-to-minority transfer policy, continuing programs to meet the special needs of children with educational deficiencies, as well as continuing bilingual programs. The settlement also allowed the case to be reopened through January 3, 1986, if a substantial change in the current student reassignment plan was found, and if the change unlawfully discriminated against students on the basis of race, color, or national origin.[11]

The three plaintiffs in the school desegregation case—the NAACP, MALDEF, and the U.S. Justice Department, gave written approval of the plan. But both Hall of the NAACP, and Amatra Mendoza of the Mexican American Coalition for Desegregation, expressed misgivings. They did not believe the district had obtained perfect unitary status. However, they went on to say that their groups were willing to give the district a chance to demonstrate that it would continue its commitment to equal education.[12]

But Volma harbored very serious misgivings about the agreement. He told news reporters that he was wary of board promises, and had seen the case bounced from court to court, including two trips to the U.S. Supreme Court, for more than a decade.[13]

Dr. Peter Werner, the lone school board member to vote *against* accepting the settlement, felt that the agreement would not change the way the district operated.

"Does it mean the children who live 120 seconds from Anderson can return there? No, it doesn't," Werner said. "This doesn't change anything. Upper-middle-class families will still tend to avoid Austin schools as they have for the past several years."[14]

Wednesday, June 15, 1983, was a landmark day for the Austin school district, plaintiffs, and others. U.S. District Judge James Nowlin signed the court order giving the school district unitary status. Judge Nowlin also agreed to let the school district turn one unresolved part of the case into a separate lawsuit.

School officials estimated the expense to be $23 million. School attorney Bill Bingham said the state of Texas should bear part of the cost of desegregating the schools.

Prior to the 1954 ruling in the *Brown* case, segregation in
the Texas public school system was state law.

* * *

Although he decided not to run for the presidency of
the Austin branch NAACP again in 1982, Volma
remained active in political issues affecting the minority
community long afterwards.

On April 6, 1984, the Austin branch NAACP, under
the leadership of John Hall, filed a lawsuit in U.S. District
Court. The lawsuit alleged that Austin's at-large method
of electing its city council "discriminates against Blacks
and violates their right to equal participation in the political process."[15]

Volma had always felt that the at-large system of
electing city council members was another means of pre-
venting minorities from serving on the city council. The
at-large system was instituted for city council elections in
1953 when Arthur DeWitty, a close friend and mentor to
Volma, was almost elected to a council seat. During that
period in Austin's politics, getting elected to the council
required only a plurality to win.[16]

The NAACP's suit also "asked the court to declare the
at-large system unconstitutional, to prevent elections under
that system, and order a single member district plan."[17]

The memory of Austin voters' rejection of single-
member districts in referendums in both 1973 and 1978
was still fresh on Volma's mind as the branch decided to
go ahead with the suit.

A change from at-large elections of Austin City
Council members to the single-member-districts method
required a change in the city's charter, and would also
require a referendum or public vote. City council members decided against putting the issue to the voters in
January 1985, as they had previously planned. Instead,
they decided to enter into a settlement with the NAACP.[18]

The city council considered its options, and after two
closed door sessions with city attorney Paul Isham,
announced that it would not fight what could become a divi-

sive, expensive, and possibly unsuccessful lawsuit. Council members voted 6-1 to seek a settlement, with council member Charles Urdy making the motion to settle. City council member Mark Spaeth cast the one dissenting vote.

The Black Citizens Task Force, represented by attorney Terry Davis, was denied a temporary restraining order to stop the city council from negotiating a settlement in what would have resulted in a drawn-out lawsuit by the NAACP and MALDEF. Davis said the decision by the council to seek a settlement would result in a change in the city charter, which only voters were allowed change. Davis also said the district plan would reduce Black voting strength from one of seven council members under the present at-large plan to one of nine.[19]

Other observers were incensed that the council vote to settle the issue came at one in the morning, when practically no one was present.

Others felt the map of proposed single member districts drawn up by political consultant Peck Young and backed by the NAACP favored liberals over conservatives, appearing to give them seven of the eight districts.[20]

Councilman Urdy said if the trial were held, the first witnesses for the prosecution would be council members. "In our campaigns we supported single-member districts, so I don't think we have a chance of defending ourselves," he said.[21]

The plaintiffs' settlement offer, negotiated by NAACP attorney David Van Os, called for eight council districts with the mayor elected at-large.

Van Os said that "It would have been a very intense and divisive courtroom fight, and no matter who won at the trial court, it would have become a long, drawn-out litigation similar to the school desegregation case."[22]

The prospect of implementing single-member districts for city council races in Austin brought out proponents and critics alike.

Gary Witt, who at one time served as chairman of the Charter Revision Commission, felt single-member districts would mean anyone, regardless of financial status, could run for election to a city council seat. "In one vote, they have spared the city major civil rights divisiveness, saved the taxpayers a million dollars in legal fees, and brought public service back down to the reach of the average citizen," Witt said. "No longer will you have to be rich or have rich friends to serve the citizens of Austin on the city council."[23]

Peck Young, a political consultant whose firm, Emory Young & Associates, drew the preliminary district map for the plaintiffs' case, also expressed support for the council vote: "Fundamentally the history of the city shows a deliberate attempt to deny minority representation and then to restrict that representation to two seats," Young said. "You would have a lot of accusations of racism, prejudice and bigotry and we still would have ended up with single-member districts."[24]

Young also felt the issue of whether to institute single-member districts should not be decided by the voters. "This is a civil rights issue, and there's no inherent right for the voters to settle it by referendum," Young said. "I'm not sure that majority rule gets to decide civil rights. The courts are there to protect people who cannot obtain the support of the majority."[25]

However, critics of the proposed plan abounded, and Volma found they were not all non-minority. Dorothy Turner, community activist and president of the Black Citizens Task Force, was firmly against single-member districts. "We want to take it to the polls," Turner said of the proposed referendum on the issue. "We are opposed to single-member districts. It dilutes the power of the mass of Black people in Austin. Now, everybody on the council is accountable to everybody else. With single-member districts, there'll be one Black district in East Austin. Well, Blacks are scattered everywhere around Austin. Who represents them?"[26]

Volma strongly disagreed with Turner's reasoning. He felt that Blacks needed someone vitally interested in Black determination and Black issues. He believed all council members should be interested in the good of the Black community, but more often than not, only the minority council members expressed an interest in Black issues.

Ray Mariotti, editor and columnist for the *Austin American-Statesman*, felt the powers that be which ran Austin politics were simply using minorities to tighten their grip on the city's voting patterns. Mariotti wrote:

> The folks who own City Hall made their big bold move last week to secure their holdings. Their hirelings on the Austin City Council voted 6-1 to take a dive in a federal lawsuit . . .
>
> Hiding sanctimoniously behind the skirts of the blacks and browns of the community, the powerful political organization that controls local politics is cementing its control in the face of declining voter advantage. As usual, it is an abuse and misuse of the plight of racial minorities . . .[27]

But what some observers thought would be a shoe-in turned into something altogether different when U.S. District Judge James Nowlin refused to sign the proposed settlement. Nowlin stated he would not accept the settlement agreement until he was convinced that the present system was discriminatory.[28] "Let me make this clear," Nowlin said, "The court will not blindly approve something just because it is labeled a settlement. Regardless of what the parties agree to, the court must determine whether or not there is a federal issue here."[29]

Judge Nowlin's refusal to sign the agreement between the city and the intervenors created a wealth of problems for everyone. Several individuals and organizations, dissatisfied with Peck Young's map, began drawing their own redistricting maps. The Austin Association of Builders submitted a map.[30]

The case grew increasingly complicated as both major and minor players jockeyed for position.

American Statesman columnist Ray Mariotti continued to criticize the single-member districting plan, calling it "the Great Austin Districting Rip Off."[31]

The city council set a date for a public hearing on the issue, only to later postpone it.

University of Texas students, in a bid to assure that their voting power would not be diluted, began talks with the city council to create a single-member district encompassing the school.[32]

The NAACP, through its lawyer Leonard Schwartz, tried a new tact. The organization requested that the U.S. Fifth Circuit Court of Appeals *order* District Judge Nowlin "to sign the agreement between the NAACP and the city council without a hearing."[33]

The NAACP also drew up a new agreement, called a "milder version of the one the city council approved," to settle the lawsuit with the city council. This new agreement cut out references to the constitutionality of the issue.[34]

"We think the judge can sign this," David Van Os, attorney for the NAACP, said. "It does not require the court to find that the city is currently acting unconstitutionally."[35]

Councilman Mark Spaeth also entered the fray. Spaeth became an individual intervenor in the suit when he filed suit in district court on September 12, 1984, opposing single-member districts. Spaeth contended that since the question of constitutionality had been removed from the suit, Austin's election could now be changed by charter revision only. This meant the voters would have to determine the issue in a referendum. Spaeth also favored a mixed plan, with both single-member and at-large districts.[36]

In another development, U.S. District Judge Nowlin cancelled the hearing previously scheduled for December 3, 1984, indefinitely until the Fifth U.S. Circuit Court of Appeals could issue a ruling on the intervenors' suit ordering Judge Nowlin to sign the agreement.[37] This action placed the issue back in the hands of the city council, which favored putting it before the voters on the January 19, 1985, ballot.

Since the city charter could only be changed once every two years, and an issue had already been approved to be placed on the ballot to change the charter, the issue of single-member districts would have to be voted on immediately or the city council would be forced to wait another two years to vote.

However, the NAACP was thwarted in its effort to appeal to a higher court for a more favorable ruling. In a stinging rebuke, the Fifth Circuit Court of Apeals found that Judge Nowlin had the right to have a hearing before deciding if Austin's at-large system was discriminatory. Judge Will Garwood wrote that Nowlin had the discretion, if not the duty, to schedule settlement hearings.[38] The appeals court decision meant that the decision on whether to change to single-member districts would go to the voters by referendum.

Just prior to the election, lawyers for the NAACP, MALDEF and LULAC (League of United Latin American Citizens) went to U.S. District Court and successfully blocked citizens in areas recently annexed by the city of Austin from voting in the January 19, 1985, election.

On November 16, 1984, the Austin City Council voted to annex an area between Ranch Road 620 and Loop 360, north of RR 2222 and south of U.S. 183. Also annexed was an area earmarked to become a park in South Austin, the Woods of Westlake subdivision, an area between Manchaca Road and IH 35 south of William Cannon Drive, an area along RR 620 and RR 2244, and land next to IH 35 in the Walnut Creek subdivision.[39]

The intervenors felt the city's newly annexed areas would "dilute the minority vote by adding 18,000 new Anglo voters to city voting rolls." Joe Garza, attorney for MALDEF, said, "Clearly, in a close election, allowing these folks to vote might change the outcome of the election."[40]

The city council placed the issue of single-member districts on the January 19, 1985, ballot. However, the issue that Volma felt to be of just as much importance for the minority community as the school desegregation lawsuit was placed on a ballot with a total of nineteen proposals.[41]

Proposals to create a metropolitan transit authority, the relocation of Mueller Airport, two bond proposals for cultural arts facilities, a proposed city charter change that would allow the city council to issue revenue bonds without voter approval, and eleven items that involved charter changes, all appeared on the ballot.

Volma felt the sheer number of issues on the ballot was detrimental to single-member districts. Conservative voters who might not have otherwise voted came out of the woodwork to defeat the issue.

The Austin branch NAACP felt the issue was of such importance that they ran a campaign to get voters to the polls. They put out fliers and offered rides to the polls on election day to get out the minority vote.

But they were sadly disappointed when the votes were counted. The single-member districting plan was overwhelmingly defeated. The vote was 44,892 against and 34,382 for the proposal.[42]

The defeat forced the issue back to Judge Nowlin's court. It also forced the city council to take a fresh look at the issue of single-member districts. After a three-hour session, the Austin City Council, in a complete about-face, voted 6-0 to order its attorney to defend the at-large issue instead of defending single-member districts in the upcoming trial in Judge Nowlin's court. The trial was set for February 1985.

Volma was discouraged by the vote, but he would not give up.

NAACP Attorney Van Os termed the council's about-face "gutless," and a breach of faith. "You're going to find out that Austin has a sordid history of vicious racial discrimination and that people who live in East Austin are still suffering the effects of that," Van Os said.[43]

* * *

Proponents and critics of single-member districts crowded into Judge Nowlin's courtroom in Austin in early February 1985. What followed was a week-long trial rife with charges of voting bias, Anglo control of council slates, and voting limits on minority candidates.

The NAACP, LULAC, and MALDEF, groups well seasoned in civil rights battles, sought to show that Austin's at-large system of electing members for the city council diminished the voting power of Blacks and Mexican Americans, thereby violating the Voting Rights Act.[44]

Charles Miles, now executive director of the Austin Housing Authority and first witness for the plaintiffs, said Black candidates must concentrate on issues such as the environment or the South Texas Nuclear Project, which are of little concern to the Black community, in order to get elected.[45]

NAACP Attorney Van Os claimed that Austin's political power brokers "had devised a paternalistic system under which blacks can win only through white benevolence." The reason a Black had been elected to the council since 1971 and a Hispanic since 1975 was the result of the gentlemen's agreement devised by Anglos, Van Os said.[46]

He contended that Anglos allowed Blacks to win one of the seven council seats as long as the black candidates were willing to receive ninety percent of their funding from whites, make promises necessary to receive that funding, and understood that their ability to speak out for their constituency was secondary to the desires of the Anglo majority.[47]

Volma also testified for the plaintiffs' case, along with Ernest Perales, past president of LULAC, and Milton Gooden and Iola Taylor, both members of the Austin branch NAACP.

The plaintiffs' allegations were disputed by Steve Bickerstaff, a private attorney conducting the rebuttal case for the city. Bickerstaff contended that "the city's at-large system is working."[48] He pointed to the city's good record of minority employment, adoption of a fair housing ordinance, and the declaration of Martin Luther King, Jr.'s, birthday as a city holiday.

But the second day's testimony brought out a strong witness for the plaintiffs' case. Ed Wendler, a city hall lobbyist and member of the liberal Austin Progressive

Coalition formed in 1970, had been involved in liberal issues since 1951 when he was a campaign worker for Arthur DeWitty's unsuccessful run for city council. The Austin daily described Wendler as walking "a tightrope between the liberal and conservative communities . . . as a man with liberal leanings, he has been an active participant in liberal politics and causes for years. As a lawyer-lobbyist for conservative builders and developers, he appears in city hall in defense of many of their projects."[49]

Wendler's testimony turned out to be a strong indictment against at-large elections in Austin. He said conservatives and liberals controlled elections by endorsing separate slates of candidates: "Since 1971 it has been virtually impossible for anyone to get elected without being on one of those two slates." The slates of candidates were made with little minority participation, Wendler said. Although minorities sometimes helped choose minority candidates, they did not participate in selecting other candidates. Even Burl Handcox, the first Black to win election to the Austin City Council, was selected to run without input from the Black community.[50]

Beginning in 1975 the gentlemen's agreement limiting Place 5 on the city council for a Mexican American, and Place 6 for a Black was understood. Acquiring endorsements and getting on a slate provided candidates with credibility, name identification, and volunteers. Mike Guerro, a candidate for Place 1 on the city council in 1981, said he felt he did not get vital endorsements because he was a Mexican American not running for Place 5. Another Mexican-American candidate, Marcos de Leon, ran for Place 3 on the council and was also defeated. Wendler testified, "It's a liability in this community to have more than one Black or more than one brown on your slate, and it's impossible to raise money."[51]

In 1983 Wendler's coalition endorsed Sally Shipman, an Anglo, over Hector de Leon. "We gave Hector no opportunity. We had made the mistake once and we weren't going to make it again," Wendler told the court.[52]

According to Wendler, the Black Voter Action Project

(B-VAP) was the only minority group that had input into a slating process that existed only because of the at-large system. "It is how the side that I am on has to deal effectively with the at-large system," Wendler said. "The process demands that we have to do certain things and we're not proud of them."[53]

Political consultant Peck Young also testified that Anglos decided which minorities would be selected for a slate by the Austin Progressive Coalition.

In 1981 the organization selected Dr. Charles Urdy over Bertha Means, even though "Means had won awards in East Austin as an outstanding community leader." Also, Urdy was willing to support issues backed by the Progressive Coalition, such as environmental protection and controlled growth.[54]

Jimmy Snell, a Black who served as a three-term city councilman, as well as Travis County commissioner, said his need for the support of Anglos restricted him from strongly espousing minority issues.[55] Snell became acutely aware of white fear of the possibility of a Black running for mayor of Austin. Although he was elected mayor pro tem by a vote of his peers in 1975, Snell saw the system soon change in 1977 to the mayor pro tem position being rotated among council members every three months. The rotation system was changed back to a two-year term when Snell left the council. "The white community thought it was my interest to run for mayor, so they put pressure on the rest of the council to rotate the position every three months," he said.[56]

Other minorities also testified that they were denied endorsements and funds when they chose to run for a place not designated for their ethnic group.

Insurance executive Marcel Rocha testified his run for a Place 1 council seat in 1975 was stymied by a lack of endorsements outside the Mexican-American community and a lack of funds because he ". . . wasn't aware I was supposed to be on a slate and as a Mexican American I was supposed to be in Place 5."[57]

Carlos Velasquez, vice president of Roy's Taxi, testified he got the "cold shoulder" in 1983 when he ran for Place 4.[58]

However, defendants' testimony during the trial refuted many parts of the plaintiffs' case. The city attorneys disputed the testimony of Ed Wendler, maintaining that he admitted no participation in conservative group meetings and had had no involvement in the Austin Progressive Coalition, a liberal group, since 1977.[59]

Terry Davis, counsel for the Black Citizens Task Force who came within 584 votes of defeating incumbent councilman Dr. Charles Urdy in a council race in 1983, said he almost won with limited endorsements. "I believe the at-large system allows access for the black community," he said. "I feel the testimony given by Mr. Wendler was greatly exaggerated."[60]

Dorothy Turner, president of the Black Citizens Task Force, stated she felt Blacks had access to the at-large system, but simply didn't use it. However, Turner also stated under cross-examination that Black problems were not being addressed by the city council.

Council member Mark Spaeth also testified he was successfully elected in 1983 without being on a slate or getting many endorsements.

Bob Binder, elected city councilman in 1973 and defeated for mayor of Austin in 1981, testified he received support from the Austin Progressive Coalition. Binder said the endorsement of the coalition was important, but did not guarantee that a candidate would be elected.

Marcos de Leon, who lost to Sally Shipman in a council bid in 1983, said he believed his loss was not related to the fact that he was a Mexican American running for a seat other than Place 5.

In written arguments, both sides summed up their cases. A brief filed by city attorney Paul Isham and private attorney Steve Bickerstaff in support of at-large voting stated, "The system has resulted in the consistent election of minority representatives on the council and a city policy that is among the most progressive and responsive in the nation . . . Segregated housing patterns are gradually breaking down as the minority population is moving out of traditional geographic areas and dispersing throughout a much larger part of the city. Austin's experience under its at-large system has been unique."[61]

In his brief in support of single-member districts, David Van Os, attorney for the NAACP, countered the city's position with the statement:

> The evidence is strong that the election of three blacks and John Trevino has not been the product of minority voters' choice of effective access to the process, but rather of the machinations of a paternalistic Anglo electorate and its kingmakers.
>
> They choose the spot for minorities, ideally the campaign issues, and monopolize their time after the election.[62]

In mid-March 1985, Judge Nowlin released a fifty-five-page opinion which found the at-large system of electing the Austin City Council to be "not unconstitutional or unlawful."[63] Volma felt Nowlin's ruling smacked of the same conservative philosophy that had always dogged NAACP court cases.

The NAACP planned an appeal before the Fifth U.S. Circuit Court of Appeals, but did not expect a ruling before 1986. However, in August 1986, the plaintiffs—the NAACP, MALDEF, and LULAC—had cause for celebration.

In a reversal, the Fifth Circuit Court of Appeals ordered Judge Nowlin to reconsider Austin's single-member districts case because of a Supreme Court ruling that set new criteria for voting rights cases.[64]

However, Van Os found that a change in city leadership worked against immediate acceptance of a change in Austin's voting method for electing city council members.

In early March 1987 Mayor Frank Cooksey seemed unfriendly to Van Os' presentation before the council to institute single-member districts. Mayor Cooksey asked Van Os and Jose Garza, lawyer for MALDEF, to end their presentation because, "We had a situation where lawyers for the other side were coming directly to us rather than talking to us when our lawyers were present. As a lawyer, that doesn't set right with me."[65]

But Van Os called the mayor's actions a farce: "Mayor Frank Cooksey exerted every effort to limit our presentation. He displayed open hostility, making it clear beyond a shadow of a doubt that he is not interested in any discussion of this case."[66]

Mayor Cooksey later told the Austin daily that a referendum was the only way to change the city charter.

NAACP Attorney David Van Os saw a ray of hope for single-member districts in the results of the April election. "Terry Davis got an overwhelming black vote," Van Os said of the Black candidate, "but it was an exercise in futility."[67] Davis came in fourth among seven candidates.

Once a staunch critic of single-member districts, the election results left Davis with a change of heart. Davis said he would be willing to look at a combination of districts and at-large plan if elected.

Gilbert Martinez, a Hispanic candidate who went into a run-off election on May 2, 1987, with a lead, also suffered defeat. He was beaten by Max Nofziger, described as a flower salesman with no political experience.

Peck Young, a political consultant, blamed Martinez' defeat on pure racism. "Martinez did a service to the community," Young said. "Here you had a Hispanic with a lead going in, well financed and well qualified" who still could not get elected.[68]

A win by Terry Davis and Gilbert Martinez would have upset the so-called gentlemen's agreement, in which places five and six were reserved for minority candidates. Since Charles Urdy, a Black, and John Trevino, a Hispanic, already occupied those places, the minority quota on the council was full.

American Statesman political columnist Pedro Ruiz

Garza put it bluntly. He theorized in an *American Statesman* column that the white liberal voter—an enlightened conscientious voter—in the absence of a minority member on the council, would vote for a minority candidate. Once the quota was filled, however, the door slammed shut.[69]

A Single-Member Districts '87 Committee was created.

The six city council members (Mayor Pro Tem John Trevino, Sally Shipman, Smoot Carl-Mitchell, George Humphrey, Charles Urdy, and Max Nofziger) expressed support for single-member districts, while Mayor Frank Cooksey expressed a preference for some at-large seats and some single-member district seats.

But amid all the criticism, opinions, council machinations, and public outcry, Judge Nowlin's ultimate ruling was the only one that counted. On Tuesday, September 15, 1987, Judge Nowlin released a long awaited ruling that let stand his 1985 ruling "that the current at-large method of electing city council members does not discriminate against minorities."[70]

Nowlin said because the present election system did not violate federal voting rights laws, the decision of whether to replace the at-large method with single member districts rested with the council and voters and not with the court.

Nowlin said in his decision, "The NAACP and legal defense fund failed to prove that Hispanics and Blacks have been allowed to serve in Places 5 and 6, respectively, only because Anglo power brokers agreed that those two places should be reserved for minorities."[71]

The ruling also said that in the 1985 and 1987 council elections for Places 4 and 1, respectively, candidate Gilbert Martinez carried more Anglo precincts than his opponents, even though he lost both races.

The plaintiffs failed to prove that the Anglo majority voted as a bloc to defeat minority-preferred candidates, Nowlin's ruling further stated. Minority-preferred candidates "have enjoyed a longstanding history of success in

Austin. There have been roughly proportional minority representation of Blacks on the council for sixteen years and roughly proportional representation of Mexican Americans for twelve years." Nowlin concluded, "Under the circumstances, the question of whether or not to adopt a single-member district council system remains a political or policy decision to be made by the elected representatives on the council and the qualified voters of Austin."[72]

Supporters of single-member districts were upset with Nowlin's ruling. "We think the judge was in error in the ruling he made this week," NAACP attorney David Van Os said.[73]

The organization was back to square one with vivid memories of three previous defeats in 1973 (defeated by sixty-three percent), 1975 (twenty-seven percent in favor of single-member districts) and 1985 (fifty-six percent of voters against single member districts).[74]

Nowlin's ruling was the second failed attempt "to get the measure sanctioned by the courts." But this time, backers of single-member districts appealed Nowlin's decision to the U.S. Fifth Circuit Court of Appeals, an action that everyone concerned knew would take a long time.

Prior to Nowlin's ruling, all the city council members went on record as being in favor of single-member districts. However, once Nowlin's ruling was publicized, council follow through became non-existent. "None of them (council members) has made establishing single-member districts a political priority," a September 1987 article in the Austin daily said.[75]

Despite the previous defeats, backers of single-member districts (including the NAACP, the Black Arts Association, and Austin Black Lawyers Association) supported it for a public vote once more. They gathered at the Arthur B. DeWitty Center in East Austin to support the measure that was up for consideration for a fourth time on May 7, 1988, while Mexican Americans gathered at the Pan American Recreation Center.

Opponents of single-member districts included

Dorothy Turner, president of the Black Citizens Task Force, and community workers Ada Anderson and Rev. Freddie Dixon, who were concerned that Blacks were not concentrated enough to benefit from single-member districts.[76]

Despite the gigantic effort, the single-member districts measure failed again. Voters defeated it by what the Austin daily estimated at "roughly fifty-seven percent to forty-three percent."[77]

Low voter turnout in the minority community, as well as lack of funds to promote the benefits of single-member districts to the public, appeared to be the major reasons for the fourth defeat.

Polling places in East, Southeast, and Central Austin, although drawing strong support for single-member districts, did not draw large numbers of voters to the polls.[78] The Montopolis precinct (#428) in southeast Austin drew only twelve percent of the voters. Only four percent of University of Texas students at Jester Center voted, while Northwest Austin drew thirty-four percent of registered voters at the box at Hill Elementary School (#246), who voted three to one against single-member districts.[79]

Austin branch NAACP President Gary Bledsoe attributed the defeat to opponents distorting the issues during the final month. He also blamed "unfounded fear that the U.S. Justice Department, which must approve any changes to the city's voting system, would require an even larger council than the nine members called for in the proposal."[80]

David Van Os, in addition to blaming members of the news media who "did not scrutinize the opposition's arguments closely enough," also blamed all the city council members.

"The city council put it on the ballot and then disappeared," Van Os said. "We were suspicious they would only give lip service to it and our suspicions were confirmed."[81]

Black council member Charles Urdy, who was re-elected, did not feel the issue should have been a part of the same ballot as political candidates. He felt the single-member districts issue "puts them (candidates) on the spot with voters."[82]

Urdy also felt that the single-member districts campaign was nonexistent. "There was no campaign," Urdy said. "It was probably the worst campaign we've had. There was no money." Even opponents of single-member districts waged a "low-key contest with little business support."[83]

* * *

In early May 1989 backers of single-member districts for the Austin City Council were again disappointed. Judge James Nowlin's ruling that held that at-large voting in Austin was legal was upheld. On May 2, 1989, the U.S. Fifth Circuit Court of Appeals upheld Judge Nowlin's ruling "that the city's system of at-large elections is legal."[84]

The court's findings said, in part, that Austin "has repeatedly elected Black and Mexican-American council members during the past seventeen years." Using the NAACP's calculations,

> Winning minority candidates frequently received well over fifty percent of the Anglo vote and were also the preferred candidate of the minorities. Ample evidence in the record supports [Nowlin's] finding that the wide open and vigorous Austin political system is not manipulated by any one group and is certainly not manipulated for racial reasons.[85]

That ruling all but destroyed hopes of instituting city council elections by single-member districts for Austin through the courts. Supporters of single-member districts predicted another court fight, but most realized it would be several years before another effort would be launched.

In early April 1990 the city council geared up to tackle single-member districting again. The council planned to appoint a seven-member charter revision commission to recommend changes in the city charter, including a possible change in the way council members were elected: concurrent terms instead of staggered terms;

changing the number of years council members serve, and other issues.

Council member Sally Shipman perhaps put it best when she stated her reasons for supporting the appointment of a charter revision commission. She said of the seven current council members "five live within walking distance of one another" in West Austin.[86]

* * *

Volma was happily retired and enjoying a life filled with golfing and ballroom dancing when a serious attack on the busing issue began in 1986.

Bernice Hart, a school board member first elected in November 1982 in a run-off election, was to have a profound effect on the way Austin integrated its public schools at the elementary level. She drew enough controversy to make her name a household word among many Austin parents.

Hart, a homegrown East Austinite and advocate for children's issues, spent thirty years in the educational system in Austin as a classroom teacher and counsellor. In 1961 she accepted a job with Camp Gary Job Corps as coordinator of mathematics and general education, where she spent five years.[87] Hart's campaigns garnered the backing of the Austin Association of Teachers and the Austin Federation of Teachers.

In her 1986 re-election campaign, Hart said she felt the busing for desegregation program needed improving. Hart said she voted in favor of a proposed study sponsored by the AISD by an independent consultant "to look at busing and I am agreeable to cutting long distances and times. It seems some schools could be paired with closer schools."[88]

In July Hart joined minority school board members Abel Ruiz and Lydia Perez in criticizing white school board members' vote to table the study. After the school board voted approval for criteria used in the study, white board members voted to take the study criteria which "would have resulted in a plan to keep Anglo enrollment between forty and sixty percent at all schools yet would not bus students before sixth grade longer than forty-five minutes or more than ten miles each way."[89]

Hart and the other two minority trustees lost trust in their fellow white board members. Hart felt the judicial system might be the only alternative to the situation. "I think some of the trustees want to eliminate busing," she said. "But if that's what they want to do, then let's not fool around with criteria or hiring a consultant. Do away with it, then let's get back in the court and let the court tell them they're wrong."[90]

Volma was concerned that the ten-year effort to end desegregation in Austin's public schools would be for naught. White board members always have "tried to eliminate busing; this is not new," Volma said. "Once they got out from under the decree (in 1983) they felt they could do anything they wanted."[91]

East Austinites were pleased with Hart's firm stance on busing. The NAACP was also pleased. In late November 1986, Hart, then in her second term on the school board, was presented the NAACP's highest honor—the Arthur B. DeWitty Award at its annual banquet held at the Capitol Marriott Hotel.

Volma presented the award, lauding Hart as being responsible for a Black agenda for the Austin school district—which had been the target of complaints that it was ignoring the concerns of Black students.[92]

However, by February 1987, Hart had completely changed her position on the busing issue. In a school board meeting in late February, Hart went along with the majority in suggesting changes to the busing plan that would "shorten students' time spent on the bus and reduce the number of years bused outside the neighborhood and create middle schools."[93]

"I really believe, as I analyze it, that even though we cut down on busing at the elementary level, we got a better [ethnic balance at the junior and senior high schools]," Hart said. "I know a lot of people believe it is better to mix [the races] early, but it hasn't really been an advantage. I really do feel, given the possibilities, that this is one of the best plans we could have come up with."[94]

She also pledged to support the sixteen elementary schools located in low-income areas with special counsellors, nurses, and special programs. These schools became known as priority schools.

On April 15, 1987, Hart made history, winning supporters to her cause, yet angering minority school board members and many individuals in the Black and Hispanic communities. Hart cast what was termed the "critical" vote for a new AISD student assignment plan that effectively eliminated busing at the elementary school level. Her vote was termed critical because white board members did not want the political fall-out that a vote along racial lines would bring.

Hart's supporters included members of the Black Citizens Task Force. Dorothy Turner, president of the organization, said, "The Black Citizens' Task Force is so very proud of Bernice Hart. She took some abuse, but she had those little children's interests at heart. That was her sole interest, and we are proud of her."[95]

The welfare of young children and the support of some Black parents seemed to be Hart's main impetus for her controversial vote. She felt forced busing did not benefit Black children, who were not achieving under the plan.

"My main concern was to get our little bitty babies off those buses at seven A.M.," she said. "Their [white] kids were not bused until they were older. For the most part, I would have really preferred eliminating busing just for grades kindergarten through three, but there were not enough votes to support that."[96]

The NAACP invited Hart to a branch meeting. No one said she was called on the carpet, but that's exactly what it was. They shut the door. When Hart reappeared later, she was unruffled and still standing by her vote as being the best decision for East Austin's children.

Hart not only went against the grain of the most powerful civil rights organization in the country, she also nullified the ten-year NAACP-led court battle to complete school integration in Austin. Hart found herself facing an opponent in her next election. The NAACP could not officially sponsor a candidate since it was mandated not to take sides in political contests. But Volma and many others supported a young man to run against Hart in the next school board election. He failed miserably; Hart won the election handily.

EPILOGUE

A mixed crowd of over 600 people filled the ballroom of the posh Stouffer Hotel in West Austin. The occasion was the 1996 Annual Equal Opportunity Day Banquet sponsored by the Austin Area Urban League.

Volma sat on the dais with dignitaries from throughout the city. After the requisite baked chicken had been devoured by well-dressed guests, Herman Lessard, Jr., president and chief executive officer of the Austin Area Urban League, rose to make the presentation of the annual Whitney M. Young, Jr., Award.

Whitney Young was a recognized leader in the Civil Rights Movement. He became leader of the National Urban League in 1961, and retained that position until his accidental drowning death in 1971. Young led the organization through the turbulent 1960s and was on hand for many of the high-level civil rights meetings, marches, and conferences between U.S. presidents and civil rights leaders. He spoke at the march on Washington and the march on Selma, and was a powerful advocate for Black equality in a nation which had overlooked Black rights far too long.

When Lessard named Volma as the 1996 recipient of the Whitney M. Young, Jr., Award, there was polite applause. Then Lessard directed everyone's attention to a video produced by local television station KVUE-TV. It was all there. The camera panned to time-worn pictures of Volma as a young boy growing up in the rural community of Maha, Texas, where the homes of the Overtons were scattered for miles. There was a reference to the poor, segregated school at Maha. When Volma left Maha, he began high school at Old L. C. Anderson High School, where he was still segregated. And finally, when he went into the U.S. Marine Corps as a new recruit, it was to more segregation.

Even when he returned home from the Marine Corps, where he had not seen one day of fighting because military brass did not feel Black soldiers were fit for duty, it was to more discrimination. This time, a white bus driver asked Volma to move to the rear of the bus to make room for white passengers. A young and rebellious Volma at first refused to move. He finally got up, but did not move to the rear of the bus. He simply got off, with the determination that he would do something about the Jim Crow practices that were taken for granted in Austin and throughout the South.

The video showed Volma as president of the National Alliance of Postal Workers, and later as president of the local branch of the NAACP in Austin.

It was to be the NAACP that offered the country boy from Maha the opportunity to show what he was made of. He made himself comfortable in a world of dignitaries, high-ranking officials, and crafty politicians.

Volma's contributions to creating a change in Austin, a city in the South, were detailed one by one: Agitation for a Human Relations Commission that was approved by the Austin City Council in 1968; leading the ten-year fight against the Austin Independent School District to complete integration of the public schools; and battling conservative forces to get single-member districts instituted. Also, Volma was responsible for filing a class action suit against the U.S. Post Office, a suit that was thrown out of court but which gave Volma the satisfaction of seeing others that came along after him gain promotions.

When the video ended, the audience stood and gave

Volma a five-minute ovation. After many years, the country boy from Maha, who's great-great-grandmother Emmaline left Travellers Rest Plantation in Tennessee in a wagon with her children and settled in the little rural community of Maha, had truly arrived.

ENDNOTES

All interviews were conducted by the author.

Chapter 1 COUNCIL SHUTDOWN

1 "Filibusterer is Willing to Take Compromise," *Austin Statesman,* April 3, 1964.

2 *Ibid.*

3 "Mayor in Hospital Near Collapse, MD Says Palmer is 'Resting,'" *American Statesman*, April 8, 1997.

4 "City May See Vote on Rights Filibusters Taking a Day-Long Recess," *Austin Statesman*, April 8, 1964.

5 "Petitions Going on Ordinance—Jaycees Need 7,000 Signatures of Voters," *American Statesman*, April 10, 1964.

6 "LaRue Calls for Cooling Off Period," *American Statesman*, April 10, 1964.

7 "A 'Long Summer' NAACP Promise," *American Statesman*, April 17, 1964.

8 "Collegians Say Militant Negroes Before Council 'Not Representative,'" *American Statesman*, April 20, 1964.

9 "City Rights Talk Tonight," *Austin Statesman*, April 27, 1964.

10 "Mayor Sees Talk Needed by Council," *Austin Statesman*, April 21, 1964.

11 "Council Rights Talks Due Early Next Week—UT Dorm Scene of a 'Sit-In,'" *American Statesman*, April 24, 1964.

12 "City Rights Talk Tonight," *Austin Statesman,* April 28, 1964.

13 "Agreement Hopes Up on Rights," *Austin Statesman*, April 28, 1964.

14 *Ibid.*

15 "No Pickets Due LBJ Talk Here," *Austin Statesman*, May 1, 1964.

16 "University Hires Negro Professor," *American Statesman,* May 11, 1964.

17 "Rights Group Plan Drafted by Council," *American Statesman*, May 12, 1964.

18 *Ibid.*

19 "Ben White Reiterates His Stand," *American Statesman*, May 13, 1964.

20 *Ibid.*

21 "Pick Rights Group, Call Sent to Council," *American Statesman*, June 10, 1964.

22 *Ibid.*

23 "Racial Barriers Dissolve," *American Statesman*, June 17, 1964.

24 *Ibid.*

25 "Protesting Negroes Given Cold Shoulder by Council, Gas Filled Balloons, Pray-In Ignored," *American Statesman*, June 18, 1964.

26 *Ibid.*

27 "Human Relations Panel Expected 'Next Week,'" *American Statesman,* June 19, 1964.

28 Interview with retired Congressman Jake Pickle, April 18, 1995, Austin, Texas.

Chapter 2 EARLY LIFE

1 Interview with Edward Doyle, July 21, 1993, Austin, Texas.

2 Interview with Vivian Prosser Smith, May 20, 1993, Austin, Texas.

3 Interview with Roscoe Overton, January 5, 1993, Austin, Texas.

4 Interview with Johnny Mae King, May 26, 1993, Austin, Texas.

5 Interview with Nicholas Overton, Jr., January 18, 1993, Austin, Texas.

6 Interview with Paine Freeman, June 19, 1993, St. Mary's Colony, Bastrop County, Texas.

7 Buchanan, A. Russell, *Black Americans in World War II*, Clio Press, Oxford, England, 1977, p. 14.

8 *Ibid.*, p.23.

9 Interview with Oneta Overton Batie, July 20, 1993, Austin, Texas.

Chapter 3 A TIME OF CHANGE—THE SIXTIES

1 Hine, Darlene Clark. *Black Victory: The Rise and Fall of the White Primary in Texas*. KTO Press, Millwood, NY, 1979, p.46.

2 *American Statesman,* August 22, 1919, Austin, Texas.

3 "Non Segregation Finds Austin Widely Divided on Outcome, Citizen Opinion Varied But Strongly Asserted," *Austin Statesman*, May 18, 1954.

4 *Ibid.*

5 *Ibid.*
6 *Ibid.*
7 *Ibid.*
8 *Ibid.*
9 "Agency Reiterates School Segregation," *American Statesman*, July 21, 1954.
10 *Ibid.*
11 "Schools Risk Fund Loss by Integration," *Austin Statesman*, August 21, 1955.
12 "Full Integration Effect Uncertain, Change Starting at Top," *Austin American-Statesman*, August 9, 1955.
13 "Junior High Not Changed," *Austin American*, June 12, 1956.
14 "Integration at the University of Texas," *The Alcade*, April 1961, p. 8.
15 *Ibid.*
16 "Regent Sees Limit by UT in Integration," *Austin Statesman*, July 26, 1961.
17 *Ibid.*
18 *Ibid.*
19 Duren, Almetris Marsh, *Overcoming: A History of Black Integration at the University of Texas at Austin,* UT Press, 1979, p. 11.
20 *Ibid.*
21 Haskins, James, *The March on Washington,* HarperCollins Publishers, New York, 1993, p. 117.
22 Film *Opening Doors*, produced by the Austin branch NAACP, 1978, published by KTVV-TV, Austin, Texas.
23 Interview with Retired Congressman Jake Pickle, April 18, 1995, Austin, Texas.
24 Letter dated March 12, 1963, from J. Phillip Crawford, attorney for the Austin branch NAACP, to Mr. Weldon Berry, attorney at law in Houston, NAACP Archives, Huston-Tillotson College, Austin, Texas.
25 Garrow, David J., *Bearing the Cross*, William Morrow and Co., Inc., New York 1986, p. 267.
26 "Connally Opposes JFK Over Rights, Property Plan Seen as Danger," *American Statesman*, July 20, 1963, written by Raymond Brooks, capitol staff.
27 *Ibid.*
28 *Ibid.*
29 "Negro Given Appointment, Ends Sit-In," *Dallas Morning News*, July 31, 1963.
30 "Integrationist Admits Record, Plans March on State Capitol," *Austin Bureau of The News,* August 8, 1963.
31 Haskins, James. *The March on Washington.* New York: HarperCollins Publishers, 1993, pp. xii-xiii.

32 Washington, James M., *A Testament of Hope—The Essential Writings and Speeches of Martin Luther King, Jr.* San Francisco: Harper, 1986, pp.217-220.

33 Duren, Almetris Marsh, *Overcoming: A History of Black Integration at the University of Texas at Austin,* UT Press, 1979, p. 13.

34 Wilkins and Matthews, *Standing Fast—The Autobiography of Roy Wilkins,* Viking Press, 1982, p. 243.

35 "Three Negroes, Austin Faculty is Integrated," *Austin American,* September 11, 1964.

36 "Conflict Growing Inside HEW, School Desegregation Guidelines Under Study," *American Statesman*, June 26, 1969.

37 "SDS Pickets Protest Cowboy Blackfaces," *The Daily Texan*, November 11, 1964.

38 *Ibid.*

39 "Black Face Mimicry," *The Daily Texan,* November 11, 1964.

40 "Civil Rights, Local Leaders Pleased by Rule," *American Statesman*, December 16, 1964.

41 "Negro Leader Hits Tokenism," *American Statesman*, December 14, 1964.

42 *Ibid.*

43 Garrow, David J., *Bearing the Cross*, William Morrow and Co., Inc., New York, 1986, p. 358.

44 Letter from Volma Overton to Clarence Laws dated February 15, 1965, NAACP Archives, Huston-Tillotson College, Austin, Texas.

45 Letter from Volma Overton and NAACP branch dated March 11, 1965, NAACP Archives, Huston-Tillotson College, Austin, Texas.

46 Letter from Volma Overton to KHFI-TV dated March 12, 1965, NAACP Archives, Huston-Tillotson College, Austin, Texas.

47 *Ibid.*

48 Wilkins, Roy, and Mathews, Tom, *Standing Fast—The Autobiography of Roy Wilkins,* Viking Press, 1982, p. 302.

49 *Ibid.*

50 Watson, Denton L., *Lion in the Lobby, Clarence Mitchell, Jr.'s Struggle for Passage of Civil Rights Laws,* William Morrow and Company, Inc., New York, p. 657.

51 *Ibid.*

52 Letter from Volma Overton to the Department of Justice dated June 4, 1965, NAACP Archives, Huston-Tillotson College, Austin, Texas.

53 Letter from Volma Overton to R. Sargent Shriver dated June 10, 1965, NAACP Archives, Huston-Tillotson College, Austin, Texas.

54 Letter from A. W. Stratton to Volma Overton dated October 27,

1965, NAACP Archives, Huston-Tillotson ˙College, Austin, Texas.

55 "Tax Collector Criticized for Not Hiring Negroes," *American Statesman*, December 8, 1965.

56 *Ibid.*

57 "Civil Rights Complaint Filed, Teacher Credit Union Under NAACP Fire," *American Statesman*, January 20, 1966.

58 Letter from John T. King to Volma Overton dated December 14, 1966, NAACP Archives, Huston-Tillotson College, Austin, Texas.

59 *Ibid.*

60 Letter from Volma Overton to U.S. Attorney Nicholas Katzenbach dated March 12, 1966, NAACP Archives, Huston-Tillotson College, Austin, Texas.

61 "NAACP To Boycott Rights Corporation," *American Statesman*, July 28, 1966.

62 *Ibid.*

63 Letter from Volma Overton to Robert L. Carter dated July 27, 1966, NAACP Archives, Huston-Tillotson College, Austin, Texas.

64 Letter from Beverly S. Sheffield to Volma Overton dated August 11, 1966, NAACP Archives, Huston-Tillotson College, Austin, Texas.

65 Letter from Arthur A. Chapin to Volma Overton dated September 14, 1966, NAACP Archives, Huston-Tillotson College, Austin, Texas.

66 "NAACP Claim Gets Answer from Barclay," *American Statesman*, October 26, 1966.

67 *Ibid.*

68 *Ibid.*

69 Letter from Stephen N. Shulman to Volma Overton dated November 25, 1966, NAACP Archives, Huston-Tillotson College, Austin, Texas.

70 Memorandum from Roy Wilkins, NAACP National Office, to all branches dated November 25, 1966, NAACP Archives, Huston-Tillotson College, Austin, Texas.

71 *Ibid.*

72 Letter from Volma Overton to Leon Lurie dated November 30, 1966, NAACP Archives, Huston-Tillotson College, Austin, Texas.

Chapter 4 CITY COUNCIL BID

1 Letter from Charles Wadley to Mr. Ashby G. Smith, President, National Alliance of Postal and Federal Employees, Washington,

D.C., dated February 14, 1967, NAACP Archives, Huston-Tillotson College, Austin, Texas.

2 Undated letter by Volma Overton, NAACP Archives, Huston-Tillotson College, Austin, Texas.

3 Austin branch NAACP minutes from membership meeting held April 27, 1967, NAACP Archives, Huston-Tillotson College, Austin, Texas.

4 "House Gets Protest on Negro Salon's Ouster," *American Statesman*, May 4, 1967.

5 Letter from Robert Kennedy to Volma Overton dated April 4, 1967, NAACP Archives, Huston-Tillotson College, Austin, Texas.

6 Letter from Volma Overton to Mrs. Daisy Bates dated May 22, 1967, NAACP Archives, Huston-Tillotson College, Austin, Texas.

7 Letter from Volma Overton to the Honorable John Connally dated May 23, 1967, NAACP Archives, Huston-Tillotson College, Austin, Texas.

8 Letter from Governor John Connally to Volma Overton dated May 25, 1967, NAACP Archives, Huston-Tillotson College, Austin, Texas.

9 Letter from Volma Overton to Mayor Louie Welch dated May 31, 1967, NAACP Archives, Huston-Tillotson College, Austin, Texas.

10 Letter from Houston, Texas, Mayor Louie Welch to Volma Overton dated June 6, 1967.

11 *Bergstrom Air Force Base,* Marcoa Publishing, 1984, San Diego, California, p. 9 (no author cited).

12 Letter from Volma Overton to Secretary of Defense Robert McNamara dated August 3, 1967, NAACP Archives, Huston-Tillotson College, Austin, Texas.

13 Letter from Volma Overton to Clarence Mitchell, Director, NAACP Washington Bureau, dated September 5, 1967, NAACP Archives, Huston-Tillotson College, Austin, Texas.

14 Letter from Volma Overton to the Office of Economic Opportunity, Washington, D.C., dated August 10, 1967, NAACP Archives, Huston-Tillotson College, Austin, Texas.

15 Letter from Volma Overton to Mr. Richard F. Brown, Publisher, *Austin American-Statesman*, NAACP Archives, Huston-Tillotson College, Austin, Texas.

16 Letter to Volma Overton from Jack Moskowitz, Deputy Assistant Secretary, Assistant Secretary of Defense, dated October 3, 1967, NAACP Archives, Huston-Tillotson College, Austin, Texas.

17 "The Human Relations Commission: It Shall," *Austin American-Statesman*, September 29, 1968.

18 *Ibid.*

19 "The Humans, They Are the City's Human Relations Commission Members," *Austin American-Statesman*, September 29, 1968.

20 NAACP membership committee meeting minutes dated January 25, 1968, NAACP Archives, Huston-Tillotson College, Austin, Texas.

21 Announcement dated March 4, 1968, by Mrs. C. C. Robinson, NAACP Archives, Huston-Tillotson College, Austin, Texas.

22 "Interest High, UT Offers Course in Negro History," *Austin American-Statesman*, October 10, 1968,

23 Advertisement by Austin Board of Realtors, *American Statesman*, April 1968, NAACP Archives, Huston-Tillotson College, Austin, Texas.

24 Letters to council members Akin, Long, and Nichols from Volma Overton dated May 21, 1968, NAACP Archives, Huston-Tillotson College, Austin, Texas.

25 Austin branch NAACP Executive Committee minutes dated July 6, 1968, NAACP Archives, Huston-Tillotson College, Austin, Texas.

26 Wilkins, Roy, and Matthews, Tom, *Standing Fast—The Autobiography of Roy Wilkins,* Viking Press, 1986, pp. 333-34.

27 Interview with Peck Young, March 3, 1995, Austin, Texas.

28 "Rat Infestation Problem Grows," *Austin American-Statesman,* August 15, 1968.

29 Interview with Larry Jackson, March 2, 1995, Austin, Texas.

30 Letter from Volma Overton to Former President Lyndon Johnson dated November 11, 1969, NAACP Archives, Huston-Tillotson College, Austin, Texas.

31 Letter from Volma Overton to O. N. Bruck, Postmaster, dated November 12, 1969, NAACP Archives, Huston-Tillotson College, Austin, Texas.

32 Letter from Postmaster O. N. Bruck to Volma Overton dated November 13, 1969, NAACP Archives, Huston-Tillotson College, Austin, Texas.

33 "Rights Agency Aide Honored," *Austin Statesman*, December 7, 1969.

34 *Ibid.*

35 *Ibid.*

36 "The Board's Plan, Austin School Desegregation," *Austin American-Statesman*, June 20, 1969.

37 "Desegregation, School Board to Follow HEW Steps," *Austin American-Statesman*, August 15, 1968.

38 *Ibid.*

39 "School Integration Said Going Well," *Austin American-Statesman*, September 19, 1969.

40 "City Integration Hearing Set," *Austin American-Statesman*, January 19, 1970.

41 "De Facto Segregation Attacked, NAACP Head Chides Austin Schools," *Austin American-Statesman,* February 16, 1969.

42 *Ibid.*

43 "Third Desegregation Proposal Attempt Due," *Austin American-Statesman*, May 8, 1969.

44 "Examiner to Hear Austin Plan," *American Statesman*, October 10, 1969.

45 "Black Into White is Integration Pattern," *American Statesman*, July 26, 1969.

46 "Eastside Schools Face Shutdown, Trustees Seek HEW Blessing," *Austin American-Statesman*, June 10, 1969.

47 "Prospects Slim on Two Way Busing; Board Meets June 23," *Austin American*, June 17, 1969.

48 *Ibid.*

49 "NAACP Supports School Plan," *American Statesman*, June 21, 1969.

50 "3 School Closing, Bus Plan Dropped, Two Way Bus Idea Also Dies," *Austin American-Statesman,* June 24, 1969.

51 *Ibid.*

52 "Year of Grace to Follow Rejection of Busing Plan," *American Statesman*, June 25, 1969.

53 *Ibid.*

54 "Editorials, A Chance (Slim) for School Plan," *Austin American-Statesman*, July 10, 1969.

55 "Nixon Said 'Breaking' the Law," *American Statesman*, July 4, 1969.

56 "Letter from HEW," *American Statesman*, July 14, 1969.

57 "School Board States Case to HEW," *American Statesman,* January 25, 1970.

58 "2 Strands Holding City School Funds," *American Statesman,* July 10, 1970.

59 "Integration Suit Filed on Austin," *Austin American- Statesman*, August 8, 1970.

60 "School Officials Prepared to Hear Desegregation Team," *Austin American-Statesman*, July 27, 1970.

61 *Ibid.*

Chapter 5 Nixon

1 "Minimum Busing Plan is Appealed—Nixon Tells His Position," *American Statesman*, August 4, 1971.

2 "An Analysis of the Busing Controversy—How the White House Okayed, Then Rejected HEW Plan," *American Statesman*, August 9, 1971.

3 *Ibid.*

4 *The United States District Court for the Western District of Texas, United States of America, Plaintiff Dedra Estell Overton, et. al, Plaintiffs-Intervenors v. Texas Education Agency, et. al,* AISD Post Trial Brief of the U.S.

5 "2 Groups in School Appeal," *American Statesman*, August 25, 1971.

6 *Ibid.*

7 "School Case, Nine-Day Extension Granted," *American Statesman*, August 26, 1971.

8 "Schools Have Only Routine Problems," *American Statesman*, August 31, 1971.

9 "School Generally Peaceful, *American Statesman*, September 4, 1971.

10 "Moves to Stop Race Strife Working in Austin Schools," *American Statesman*, September 8, 1971.

11 *Ibid.*

12 *Ibid.*

13 *Ibid.*

14 "Burger Says Race Balance Misused," *American Statesman,* September 1, 1971.

15 *Ibid.*

16 "Race Tension Sparks Clash," *American Statesman*, September 2, 1971.

17 *Ibid.*

18 *Ibid.*

19 "Tension Easing in City Schools," *American Statesman*, September 3, 1971.

20 *Ibid.*

21 "One Race Busing ACLU Brief Topic," *American Statesman,* September 5, 1971.

22 "Minorities Get Most Discipline," *Austin American,* October 3, 1973.

23 *Ibid.*

24 "Officials Scolded by NAACP Head," *American Statesman,* February 12, 1972.

25 "Justice to Hear of Reagan," *American Statesman*, February 3, 1972.

26 *Ibid.*

27 "Parents, School Officials Discuss Martin Disturbances," *American Statesman*, April 21, 1972.

28 "Schools to be Harder on Fighting Students," *American Statesman*, April 12, 1972.

29 *Ibid.*

30 "Davidson Says Schools Are Geared for Trouble," *American Statesman*, April 29, 1972.

31 "The Power of Fear in Our Schools," *TV Digest*, May 13-19, 1972.

32 *Ibid.*

33 "'Key' Federal Man Coming to Austin on Fund Request," *American Statesman*, September 24, 1971.

34 "Austin Schools Answer Appeal," *American Statesman*, September 22, 1971.

35 *Ibid.*

36 "Austin, HEW Collide Oct. 28 Before Fifth Circuit Court," *Austin American*, October 5, 1971.

37 "Over 'Austin Plan'—School Appeals Bout Thursday," *Austin American*, October 24, 1971.

38 *Ibid.*

39 *Ibid.*

40 "Board Members to Attend Hearing on Desegregation," *American Statesman*, October 28, 1971.

41 "One Tells of Small Grant—HEW Letters Confuse School Officials," *Austin American-Statesman*, October 30, 1971.

42 "'Merits May Not Determine Outcome' School Board Head Fears Desegregation Fueling," *Austin American- Statesman*, November 7, 1971.

43 "Few Think Congress' Acts Will Affect Busing Pace," *American Statesman,* November 6, 1971.

44 *Ibid.*

Chapter 6 POLICE BRUTALITY AND OTHER ISSUES

1 "New Schools Named for L. C. Anderson, Lyndon Johnson, and George I. Sanchez," *Austin American-Statesman*, April 17, 1973.

2 "Letters to the Editor, School Naming," *Austin American-Statesman*, April 24, 1973, letter written by Quinton Wiles.

3 *Ibid.*

4 "Black to Lead High School, Fulfills 'Lifetime Dream,'" *The Daily Texan*, February 5, 1973.

5 "Anderson Open House, New High School Makes Its Debut," *Austin American*, August 17, 1973.

6 "East Austin Group Lodges Police Brutality Complaints," *Austin American-Statesman*, September 25, 1973.

7 "Continuing Campaign, Police Pressing Hiring Minorities," *Austin Statesman*, October 24, 1973.

8 *Ibid.*

9 *Ibid.*

10 *Ibid.*

11 *Ibid.*

12 *Ibid.*

13 "Miles Gives 'Last Gasp' Talk to Crew, Police Supervisors Hear Departing Chief," *Austin American-Statesman*, November 21, 1975.

14 "Wilkins Accepts Award With 'New World' Hope," *Austin American-Statesman*, October 8, 1973.

15 *Ibid.*

16 *Ibid.*

17 "NAACP Dinner, 2 Presented Awards Here," *Austin American-Statesman*, December 9, 1973.

18 *Ibid.*

19 *Ibid.*

20 "Black Faculty at University Less Than 1%," *Austin American-Statesman*, January 10, 1974.

21 "Harlem Theater Burns," *Austin American-Statesman*, January 20, 1974.

22 "Mayor Mum on Plan Involving Police Chief," *Austin American-Statesman*, April 2, 1974.

23 *Ibid.*

24 "Councilmen Reject Plan for Public Safety Post," *Austin American-Statesman*, April 5, 1974.

25 "County Democratic Aide Young Plans to Trim Political Duties," *Austin American-Statesman*, May 1, 1974.

26 *Ibid.*

27 "New School Plans Presented," *Austin American-Statesman*, November 20, 1973.

28 *Ibid.*

29 "School Bounds Okayed by Judge, Mexican American Challenge Loses," *Austin American-Statesman*, June 13, 1974.

30 *Ibid.*

31 "Discrimination Claimed Tied to Employment," *Austin American-Statesman*, July 2, 1974.

32 *Ibid.*

33 *Ibid.*

34 *Ibid.*

35 *Ibid.*

36 *Ibid.*

37 "AISD Hopes Salaries Will Entice Minorities," *Austin American-Statesman*, September 1, 1974.

38 "H-T Officials: AISD Discriminates in Hiring," *Austin American-Statesman,* June 25, 1975.

39 *Ibid.*

40 *Ibid.*

41 "Local NAACP Leader Wants Youth Input," *Austin American-Statesman*, October 14, 1974.

42 *Ibid.*

43 *Ibid.*

44 *Ibid.*

45 "Austin Desegregation 20 Years Later, Ruling Began Tortuous Climb," *Austin American-Statesman*, May 17, 1974.

46 "Human Relations Group Seeking Local Powers," *Austin American-Statesman*, August 27, 1974.

47 "Austin Councilmen Vote Down Employment Ordinance," *Austin American-Statesman*, January 10, 1975.

48 *Ibid.*

49 "EEO Under Human Relations Dept.," *Austin American-Statesman*, July 11, 1975.

50 "Ideas Heard on Police Relations," *Austin American-Statesman*, January 7, 1975.

51 "Police Brutality Charges Heard," *Austin American-Statesman*, January 14, 1975.

52 *Ibid.*

53 "Mrs. King Urges Full Employment," *Austin American- Statesman*, February 26, 1975.

54 "HEW Criticizes UT Civil Rights Efforts," *Austin American-Statesman*, March 1, 1975.

55 *Ibid.*

56 Letter from Glocester B. Current dated March 17, 1975 to State Conference, Branch, College Division, and Youth Council Presidents, NAACP Archives, Huston-Tillotson College, Austin, Texas.

57 World Book Encyclopedia, World Book, Inc., Chicago, 1993, p. 514.

58 "MHMR Centers Merger Eyed by Citizens Boards," *Austin American-Statesman*, July 24, 1975.

59 "Rosewood, East Austin Centers, Merger of MHMR Sites Fought," *Austin American-Statesman*, September 25, 1975.

60 "MHMR Fiscal Probe Urged," *Austin American-Statesman*, October 28, 1975.

61 "Rosewood Center Funding Increase Voted by MHMR," *American Statesman*, October 31, 1975.

62 *Ibid.*
63 "Rosewood Reps Complaint Sent Back to MHMR," *Austin American-Statesman,* November 21, 1975.
64 *Ibid.*
65 *Ibid.*
66 "MHMR Controversy Laid to Rest," *Austin American-Statesman,* January 1, 1976.
67 "Blacks Want One of Own Put on Panel," *Austin American-Statesman*, February 5, 1976.
68 *Ibid.*
69 "NAACP Leaders Ask City Jail Tour," *Austin American-Statesman*, August 27, 1975.
70 "NAACP Requests Probe of City," *Austin American-Statesman*, July 25, 1975.
71 *Ibid.*
72 "19th Street Renamed Martin Luther King Blvd.," *Austin American-Statesman,* April 11, 1975.
73 *Ibid.*
74 "Black Educator Collapses, Dies While Defending King Boulevard," *Austin American-Statesman,* May 2, 1975.
75 "Groups Ask to Join 19th Street Hearing," *Austin American-Statesman*, September 20, 1975.
76 "4 on Council Want to Fight 19th Street Ruling," *Austin American-Statesman*, November 21, 1975.
77 *Ibid.*
78 "19th Street Payoff Alleged," *Austin American-Statesman*, May 8, 1975.
79 *Ibid.*
80 *Ibid.*
81 "19th Street Renamed Again," *Austin American-Statesman*, June 24, 1976.
82 "Givens Park Citizens View Plans for Center," *Austin American-Statesman*, November 19, 1975.
83 Undated Notes Written by Volma Overton, NAACP Archives, Huston-Tillotson College, Austin, Texas.

Chapter 7 SCHOOL DESEGREGATION PLAN—BACK TO SCHOOL DISTRICT

1 "Austin Trustees Approve Plan on District Desegreation," *American Statesman*, April 26, 1973.
2 "Witnesses Testify About School Life," *American Statesman*, May 8, 1973.
3 *Ibid.*

4 *Ibid.*
5 "Prof Outlines School Plan," *American Statesman*, May 9, 1973.
6 "Johnston Issues Heard at Trial," *American Statesman*, May 10, 1973.
7 *Ibid.*
8 *Ibid.*
9 *Ibid.*
10 "School Conditions Poor, Segregation Trial Told," *Austin American*, May 11, 1973.
11 *Ibid.*
12 *Ibid.*
13 *Ibid.*
14 "Housing Pattern Linked to Deeds," *Austin American-Statesman*, May 12, 1973.
15 *Ibid.*
16 *Ibid.*
17 *Ibid.*
18 "Johnston Issues Heard at Trial," *American Statesman,* May 10, 1973.
19 "School Locations Defended," *American Statesman*, May 15, 1973.
20 *Ibid.*
21 *Ibid.*
22 "Expert Scorns Austin School," *American Statesman*, May 17, 1973.

Chapter 8 SCHOOL SUIT CONTINUES

1 "Decision to Limit Citizen Say in Police Chief Choice Attacked," *Austin American-Statesman*, January 13, 1976.
2 *Ibid.*
3 Program Notes, greeting from Mayor Edward A. David, official program of the 70th Annual Alpha Phi Alpha Convention, Monrovia, Liberia.
4 World Book Encyclopedia, 1983, World Book, Inc., Chicago, p. 205.
5 Interview with Fay Willis, March 3, 1995, Austin, Texas.
6 Interview with Dean Stitt, Arthur Murray Dance Studio, August 30, 1995, Austin, Texas.
7 "City Gets EEOC Funding," *Austin American-Statesman*, February 10, 1976.
8 *Ibid.*
9 "Focus on Juvenile Crime, Dyson Favors 'Team Methods,'" *Austin American-Statesman*, April 21, 1976.
10 *Ibid.*

11 "Postal Agency Hit for Discrimination," *Austin American-Statesman*, June 25, 1976.

12 *Ibid.*

13 "U.S. Move to Enhance School Suit," *Austin Citizen*, October 7, 1976.

14 *Ibid.*

15 *Ibid.*

16 *Ibid.*

17 "UT Prof to Debate Success of Busing," *Austin Citizen*, November 5, 1976.

18 "Graglia Defends Anti-Busers," *Austin Citizen*, November 8, 1976.

19 "Minorities Set Deseg Deadline," *Austin Citizen*, November 5, 1976.

20 *Ibid.*

21 *Ibid.*

22 "White School Enrollment Dips Sharply," *Austin Citizen*, November 10, 1976.

23 *Ibid.*

24 *Ibid.*

25 *Ibid.*

26 "A Squak From Austin," *Christian Science Monitor,* December 29, 1976.

27 "Order Limits Mass Austin Busing—Supreme Court Overturns Fifth Circuit Ruling," *Austin American-Statesman*, December 7, 1976.

28 *Ibid.*

29 "A Squak From Austin," *Christian Science Monitor,* December 29, 1976.

30 *Ibid.*

31 *Ibid.*

32 "Judges' Segregation Decision Viewed with Mixed Feelings," *The Daily Texan*, December 7, 1976.

33 *Ibid.*

34 "School Board President Explains Decision," *The Daily Texan*, December 9, 1976.

35 *Ibid.*

36 *Ibid.*

37 "Judges' Segregation Decision Viewed with Mixed Feelings," *The Daily Texan*, December 7, 1976.

38 "A Squak From Austin," *Christian Science Monitor,* December 29, 1976.

Chapter 9 MORE CHANGES—1977

1 "Ouster of School Official Sought," *Austin Citizen*, April 28, 1977.

2 *Ibid.*

3 *Ibid.*

4 Wilkins and Matthews, *Standing Fast—The Autobiography of Roy Wilkins*, Viking Press, 1982, p. 340.

5 "Court Hits School Segregation," *Austin Citizen,* November 22, 1977.

6 *Ibid.*

7 *Ibid.*

8 *Ibid.*

9 "Schools Appeal Deseg Ruling," *Austin Citizen*, November 29, 1977.

10 *Ibid.*

11 "Groups Plan Joint Desegregation Push—Chicano Unity Sought on School Issue," *American Statesman*, February 5, 1978.

12 *Ibid.*

13 "Overton Charges City With Bias in Hiring for Federal Programs," *Austin American-Statesman*, January 10, 1978.

14 *Ibid.*

15 "Austin Awaits Guidance From Desegregation Suit," *Austin Citizen*, April 24, 1979.

16 *Ibid.*

17 "Back to Court? AISD Accused of Bad Faith in Desegregation," *Austin Citizen*, May 30, 1979.

18 "Court Denies Appeal by AISD Board," *Austin Citizen*, July 2, 1979.

19 *Ibid.*

20 *Ibid.*

21 *Ibid.*

22 *Ibid.*

23 *Ibid.*

24 "Chicken-and-Egg-Dispute—AISD Desegregation 'Remedy Trial' Begins," *Austin Citizen*, July 11, 1979.

25 *Ibid.*

26 "AISD Tactics Draw Justice Objections," *Austin Citizen*, July 12, 1979.

27 *Ibid.*

28 "Over Justice Objections—School Sites Defended," *Austin Citizen*, July 13, 1979.

29 *Ibid.*

30 "AISD Tactics Draw Justice Dept. Objections," *Austin Citizen*, July 12, 1979.

31 *Ibid.*

32 *Ibid.*

33 "District Disputes its Policies Spurred Housing Segregation," *Austin Citizen*, July 24, 1979.

34 *Ibid.*

35 *Ibid.*

36 "AISD Remedy Trial—Parties Parry Over Sites," *Austin Citizen*, July 16, 1979.

37 *Ibid.*

38 *Ibid.*

39 *Ibid.*

40 *Ibid.*

41 "AISD to Blame? Economics Said Root of Segregation," *Austin Citizen*, July 17, 1979.

42 *Ibid.*

43 *Ibid.*

44 "AISD Segregation Hearing Continues," *The Daily Texan*, July 18, 1979.

45 "Fourteen 'Segregative' Schools Indicated in Trial," *Austin Citizen,* July 19, 1979.

46 *Ibid.*

47 *Ibid.*

48 *Ibid.*

49 "Desegregation Planning Viewed—Superintendent Davidson Defends School District's Post—'76 Policies," *Austin Citizen*, July 20, 1979.

50 *Ibid.*

51 "AISD Hearing—Judge Denies Motion to End School Segregation," *The Daily Texan*, July 23, 1979.

52 *Ibid.*

53 *Ibid.*

54 "Desegregation Plan Author Gives Views," *Austin Citizen*, July 26, 1979.

55 "We're Gonna Take Time, 'Deseg Ruling Won't Be Swift,'" *Austin Citizen*, July 30, 1979.

56 "Evers' Widow Cites Problems," *Austin American-Statesman*, December 4, 1977.

Chapter 10 JUDGE ROBERTS ISSUES FINAL ORDER—1979

1 "Anglo Enrollment Must Be in Proportion: Roberts—Judge Orders Austin Deseg Plan," *Austin Citizen*, November 5, 1970.

2 "AISD Ordered to Implement Desegregation Plan," *Austin American-Statesman,* November 6, 1979.

3 *Ibid.*

4 *Ibid.*

5 Editorials, "Austin Schools—Busing Will Aid Desegregation," *The Daily Texan*, November 7, 1979.

6 "AISD Ordered to Implement Desegregation Plan," *The Daily Texan*, November 6, 1979.

7 *Ibid.*

8 "Student Busing to Increase," *Austin Citizen*, November 6, 1979.

9 *Ibid.*

10 "NAACP to Appeal Decision—Group Will Respond to AISD Desegregation Plan," *The Daily Texan*, November 9, 1979.

11 "Deseg Order for Speed Brings Objections—Chaos, School Shutdown Feared," *Austin Citizen*, November 15, 1979.

12 *Ibid.*

13 *Ibid.*

14 "AISD To Propose Deadline Extension," *The Daily Texan*, November 16, 1979.

15 *Ibid.*

16 *Ibid.*

17 "School Trustee Blasts Desegregation Demands," *American Statesman*, December 5, 1979.

18 *Ibid.*

19 "Anti-Busing Group Says Ignore Order," *Austin Citizen*, December 4, 1979.

20 "2000 Jeer Desegregation, Board," *Austin Citizen*, December 11, 1979.

21 "300 Storm Carruth Building—Students: 'We Won't Go,'" *Austin Citizen*, December 10, 1979.

22 "15,000 to be Bused, Deseg Agreement Reached, Judge Roberts to Get Proposal," *Austin Citizen*.

23 "Protesters Unhappy With AISD Vote," *Austin American-Statesman*, December 17, 1979.

24 "Board Vows to 'Obey the Law,'" *Austin Citizen,* December 17, 1979.

25 "New Busing Plan Baffles Coaches—Johnston, Anderson Consolidation Sparks Controversy," *American Statesman*, December 19, 1979.

26 *Ibid.*

27 "Catholics Freeze Enrollment of Schools," *American Statesman*, December 19, 1979.

28 *Ibid.*

Chapter 11 RETIREMENT—THE EIGHTIES

1 "Judge Gets New Plans to Deseg," *Austin Citizen*, January 2, 1980.

2 *Ibid.*

3 "Judge Puts OK on AISD Busing Plan," *Austin Citizen,* January 3, 1980.
4 "South, North Residents Divided Over Desegregation Proposals," *Austin Citizen*, January 8, 1980.
5 "Former Foes Vow to Make 'A' Busing Formula Work," *American Statesman*, January 15, 1980.
6 "Pickle Conference Leaves Anti-Busers Frustrated," *Austin Citizen*, January 21, 1980.
7 *Ibid.*
8 "Busing Issue Critical in School Board Election, Defeated Incumbent Attributes Loss to Controversy, Low Voter Turnout," *The Daily Texan*, April 7, 1970.

Chapter 12 END OF OVERTON ERA WITH NAACP—1983

1 "Former NAACP Leader Recalls Efforts—Volma Overton Worked for 20 Years to Bring About Changes in Austin," *Austin American-Statesman*, January 13, 1983.
2 "New NAACP Leader Says Struggles Remain," *Austin American-Statesman*, January 2, 1983.
3 "NAACP Seeks Extended Check in New Schools," *Austin American-Statesman*, March 9, 1983.
4 *Ibid.*
5 "NAACP Seeks Extended Check in New Schools," *Austin American-Statesman,* March 9, 1983.
6 "Rights Cases Nearly Settled in 3 Cities," *Austin American-Statesman*, March 23, 1983.
7 *Ibid.*
8 "Segregation Fears Remain: US Asked to Monitor Schools," *Austin American-Statesman*, May 17, 1983.
9 *Ibid.*
10 "Austin School Trustees Accept Desegregation Suit Settlement," *Austin American-Statesman*, June 7, 1983.
11 *Ibid.*
12 *Ibid.*
13 *Ibid.*
14 *Ibid.*
15 "Keeping a Low Profile, NAACP Challenge of City Elections Seen As Typical of Methods," *Austin American-Statesman*, April 23, 1984.
16 "Judge Holding Key to Future Character of Council Elections," *Austin American-Statesman*, August 2, 1984.
17 "City Weighs NAACP Pact in Districting," *Austin American-Statesman*, July 27, 1984.

18 "City-NAACP Settlement Stalled by Federal Judge," *Austin American-Statesman*, August 9, 1984.

19 "Bid Denied to Black Council District Plan," *Austin American-Statesman*, July 31, 1984.

20 "Public Gets Chance to Speak Mapping of Council Districts," *Austin American-Statesman*, August 7, 1984.

21 "NAACP Proposes 8 Districts," *American Statesman*, July 28, 1984.

22 *Ibid.*

23 "Single-District Plan Praised as 'Right,' But Timing Assailed," *American Statesman*, July 28, 1984.

24 *Ibid.*

25 *Ibid.*

26 "Judge to Hear Arguments, Dec. 17 Council District Hearing Scheduled," *Austin American-Statesman*, December 5, 1984.

27 "Austin Kingpins Win Their Numbers Game," *Austin American-Statesman*, July 29, 1984.

28 "Judge Holding Key to Future Character of Council Elections," *American Statesman*, August 2, 1984.

29 "City-NAACP Settlement Stalled by Federal Judge," *Austin American-Statesman*, August 9, 1984.

30 "Builder Group Studying Alternative Map for Council Districts," *Austin American-Statesman*, November 11, 1984.

31 "Here Comes Da Judge, and He Sounds Smart," *Austin American-Statesman,* August 9, 1984.

32 "UT Students Seek Council District," *Austin American-Statesman*, October 21, 1984.

33 "Federal Court Asked to Settle Austin Voting Plan," *Austin American-Statesman*, August 14, 1984.

34 "City, NAACP Try New Voting Accord," *Austin American-Statesman*, August 21, 1984.

35 *Ibid.*

36 "At-Large Voting Faces Test Today in Trial Startup," *Austin American-Statesman*, February 4, 1985.

37 "Districting Case Appears Headed for Jan. 19 Vote," *Austin American-Statesman*, December 1, 1984.

38 "Appeal Court Backs Hearing on At-Large Vote," *Austin American-Statesman*, December 4, 1984.

39 "NAACP Considers Voting Suit to Challenge City Annexations," *Austin American-Statesman*, November 17, 1984.

40 "Minorities Ask U.S. to Refuse Annexations," *Austin American-Statesman*, January 17, 1984.

41 "January Ballot to Include Mix of 19 Proposals," *Austin American-Statesman,* December 14, 1984.

42 "Defeat of District Plan Puts Election System Back in Court," *Austin American-Statesman*, January 21, 1985.
43 "Election Sways Council to Alter At-Large Stand," *Austin American-Statesman*, January 25, 1985.
44 "At-Large Voting Faces Test Today in Trial Startup," *Austin American-Statesman*, February 4, 1985.
45 "Vote Bias is Claimed in Court," *Austin American-Statesman*, February 5, 1985.
46 *Ibid.*
47 *Ibid.*
48 *Ibid.*
49 "Wendler Stretches Political Tightrope with Slate Account," *Austin American-Statesman*, February 17, 1985.
50 "Anglos Control Council Slates, U.S. Judge Told," *Austin American-Statesman*, February 6, 1985.
51 *Ibid.*
52 *Ibid.*
53 *Ibid.*
54 "Control of Elections by Anglos Disputed," *Austin American-Statesman,* February 7, 1985.
55 *Ibid.*
56 *Ibid.*
57 *Ibid.*
58 *Ibid.*
59 "Decision Looms in Suit Over At-Large Council Elections," *Austin American-Statesman*, March 2, 1985.
60 "Control of Elections by Anglos Disputed," *Austin American-Statesman*, February 7, 1985.
61 "Decision Looms in Suit Over At-Large Council Elections," *Austin American-Statesman,* March 2, 1985.
62 *Ibid.*
63 "Judge Okays At-Large Vote for Council," *Austin American-Statesman*, March 13, 1985.
64 "City Asked to Plan Single Member Election, Minorities Say Ruling Paves Way for Change from At-Large System," *Austin American-Statesman*, August 27, 1986.
65 "Minority Groups Air Council Election Plan," *Austin American-Statesman,* March 4, 1987.
66 "At-Large Election Critics Condemn City Council," *Austin American-Statesman*, March 9, 1987.
67 "Candidates Prepare for Trench Warfare in Runoff," *Austin American-Statesman*, April 6, 1987.
68 "Single-Member Proponents Note Martinez Loss," *Austin American-Statesman*.
69 "Election Hastens Day of Single Member Districts," *Austin American-Statesman*, May 11, 1987.

70 "At-Large Ballot is Reaffirmed, Issue Rests With Austin," *Austin American-Statesman*, September 16, 1987.

71 *Ibid.*

72 *Ibid.*

73 *Ibid.*

74 "NAACP Expects to Appeal Election Ruling," *Austin American-Statesman*, September 17, 1987.

75 "Districts Not on Horizon for Council, Single Member System Not No. 1 on Agendas," *Austin American-Statesman*, September 27, 1987.

76 "Single Member Districts Concept Splits Minorities," *Austin American-Statesman*, April 19, 1988.

77 "Single Member District Backers Handed Fourth Loss," *Austin American-Statesman*, May 8, 1988.

78 "Council District Backers See Loss As Sign of Discrimination," *Austin American-Statesman*, May 9, 1988.

79 *Ibid.*

80 *Ibid.*

81 *Ibid.*

82 *Ibid.*

83 *Ibid.*

84 "Court Rules Austin At-Large System Legal," *Austin American-Statesman*, May 3, 1989.

85 *Ibid.*

86 "On Charter Agenda: Single Member Issue," *Austin American-Statesman*, April 6, 1990.

87 "Kids Have A Friend on School Board," *Austin American-Statesman*, February 2, 1984.

88 "Busing Tops Concerns in Place 1, School Board Hopefuls Target Improvements," *Austin American-Statesman*, March 20, 1986.

89 "Minorities Say Vote on Busing Lowers Trust, Board Members Accused of Trying to End Integration," *Austin American-Statesman*, July 17, 1986.

90 *Ibid.*

91 *Ibid.*

92 "NAACP Honors Austinite," *Austin American-Statesman*, November 30, 1986.

93 "Trustees Applaud Plan to Cut Busing," *Austin American-Statesman*, February 25, 1987.

94 *Ibid.*

95 *Ibid.*

96 *Ibid.*

INDEX